D0303884

# Sport for Development and Peace

LIVERPOOL JMU LIBRARY

3  1111  01440  9286

# Sport for Development and Peace

## A Critical Sociology

Simon C. Darnell

BLOOMSBURY

LONDON · NEW DELHI · NEW YORK · SYDNEY

**Bloomsbury Academic**
An imprint of Bloomsbury Publishing Plc

50 Bedford Square
London
WC1B 3DP
UK

1385 Broadway
New York
NY 10018
USA

www.bloomsbury.com

**Bloomsbury is a registered trade mark of Bloomsbury Publishing Plc**

First published 2012
Paperback edition first published 2013

© Simon C. Darnell, 2012

Simon C. Darnell has asserted his right under the Copyright, Designs and Patents Act, 1988, to be
identified as Author of this work.

All rights reserved. No part of this publication may be reproduced or transmitted in any form or by any
means, electronic or mechanical, including photocopying, recording, or any information storage or retrieval
system, without prior permission in writing from the publishers.

No responsibility for loss caused to any individual or organization acting on or refraining from action as a
result of the material in this publication can be accepted by Bloomsbury or the author.

This work is published subject to a Creative Commons Attribution Non-Commercial Licence. You may
share this work for non-commercial purposes only, provided you give attribution to the copyright holder
and the publisher. For permission to publish commercial versions please contact Bloomsbury Academic.

**British Library Cataloguing-in-Publication Data**
A catalogue record for this book is available from the British Library.

ISBN: HB:    978-1-84966-344-1
       PB:    978-1-4725-3954-0
       ePDF:  978-1-8496-6590-2
       ePUB:  978-1-8496-6591-9

**Library of Congress Cataloging-in-Publication Data**
A catalog record for this book is available from the Library of Congress.

Cover design: Burge Agency

Printed and bound by CPI Group (UK) Ltd, Croydon, CR0 4YY

# Contents

# Globalizing Sport Studies
## Series Editor's Preface

There is now a considerable amount of expertise nationally and internationally in the social scientific and cultural analysis of sport in relation to the economy and society more generally. Contemporary research topics, such as sport and social justice, science and technology and sport, global social movements and sport, sports mega-events, sports participation and engagement and the role of sport in social development, suggest that sport and social relations need to be understood in non-Western developing economies as well as European, North American and other advanced capitalist societies. The current high global visibility of sport makes this an excellent time to launch a major new book series that takes sport seriously and makes this research accessible to a wide readership.

The series *Globalizing Sport Studies* is thus in line with a massive growth of academic expertise, research output and public interest in sport worldwide. At the same time, it seeks to use the latest developments in technology and the economics of publishing to reflect the most innovative research into sport in society currently underway in the world. The series is multi-disciplinary, although primarily based on the social sciences and cultural studies approaches to sport.

The broad aims of the series are to: *act* as a knowledge hub for social scientific and cultural studies research in sport, including, but not exclusively, anthropological, economic, geographic, historical, political science and sociological studies; *contribute* to the expanding field of research on sport in society in the United Kingdom and internationally by focussing on sport at regional, national and international levels; *create* a series for both senior and more junior researchers that will become synonymous with cutting-edge research, scholarly opportunities and academic development; *promote* innovative discipline-based, multi-, inter- and trans-disciplinary theoretical and methodological approaches to researching sport in society; *provide* an English-language outlet for high quality non-English writing on sport in society; and *publish* broad overviews, original empirical research studies and classic studies from non-English sources, and thus attempt to *realise* the potential for *globalizing* sport studies through open content licensing with 'Creative Commons'.

Sport (broadly defined to encompass physical activity, physical education and even physical culture) has increasingly been seen as having a role to play in contributing to the resolution of enduring societal problems, especially in the Global South or developing world. In 2003, the United Nations (UN) adopted resolution 58/5, which formally recognized the contributions that sport can make to meeting international development goals, and followed this with the international Year of Sport and Physical Education in 2005. Sport has since gained both international recognition and political traction within development initiatives, notably the United Nations' millennium development goals that seek, for example, to eradicate extreme poverty and achieve sustainable gender equality – particularly in the Global South – by 2015. There are currently dozens of sport-based international development programmes and non-governmental organizations (NGOs) listed on the International Platform for Sport and Development, and organizations like Right to Play enjoy a strong international profile and support from government, multinational corporations and celebrity athletes.

*Sport for Development and Peace: A Critical Sociology* brings a sociological view to bear on such initiatives and the momentum behind 'sport for development and peace' (SDP). Simon Darnell does not seek to discredit or, as he says, 'derail' SDP, the related notion of sport-for-development (SFD), or any of the contributions that sport might make in meeting development goals, but rather raises critical questions about the political and social implications of SDP. The book considers the institutionalized relationship between sport and international development by using insights drawn from critical sport sociology and critical development studies.

Chapter 1 examines the ways in which sport, and SDP in particular, can be understood through contemporary social theories (notably Gramscian, Foucauldian and post-colonial theory), and Chapter 2 outlines a brief history of the politics of international development. Chapters 3 and 4 employ the theoretical perspectives outlined there to analyse data from original research into the experiences of young people on an international development programme and interviews with various stakeholders and programme officials working within SDP organizations. Chapter 5 shifts the focus to consider the role of sports mega-events in the field of SDP, particularly as they are increasingly hosted by cities and nations in the Global South. Darnell assesses the claims that sustainable international development can be ascribed to such events. Chapter 6 looks specifically at the phenomenon of sporting celebrity and offers analysis of the implications of celebrity athletes as SDP activists and stakeholders. In Chapter 7, Darnell argues for a commitment to solidarity with marginalized people as preferable to the discourse of empowerment that aligns with, and is susceptible to, the hegemony of neoliberal development philosophy.

Darnell suggests that those interested in SFD and SDP need to consider the implications of linking sport to the development paradigm and asks questions such as who are the targets of SDP, what kind of world view is championed through SDP, and what inequalities exist and how does SDP respond?

'Sport for development and peace', 'sport-for-development' and associated slogans have risen in popularity in the past 20 years; this is the first coherent book-length attempt to understand some of the implications, assumptions and ideologies underpinning these developments.

**John Horne, 2012**

# Acknowledgements

This book came into existence in large part through the support I received from the following people.

Bob Sparks and Brian Wilson at the University of British Columbia first introduced me to the role of the cultural researcher and intellectual and to methods for thoughtful and cogent social analysis. Their lessons have stayed with me to this day. Peter Donnelly and Bruce Kidd at the University of Toronto facilitated my grounding in the critical study of sport, policy and the public good. Sherene Razack from the Ontario Institute for Studies in Education moved me towards post-colonial theory and studies of Whiteness by modelling her thorough and rigorous critique. Special mention is owed to Margaret MacNeill who not only supervised my doctoral research but also consistently supported my scholarly ambitions and confidence. During my time as a postdoctoral researcher at Dalhousie University, David Black and Owen Willis helped to confirm for me the importance and legitimacy of studying sport and its place in social and political life. Finally, John Horne showed interest and faith in this project through its various stages. His editorial guidance, and the feedback of anonymous reviewers, proved essential.

Academia has also given me many important friends whose support has been instrumental and whose insights can be found throughout this book. Ted Alexander was my first grad student colleague and somehow understood from the beginning that a commitment to sociology and to fantasy sports is not incommensurate. Janelle Joseph, Russell Field, Yuka Nakamura, K. Y. Kim, LeAnne Petherick, Ted Norman, Cora McCloy and Lindsay Hayhurst all shared in the daily grind of life as a doctoral student and served as social support as I made it through to the end. Most recently, Bob Huish and Rachel Brickner provided unconditional understanding and regular pep talks through the tumultuous experience of completing a manuscript while being 'on the market'.

Finally, there is my family. The Darnell-Campbells in Mahone Bay offered nourishing weekend retreats during the completion of this text. My Dad, Bill, has always supported my belief in the importance of this work and the understanding that inequalities demand attention. My brother Jesse is the most reliable person I know. My mother, Elaine, taught me to be organized and disciplined but also imaginative and flexible, a combination that proved invaluable for the writing of this book.

And last, but by no means least, there is Sandy, with whom everything in life seems possible and for whom I am forever thankful.

# Acronyms

Brazil, China, Russia and India (BRIC Nations)
Business International Non-governmental Organizations (BINGOs)
Canadian International Development Agency (CIDA)
Commonwealth Games Canada (CGC)
Corporate Social Responsibility (CSR)
Fédération Internationale de Football Association (FIFA)
Football Association (FA)
General Agreement on Tariffs and Trade (GATT)
Human immunodeficiency virus and/or acquired immunodeficiency syndrome
   (HIV/AIDS)
International Development through Sport program (IDS)
International Financial Institutions (IFIs)
International Monetary Fund (IMF)
International Olympic Committee (IOC)
Kicking AIDS Out! (KAO!)
Low- and middle-income countries (LMICs)
Mathare Youth Sport Association (MYSA)
Millennium Development Goals (MDGs)
Monitoring & evaluation (M&E)
National Basketball Association (NBA)
New Partnership for Africa's Development (NEPAD)
Non-governmental organizations (NGOs)
Olympic Advocates Together Honourably (OATH)
Open Fun Football Schools (OFFS)
*Sociology of Sport Journal* (SSJ)
Sport-for-development (SFD)
Sport for development and peace (SDP)
Sport-in-development (SID)
Sports Sans Frontières (SSF)
United Kingdom (UK)
United Nations (UN)
United Nations General Assembly (UNGA)
United Nations Inter-agency Task Force on Sport for Development and Peace
   (UNITSDP)
United Nations Office on Sport for Development and Peace (UNOSDP)
United States (US)
World Trade Organization (WTO)

ascribed particularly to football, given its popularity across diverse social and geographical contexts and its construction as a 'universal language'.

Two, the resolutions referenced the enduring and often seemingly interminable and intractable challenges of international development and its traditional failings, and invoked the role of sport as a response. From this perspective, sport is increasingly understood to be able to make a contribution to the enduring global problems that have yet to be solved in the 'development era'. One may take the starting point for this era to be the colonial impulses and practices of nineteenth-century Europe or the modernist version of contemporary development most often attached to United States (US) President Harry Truman who argued for the northern, 'developed' states to usher in a new era of post-war prosperity by participating in the development of the 'Third World'. In either case, much of the efforts ascribed to and mobilized through the efforts of international development have failed to achieve the long-term and sustainable changes imagined, if not promised. Thus, the current mobilization of sport-for-development (SFD) can be understood as a response to the failure of development's traditional orthodoxy and a role for sport in filling a development void (Levermore and Beacom 2009).

Three, particularly with regard to the FIFA World Cup in South Africa, the resolutions spoke to the importance of the Global South, geographically, politically and even discursively in relation to Global sport. In this sense, even in the cases where the notions of development as a southern issue, or a project of benefits to be delivered from the North to the South, has been contested or rejected, there is still a sense of the South, both materially and metaphorically, as the quintessential site of development. On the one hand, there are objectively higher levels of, for example, poverty in the southern hemisphere and therefore the South is, in the materiality of the everyday, a disproportionate site for development initiatives and struggles. On the other hand, the South continues to be the site of the North's 'development imagination', one that is regularly informed by stereotypes as well as the relations of power that serve in the construction and maintenance of the political economy and a process of Othering. It is revelatory, then, that development (in this case through sport) is most oft-constituted or referred to as 'international development', given that it invokes the notion of development as a process required and performed in 'Other' parts of the world.

Four, the resolutions spoke to, or captured, the instrumental or functional notion of sport in relation to international development (see Coalter 2009). From this perspective, sport is increasingly positioned as a 'tool' or a means by or through which to achieve development goals. This stands in distinction to the notions of sport as an activity or pastime, sport as a sociocultural construction and/or sport as an intimate part of the processes by which the social and political world is negotiated and formed. From the functionalist perspective, sport is recognized by the cultural role it fulfils and, in the case of the UN resolutions, considered a relatively benign cultural institution that serves to bring people together or even transcend the dogged social and political challenges of international development that have largely prevented the achievement of development goals. From a critical perspective, its function is but one way to theorize sport in society.

Five, the resolutions invoked the idea that sport may be a politically palatable, non-threatening and/or effective tool for bringing together diverse people within and across the borders of nation states. The connection between sport, nationalism and the building of nations in this sense is positioned as an opportunity to work towards the inclusive and peaceful achievement of a functioning and prosperous nation-as-community, one that bypasses or usurps racism, patriarchy or material inequalities that have so often proved difficult in the construction and operation of inclusive and peaceful communities and nations.

Six, the incredible popularity of sport around the world, as the focus of physical and consumer activities, was recognized in the resolutions as part of its utility and contribution to meeting international development goals. From this point of view, sport as a popular dimension of culture, and a dimension of popular culture, holds social significance and sport organizations enjoy undeniable political clout. Put differently, given that sport is such an important part of the social experiences of so many around the world, sport is understood to have a potential role in improving the lot of marginalized people in different geopolitical contexts and contributing to the process of overcoming the dogged development challenges of our time.

Seven, the resolutions recognized the increasing development potential and importance attached to major games or sports mega-events. Whereas previously understood as a means primarily or even exclusively to celebrate athletic achievement and a way by which cities and nation states can establish and assert their international reputation, increasingly sports mega-events like the Olympic Games and FIFA World Cup are understood to serve a development purpose both soft – building social cohesion, increasing community participation, positive national identification etc. – and hard – mobilizing public funds, improving infrastructure, attracting foreign investment etc. From this point of view, sports mega-events, their organization and funding are intimately tied to international development issues.

All of these dimensions of the two UN resolutions speak to the social and political challenges of mobilizing sport to meet international development goals, particularly the attainment of equitable, sustainable, healthy and self-determined livelihoods for the world's disadvantaged peoples. These kinds of initiatives are now often described as SFD programmes, given that they explicitly engage and organize sport to improve the lives and life chances of the world's poor and marginalized, often in the Global South. The purpose of this book is to bring a sociological view to bear on such initiatives and the burgeoning 'sport for development and peace' (SDP) sector that is made up of many of these international organizations that support and implement SFD programmes.

The text takes as its starting point that while important socio-managerial work has been, and will continue to be, done regarding what the mobilization of sport can do to effect sustainable social change in various contexts around the world, there are important theoretical and critical questions that need to be asked of the SDP sector. These are not questions that seek to discredit or derail the momentum of SDP, the notion of SFD or any contributions (potential or actual) of sport to meeting development goals, but rather questions that are concerned with the political and social implications of SFD and SDP. These questions also proceed from an idea central to critical development scholarship, namely that questions and critical analyses of power and politics make for better policies and programmes (Nustad 2001).

The book is written from the perspective that every scholarly endeavour is beholden to the political and practical utility that it creates or attempts to carve out for itself. As Alcoff (1991) has argued, where a text goes, for whom it is intended and why it is needed are of central importance to the activity that is critical scholarship. While this text is not written as a manual or set of best practices for how to do SDP work, it is inextricably linked to the question of what sport, physical activity and sport culture can do to make the world a more just and equitable place, and it is these concerns for social justice that inform the analyses. A sociological understanding of power is key. Relations of power underpin sport and international development, respectively, and are therefore of central importance to the study of SDP. This is the 'praxis' of the book, by which I refer to the mobilization of theory and analysis towards critically informed practice.

The main argument of the book then is twofold. One, from a sociopolitical perspective, I suggest that those interested in SFD and SDP would be well served to think of the sector as more than a process requiring 'monitoring & evaluation' (M&E) or managerial refinement in order to determine how best it works. While M&E is no doubt important, I argue that without an associated critical analysis, a strictly managerial approach can slip into the theory of development as a process of linear improvement or modernization, which has serious limitations given that it regularly fails to challenge the relations of power, privilege and dominance that result in a small number of international haves and a large number of international have-nots. Rather, I argue that we need to think of the implications of hitching sport to the development paradigm and ask social questions (e.g. who are the targets of SDP?), political questions (what kind of world view is championed through SDP?) and material questions (what inequalities exist and how does SDP respond?) of the SDP sector.

Two, from a perspective of theory and research, there is genuine potential to consider the implications of the increasingly institutionalized relationship between sport and international development by deliberating on the insights of critical sport and critical development studies, both respectively and in conjunction. That is, the critical study of SDP need not reinvent the theoretical or methodological wheel in order to construct a sound, comprehensive and cogent framework for analysis. We need, rather, to consider the potential connections and synthesis between critical studies of sport and development, a modest contribution that I take on in the following pages.

To do so, I do focus primarily on the activities within SDP as they are currently mobilized along the traditional lines of northern organizations and southern beneficiaries. I am not proposing, in this short text, to explore all of the possibilities, theoretical and practical, of connecting sport to development initiatives, though much important work remains to be done in this regard. Rather, I am most focused in this book on the international bodies and non-governmental organizations (NGOs) that have taken an increased interest in SFD in recent years. While this does something of a disservice to the myriad conceptions of development itself that are possible in relation to sport, a notion that I explore to a degree throughout the text (also see Hartmann and Kwauk 2011), this focus is justifiable and important for at least three reasons: One, this focus on northern organizations is where critical scholarly attention has lacked in recent years, given the propensity to focus on the recipients or targets of SDP initiatives and to do so, in some cases, at the expense of broader relations of power. Two, this focus does not undermine southern agency, given that southern agency is rarely included in northern representations and regimes of power in development (see Biccum 2010). And three, it provides a basis from which to theorize new or previously unexamined connections between sport and international development to the benefit of future research, practice and activism.

In sum, the text is guided by an ethical and political investigation of SDP and the current mobilization of SFD. I follow Gasper (2004: xii) in this regard who argues that the ethics of development can be conceptualized in three stages: ethical concerns about development policies and the experiences they afford, ethical examinations of the core concepts and theories employed to understand those experiences and actions, and then the ethics of development practice. Also similar to Gasper, this text focuses primarily on the first two stages, with the third (which speaks more to 'development ethics' than 'the ethics of development') largely beyond the scope of the book and requiring a methodology (i.e. ethnographic fieldwork) beyond the historical, textual and interview methods employed here. This is not to suggest that the development ethics of SDP are not important; indeed it is hoped that the analysis offered in this book will go some way towards a more theoretically and critically informed body of future SDP research.

The remainder of this introductory chapter proceeds in seven parts. Next, I offer a brief discussion of key terms and tenets in SDP, and the major stakeholders involved. This is followed by a short historical/political overview of the momentum underpinning SDP, particularly at the supra- and international level. I follow with an introduction to the theoretical framework employed in the text, an outline of some of the social and political paradoxes that underpin SDP and a discussion of SDP amidst theoretical understandings of social movements. The Introduction concludes with a preview of subsequent chapters.

## SDP: Terms and tenets

In general, sport-for-development – sometimes used interchangeably with sport-in-development (SID) – describes the specific mobilization and implementation of sport as a means of meeting the goals and challenges of international development. Important here is the understanding that SFD and SID are distinct from 'sports development', which refers to the social and political processes by which the organizational and institutional world of sport is formed. Whereas sport development is principally concerned with improving the world of sport (from which broader social development is often presumed to follow), sport-*for*-development takes issues of development as its primary focus and sport as a means of tackling them.[2]

Coalter (2009, 2010a, 2010b) has described this distinction as 'sport plus' versus 'plus sport', where a sport plus approach focuses on sport development and plus sport takes development as its goal and positions sport in support of achieving development. While both sport development and SFD (or sport plus and plus sport) can and do find their way into the topics and examples covered in this text, the book is focused primarily on SFD and plus sport. I am interested in unpacking and analysing the implications of positioning and mobilizing sport as a means of achieving development, a perspective not necessarily captured in and through sport development processes, policies and literatures.

To that end, throughout the remainder of the text, I follow Kidd by using the term 'sport for development and peace' to describe the momentum and organization of and interest in SFD. I am in favour of this term for several reasons: First, it captures the SFD or plus sport perspective under a tidy title. Second, it includes a distinct reference to peace building or conflict resolution, a topic that needs to be included within international development but is not reducible to international development. And third, it considers SDP, in the manner constructed and described by Kidd, in relation to New Social Movements, an important characteristic and one that I analyse in more detail below.

It is also important to acknowledge the diversity of programmes and policies that exist under the title of SDP. While SDP programmes range in size, scope and focus, all incorporate sport – understood, in the broadest sense, to include play and physical activity – to promote social change within a paradigm of international development. Levermore (2008: 56) has provided important classificatory analyses of SDP and posited that SDP programmes fall into seven categories defined by the development outcomes that they seek in and through the organization and mobilization of sport and physical culture. These are conflict resolution, cultural understanding, infrastructure development, educational awareness, the empowerment of marginalized groups, encouragement of physical activity and health, and driving economic development. In addition, several organizations, like Commonwealth Games Canada and Right to Play, offer internships or volunteer opportunities in low- and middle-income countries (LMICs) in the Global South.[3]

Levermore's classification illustrates the breadth of initiatives and organizations that fall under the broad catchment of the SDP title, and SDP organizations can be found that fall under each of his seven categories. For the purposes of this introduction, however, I follow the UN Inter-agency Task Force on Sport and Development and Peace (United Nations 2003: 26) that suggests that SDP programmes fall into three broad categories – social, health and economic development. As context for the analyses that follow, I provide a brief (though by no means complete or exhaustive) overview of the three categories and examples of organizations that fit therein.

## Social issues

Social issues attended to in international development and SDP include poverty, lack of education, gender inequality, human insecurity and displacement, and conflict. Arguably, Right to Play enjoys the highest profile among SDP organizations concerned with such social issues. Originally known as Olympic Aid, the organization grew out of the 1994 Winter Olympics in Lillehammer, due in part to the athletic success of its founder, Norwegian speed skater Johann Olav Koss. Koss parlayed his performance in Lillehammer into donations used to deliver sport and play opportunities for children living in poverty, primarily in Africa. In 2001, as a non-governmental organization, Olympic Aid began direct programme implementation to facilitate physical and social development among marginalized youth in the Global South. Olympic Aid transitioned to Right to Play in 2003. By the end of 2009, Right to Play was providing regular weekly sport and physical activity to 700,000 children supported by 15,000 local coaches and leaders (Right to Play 2011). The organization also benefits from an 'International Team of Athlete Ambassadors', including many celebrity athletes, that lend support and prestige to Right to Play's efforts (Right to Play 2011).

Other humanitarian organizations also hold sport as their central mandate. PLAY SOCCER Nonprofit International has been operating since 2001 and oversees a network of national organizations in Africa. Through the training of local volunteer coaches and leaders, Play Soccer programmes facilitate 'activity-based games that empower children by helping them experience, practice and acquire new healthy habits, attitudes and social skills, while they play the game' (Play Soccer 2011). Similarly, Sports Sans Frontières (SSF) views sport as an essential activity fundamental to the healthy development of children. Working in places as disparate as Afghanistan, Burundi, Kosovo and Haiti, SSF advocates for sport as 'a universal language of our time, a driver of cohesion and mobilization, a means to bring reassurance and stability … (and) a new vehicle for development, both of the individual and of the community' (SSF 2011). As well, SCORE – an NGO operating under the vision 'To Change Lives and Build Stronger Communities through Sport' – operates programmes, including Cup of Heroes and Living Sport across South Africa, that are designed to support, empower and celebrate community development and sport opportunities.

Organizations concerned with post-war reconciliation and sustainable conflict resolution have also turned to sport and play as tools of social development.[4] For example, Open Fun Football Schools (OFFS) is a cooperative project of the Danish NGO Cross Cultures Project Association, the Norwegian Football Association and the Gerlev Sports Academy. OFFS employs 'football-as-fun' as the basis of a pedagogical framework to facilitate democracy, peace and social cohesion in the former Yugoslavia and other parts of south-east Europe. Similarly, Soccer for Peace and Football for Peace have used soccer as a non-violent means of social interaction in the Middle East. For these organizations, the global popularity of the game makes soccer both a metaphor and a vehicle of peace building (Soccer for Peace 2011).[5]

## Health and education

SDP initiatives are also concerned with health issues such as the prevention of human immunodeficiency virus and/or acquired immunodeficiency syndrome (HIV/AIDS) and immunization against preventable diseases. For example, Right to Play directs resources towards HIV/AIDS prevention in places like Botswana where the population has suffered from the pandemic. Positioning their work as a supplement to government-led initiatives, Right to Play mobilizes sport to support education about HIV/AIDS, and support and promote gender equality towards reducing the spread of infections.

Right to Play is not the only SDP NGO concerned with HIV/AIDS. Grassroot Soccer (2011) also uses the interest in football and the popularity and cultural influence of famous players to support HIV/AIDS education and prevention in Zimbabwe, Zambia and South Africa. Similarly, Kicking AIDS Out! (KAO!) designs and implements sport-based educational programmes to improve awareness and prevention in African communities confronting the AIDS pandemic. Notably, KAO! is a project of the EduSport Foundation, an

NGO based in Zambia, and is designed by and for African citizens, in contrast to many SDP NGOs whose organizational roots are North American and European.

## Economic development

The third category of SDP initiatives focuses on economic issues such as the building of local capacities, employment and environmental protection. The best example is Alive and Kicking, an 'African social enterprise' started by the late Jim Cogan, which works to provide soccer balls for youth, jobs for adults and promote health education at the same time (Alive and Kicking 2011). The programme is designed to spur local economies and provide affordable sporting equipment to youth in impoverished communities in support of health promotion and physical activity. Soccer balls manufactured through the Alive and Kicking programme, for example, are labelled with educational messages about HIV/AIDS and malaria. Furthermore, according to the International Platform on Sport and Development, running races in Peru, such as the Inca Marathon, the Andes International Marathon and the Huancayo Race, have led to the development of local shoe building industries for runners (sportanddev. org 2011, Developing Local Markets through Sport).

Admittedly, a complete overview of the SDP sector and its constitutive organizations is beyond the scope of this Introduction. However, it is reasonable to argue that what unifies SDP, and what secures its political orientation or ethos, is a commitment to sport in support of egalitarian and sustainable development. Egalitarian development is understood here as supporting the access for all to basic human needs and of redressing the current cultural and political economy that prevents such access. Sustainable development is recognized by the UN Inter-agency Task Force and references the importance of social equity, economic development and environmental protection through 'development which meets the needs of the present without compromising the ability of future generations to meet their own needs' (United Nations General Assembly 1987). Clearly, no organization that can be termed to support the momentum of SDP is interested in exacerbating poverty, poor health or disempowerment or securing socio- or geopolitical dominance. The goals, then, of SDP are laudable and no reasonable analyst, critical or otherwise, would argue against the importance of development amidst sustained poverty. To that end, my arguments in the chapters that follow are not against the general tenor of SDP that supports better conditions of life for the world's poorest and most marginalized. Rather, my critical analysis focuses on the political orientation for securing change employed within SDP, the notions of sport that SDP regularly presupposes and secures, and the understandings of development politics that are embraced within the sector. I share then, with SDP organizations, stakeholders and proponents, a goal of mobilizing sport in support of sustainable development; my critical analysis is based on the contestations of the politics and means of achieving this goal.

# Stakeholders

A variety of stakeholders are involved in SDP. There are literally hundreds of organizations that are interested and active, in some form or another, in mobilizing sport towards the goals of international development. This text cannot provide an exhaustive overview or analysis of all of the stakeholders if for no other reason than they are constantly adding and being changed. Nevertheless, it is important to recognize the diversity of the organizations involved.

First and foremost, the United Nations has taken an active role in supporting the SDP sector, particularly through the organization of the United Nations Office on Sport for Development and Peace (UNOSDP) and the creation of a Special Advisor to the UN Secretary-General concerned with SDP (currently Wilfried Lemke). The UNOSDP does not implement SDP programmes or initiatives but rather supports the mobilization of SFD and facilitates the organization and communication of various other SDP stakeholders. Not to be overlooked, of course, is the extent to which UN support lends the sector cultural and political legitimacy, particularly within civil society and among advocates of non-governmental or rights-based development policy.

These kinds of advocates include non-governmental organizations (NGOs) like the ones described above, which arguably are the hub of the SDP sector as they organize and implement many of the SDP initiatives currently underway around the world. In Chapters 4–6, I draw on interviews with representatives of various SDP organizations in order to explore the political orientation and development practices of NGO-led SDP programmes. By no means, however, are NGOs the only organizations working to implement SDP programmes. Not surprising given the commodification of contemporary sporting culture, various corporations (sport-focused and otherwise) have also taken an active role in SDP. Again, Levermore (2011) has provided important classificatory analyses of this, particularly the ways in which SDP offers corporations an opportunity to implement corporate social responsibility (CSR) initiatives. While little monitoring of the impact and/or success of these SDP for CSR projects takes place (see Levermore 2011) it is important to recognize that corporate funding for SDP is available and that the relatively non-threatening politics of mobilizing SFD provide an attractive opportunity for international corporate entities to construct reputations as responsible corporate citizens.

In turn, stakeholders in SDP include key organizations and individuals from the world of high-performance, professional and elite sport. Included here are professional sport organizations like England's Football Association (FA) and the US-based National Basketball Association (NBA), which supports development and the general parameters of SDP through initiatives like Basketball without Borders (see Millington 2010). As well, the world's pre-eminent supranational sporting organizations are involved in SDP. The International Olympic Committee (IOC) now lists 'Development through Sport' as a component of 'Olympism in Action' with the mandate to '[b]uild a better world by developing programmes that provide concrete responses to social inequality'.[6] The Federation Internationale de Football Association (FIFA) operates Football for Hope, which 'supports programmes all over the world that combine football and social development'[7] – a scheme that received considerable publicity and advertising during the 2010 World Cup in South Africa.

As well, the confluence of sport, capital and media underpinning the contemporary phenomenon of athletes as cultural celebrities has found its way into SDP to the extent that famous athletes – like NBA star Steve Nash and tennis idol Roger Federer – support international development initiatives (sporting or otherwise) through their charitable foundations. Through SDP, athletes like Nash and Federer (in a manner akin to celebrity activists like rock star Bono) have become important arbiters of development funding and practice.

Finally, it is important to recognize the extent to which the state and national governments are interested and involved in SDP programming and policy. That is, even though governments tend to be less active in SDP than organizations like the United Nations or IOC or various NGOs, governments are involved in supporting the mobilization of SFD. Huish (2011), for example, has explored the role of the Cuban state in supporting the training of professional coaches across the southern hemisphere as a form of sport-based solidarity. Furthermore, the Government of Canada's Ministry of Heritage and Youth Employment Strategies support the SDP internship programme organized by Commonwealth Games Canada (see Chapter 3). Understanding the role of the state in SDP is therefore important for at least two reasons: One, it stands as a means of comparative analysis, particularly in relation to the predominance of civil society actors within the SDP sector, and two, it recognizes the calls in recent years for the state to take a more active role in SDP such that it could make SFD more publicly focused, committed and available to citizens (Kidd 2008; Njelesani 2011).

## SFD: Historical and political context

The October 2009 UN Resolutions were not the first concerned with sport. On 3 November 2003, the General Assembly of the United Nations passed Resolution 58/5, entitled 'Sport as a means to promote education, health, development and peace'. Acknowledging the Convention on the Rights of the Child, the International Charter of Physical Education and Sport, and the UNITSDP, the resolution called for various stakeholders (the United Nations, governments, sport institutions and specialized agencies) to promote sport and physical education as part of development programmes and policies. The resolution also advocated for the utility of sport-based programmes in order to meet the United Nation's Millennium Development Goals (MDGs)[8] and for a focus on partnerships and cooperation 'in order to promote a culture of peace and social and gender equality and to advocate dialogue and harmony' (UN General Assembly 2003).

These invocations of sport as a socially productive and transformative cultural form that are characteristic of the SDP sector have strong historical antecedents in European and northern cultures (Kidd 2008: 371). In the Victorian era of the nineteenth century, emergent class-informed, bourgeois sensibilities led to new understandings of sport participation focused on the development of discipline and character. No longer merely escapism or an excuse to participate in debauchery, sport became linked to 'rational recreation', characterized by organization, codification and competition (Guttmann 1978). By the end of the nineteenth century, such connections were made explicit within movements of religious reform, and masculine sport participation as a way to develop and discipline the body was encouraged by Protestant leaders in support of 'Muscular Christianity' (Bouchier 1994; Putney 2001). By the early twentieth century, a 'playground movement' emerged, in which working-class demands for access to safe recreation, coupled with owning-class desires for a productive work force, made possible the development of physical activity facilities, deemed central to social and physical health and well-being (Ingham and Hardy 1984). In all of these cases, participation in sport and physical activity was presumed to offer tangible and sustainable benefits that extended beyond just playing the game.

Resolution 58/5 in 2003 represented high-profile recognition and institutionalization of such logic. While humanitarian groups and non-governmental organizations had previously used sport and physical education within their programmes, Resolution 58/5 lent international legitimacy to SFD. It also recognized the diversity of programmes and interventions under the banner of SDP. While discussing the potential of sport, then UN Secretary-General Kofi Annan stated:

> Sport is a universal language. At its best it can bring people together, no matter what their origin, background, religious beliefs or economic status. And when young people participate in sports or have access to physical education, they can experience real exhilaration even as they learn the ideals of teamwork and tolerance. That is why the United Nations is turning more and more to the world of sport for help in our work for peace and our efforts to achieve the Millennium Development Goals. (United Nations 2004)

Implicit within Annan's remarks was the notion that the universality of sport, and sport as a cross-cultural language, is compatible with the mandate of international development based on universal human rights. However, while the acceptance and support of the universality of sport and human rights – and their compatibility – lends the SDP sector its social and political credibility, this perspective requires (and largely perpetuates) essentialist assumptions regarding culture and human organization. This is particularly significant given that SDP initiatives often take place in countries with histories of colonization and marginalization in global and geopolitics. Mobilizing sport to meet international development goals in the post-colonial world is implicated in this history.

Furthermore, as Maguire (2006: 107; 2008) has argued, mobilizing sport towards the attainment of development goals begs for analysis of sport's organization, dissemination and impact as well as critical consideration of the extent to which dominant sporting forms are conducive to meeting the goals of international development. This is called for given the regular invocations of sport's inherent positivity – what I refer to as the tendency to 'essentialize' the sporting experience in development and SDP – that are useful in substantiating the sector and, perhaps more importantly, presenting the mobilization of SFD as natural and largely apolitical. Such invocations are evident in the regularly cited (see, for example, Coalter 2010b) description of sport's contribution to development within 2005 report of the UNITSDP:

> The world of sport presents a natural partnership for the United Nations' system. By its very nature sport is about participation. It is about inclusion and citizenship. Sport brings individuals and communities together, highlighting commonalities and bridging cultural or ethnic divides. Sport provides a forum to learn skills such as discipline, confidence and leadership and it teaches core principles such as tolerance, cooperation and respect. Sport teaches the value of effort and how to manage victory, as well as defeat. When these positive aspects of sport are emphasized, sport becomes a powerful vehicle through which the United Nations can work towards achieving its goals. (United Nations 2005)

The issue is not that such romanticized notions of sport and its social, political and pedagogical values are necessarily wrong but rather that they are neither inherent nor essential to the sporting experience. In fact, the tradition of critical sports studies has forcefully illustrated the ways in which dominant sporting forms can be implicated in gendered (e.g. Burstyn 1999) and racialized hierarchies (e.g. Carrington 2010; Hylton 2009), the securing of hetero-normativity (e.g. Lenskyj 1986, 1993) as well as dominant relations of social class (e.g. Donnelly and Harvey 2007). Furthermore, critical scholarship has shown that organized sporting forms serve as regimes of discipline as much as catalysts of cultural freedom and self-expression (e.g. Shogan 1999). In turn, the ability of sport in any essential form to support sustainable development on an international scale is complicated by the extent to which the control of 'global sport' still rests primarily in dominant, northern capitalist nations (Maguire 2006: 111). Key then, for critical scholars, is the judicious application of critical theory in order to make sense of the ways in which sport and its organization, culture and politics are negotiated and organized within the contemporary SDP setting.

## A theoretical approach to SDP

Given the limits of essentializing sport, a critical analysis of SDP is called for. In the broadest sense, three distinct (but, I argue, complementary) theoretical/ philosophical/sociopolitical frameworks guide the analyses in this text to varying degrees: Gramscian hegemony, Foucauldian bio-power and post-colonial theory. In addition, I employ insights from critical pedagogy and ethics in order to argue for an approach to SDP that is self-reflexive in its understanding of sport-based interventions. Each of these major frameworks are useful for the sociological analysis of SDP because (a) they all have a tradition in the study of sport and international development, respectively, and (b) they all speak to the construction, operation and maintenance of relations of power and thus make a contribution to the analytical focal point and purpose of this text.

First and foremost, Gramscian hegemony illustrates the ways in which ideas attain a notion of common sense within relations of dominance and consent. For Gramsci (1971), this necessitated an understanding of the processes by which relatively powerful groups secure their hegemonic position in and through social and political negotiation with subordinated classes, particularly in the cultural sphere. In the study of sport, physical activity and leisure, Gramscian theory has been used to illustrate how the construction of sporting institutions, the opportunities to participate and the meanings ascribed to physical activity and recreation are mediated in and through relations of power. Sport is not a benign social institution; it is a product of interactions between the relatively powerful/powerless. Similarly, in development scholarship and theorizing, hegemony has been used to examine and understand how poor and marginalized persons and populations struggle for self-determination from relatively powerless positions. Understanding these processes is crucial, I argue, for the study of SDP because of the enduring rhetoric and positioning of sport as a universal experience that too often results in theories of sport as external to power. By extension, the use of hegemony theory reduces the tendency to obscure or subsume the relations of power that underpin development and the reasons why people are relatively 'underdeveloped' in the first place. This criticism also harkens to the fact that the act of working towards development (through sport or otherwise) is itself an act of power, an idea highlighted by theories of power in the Foucauldian tradition.

In distinction from Gramsci's theorizing of the interactions and negotiations between groups within relations of power, Foucault theorized power as productive or the ability to confer positive change and encourage action deemed appropriate and civil. Bio-power was Foucault's (1978) theoretical means of situating this power across the two poles of the body and the population. In sport and the study of the physically active body, such theorizing has been used to understand the disciplining of bodies and subsuming of freedoms that is often central to the success of athletic performance and achievement. In development studies, Foucault's theorizing has been instrumental in illustrating how the inequalities that result from the organization and maintenance of the political economy are often reduced to, or subsumed by, the bio-political or governmental focus on the conduct of marginalized people. In both cases, it is important to note that Foucault also strongly advocated for a commitment to ethics as part of the understanding of the operations of power. The moment and/or site at which positive change is conferred become a moment/site of the working of power that necessitates a concomitant analysis of the ethical implications. This understanding of ethics is a central tenet of this text's praxis.

Post-colonial theory has a tradition in both sport and development studies as well. Post-colonial theory is not only concerned with the era or epoch after southern countries were 'freed' from the institutional and economic shackles of the European colonial project. In addition, post-colonial theory focuses on the enduring regimes of power and knowledge that proceeded from the dominance of racialized persons by northern stewards through notions of prosperity, respectability and social change (see Hesse 2002). In sport studies, such theorizing has illustrated that sport and physical education were not only a central part of the civilizing mission of northern states and people but also that many of the sports that are now recognized for their global popularity, geographic reach and/or 'universality' could have only emerged in and through these colonial relations (Saavedra 2009). In development studies, post-colonial theory has pointed to the ways in which the need for development was and continues to be constituted in and through structural relations of colonization. In addition, regimes of truth and understandings of northern benevolence, stewardship and even 'helping' are often similar to, and may therefore do little to challenge, the colonial understanding of the helpless, passive, inferior Other (Heron 2007).

My point in advocating the use of these three approaches is not to conflate them; indeed, I am aware of and sensitive to the criticism that the deployment of various theoretical models within a single study or analysis is at best inconsistent and at worst irresponsible within the tradition of the social sciences (see Andrews 2000). However, I justify this use of multiple theories in two ways: One, the deployment of Foucauldian understandings of discourse and productive power in conjunction with Gramscian politics has been used to good effect, in particular by eminent post-colonial theorists like Edward

Said (1978) as well as within more contemporary ethnographic analyses of the social politics of international development (see Asher 2009; Li 2007). In turn, and two, the complementary use of hegemony and bio-power proceeds from the perspective that critical scholars can, and should, use all theoretical and methodological tools available in the study and challenge of oppression. From this compound standpoint approach, the issue is less the consistency of, and match between, the paradigms and more the utility of the paradigms to explain the workings of power and lend insights to the analysis of their implications (De Lissovoy 2008a). Of course, this approach does not afford any scholar (interested in SDP or otherwise) free reign to apply or mix and match any and all theoretical approaches but does allow a measure of freedom to approach the workings of power from a variety of perspectives.[9]

## Paradoxes of development and paradoxes in SFD

Perhaps then, the critical focus of this book is best conceptualized as a commitment to the exploration of the differing perspectives and understandings of development and sport, as well as the political dimensions of both, within SDP. Black (2010) has drawn attention to the 'ambiguity' of development in SDP, exemplified by the importance of tempering a commitment to social and political change with the critical analysis of stewardship and relations of power. Here, I would add that SDP is exemplary of a number of paradoxes that, rather than paralyze the sector, can serve as important reminders of the fraught political territory that any development initiative necessarily inhabits.

For example, Li (2007) has drawn attention to the contradictions within international development initiatives particularly as they are organized, mobilized and implemented by international organizations or NGOs. She points out the contradiction between the promotion of capitalist processes, which rest on a competitive advantage, and the concern to facilitate a better lot for the relatively marginalized and dispossessed. This is what Biccum (2010) refers to as the traditional 'dual mandate' of development – to increase the reach and profit of capitalist endeavours while championing the welfare of poor natives. This dual mandate dovetails with the contradiction within development initiatives that seek to improve partnerships between development trustees (i.e. NGOs, International Financial Institutions or IFIs, development volunteers) and the 'deficient subjects' who stand as the targets of development initiatives but serve in turn to necessarily re-inscribe these social and political boundaries (Li 2007: 31).

While not a perfect match to SDP, I submit that the critical analysis of development paradoxes and contradictions drawn out by scholars like Biccum and Li can also be seen in SDP, in at least four ways. First, there is a political contradiction within SDP, given that while few would argue that development is apolitical, sport in the service of development or peace is often presented as politically non-threatening or 'value-neutral' (see Sugden 2006). This apolitical presentation of sport is then offered as evidence of its usefulness or applicability to meeting development goals. Second, the notion of sport as universal, discussed above, raises the question of why NGOs take up the task of mobilizing SFD. If sport is universal, what knowledge are SDP NGOs imparting? Certainly, in a plus sport formulation, sport is an entry point towards promoting other ideas and pursuing other goals, but the point remains that the presumed universality of sport undermines the urgency or necessity of SDP at least to a degree. Furthermore, as I explore in subsequent chapters, the promotion of the importance of sport itself remains embedded within many SDP activities, a position that seems at odds with the universal notion of sport.

Third, there are paradoxes of power within SDP. Sport for Development and Peace – International Working Group stated in its 2006 report that governments, particularly in developing nations, need to be convinced of the importance and utility of SFD. If sport constitutes an accessible and participatory means of supporting egalitarian development, through what logic or political motivation do developing nations need convincing? Finally, I would suggest that a contradiction can be seen in the ways that sport itself is often positioned as a successful development tool within SDP, but one also beholden to the meeting of other particular conditions (such as that it be organized in an inclusive manner and/or situated as part of a broader development plan). By the essentialist logic of sport's utility, should not sport take care of these development complexities? What this suggests, I submit, is that the political commitment to egalitarian development or conflict resolution is more important than the application of sport to meeting development goals (see Darnell 2011a). This does not mean that sport offers nothing to meeting development goals but reminds scholars and activists of the limits of essentializing sport and, in turn, that struggles for development are inherently neither enhanced nor reduced by the act of organizing sporting opportunities.

## SDP as/and new social movements

Finally, then, it is necessary to address, at least briefly, the extent to which SDP in its current incarnation is representative of a New Social Movement as Kidd (2008) has suggested. Throughout this text, I resist the tendency to refer to SDP as a 'movement', though I do acknowledge the attractiveness of the term for describing the momentum and institutionalization of SDP. Such momentum is evident through the leadership and commitments made by the United Nation's Office on Sport for Development and Peace, high-profile NGOs and financial support from national governments, particularly northern donor countries like

Norway, Britain, Germany and Canada as well as corporate and charitable foundations. It is also tempting to use the term 'movement' in recognition of the ways that stakeholders themselves consider and position SDP or to situate the SDP sector at the particular intersection of civil society, international aid and development philanthropy.

However, given the questions of power and politics that are central to this text, terming SDP as a 'movement' diverges significantly and problematically from the generally accepted sociological understanding of New Social Movements, which traditionally referred to the struggles for individual and cultural reform of the 1960s and 1970s and were preceded by the socialist, workers movements of newly industrialized societies (Wieviorka 2005). In turn, as Wieviorka (2005: 8) argues, 'the era of "new social movements" is behind us now', replaced by Global Movements (most famously the Zapatista Movement in Chiapas, Mexico). These Global Movements moved beyond a fixed focus on the nation state and towards an integrated demand for cultural recognition, political reform and economic self-determination, and did so through 'a loose conglomeration campaigning against a vague, impersonal and poorly identified opponent' (Wieviorka 2005: 8).

It would be a mistake to suggest that SDP bears none of the hallmarks of Global Movements; to be sure, there are some important parallels that can be drawn between Global Movements and SDP. SDP is a relatively loose conglomeration and is concerned with reform beyond the nation state – for example, the establishment of Olympic AID/Right to Play, aligned temporally and politically with the movement among athletes and stakeholders for a renewed ethics in the Olympic Games, and the Olympic Movement itself, particularly in the wake of performance-enhancing drug use, bribery scandals and a general lack of faith in the purity of high-performance sport. In June 1999 athletes, administrators and researchers established Olympic Advocates Together Honourably (OATH) to promote ethical values and democratic reforms towards the 'peaceful fulfillment of human potential'.[10] It is reasonable to argue that such invocations of elite sporting reform led, at least in part, to the notion that sport could 'do more' to make the world a better place, an ethos that serves as a basis for many SDP initiatives.

However, as I argue throughout this text, the current political orientation and practice of much of SDP tends to align with facilitating – or 'empowering' in the parlance of SFD – the better participation of the relatively marginalized or dispossessed within the current (capitalist) cultural and political economy. This approach is qualitatively different from New Social and Global Movements that resist the machinations of global capital and social hierarchies that construct and sustain inequality. In this way, even though the 'opponent' of Global Movements tends to be vague, there tends to be no opponents at all in SDP save for the poor or improper motivation, conduct, education, health or material existence of the world's poor people. SDP, in this sense, focuses on securing upward mobility more so than challenging the structures of inequality. Such an ethos clearly limits the extent to which SDP can (or should) be considered a New Social or Global Movement.

This apparent misalignment between current or 'mainstream' SDP discourse and Global Movements of the kind described by Wieviorka does not mean that grassroots or oppositional organizations do not feature within the SDP community, or within its social and political imagination,[11] but does serve to make the point that SDP is not representative of all of the possible connections between sport and international development or, perhaps more importantly, of all of the possible political orientations towards redressing global inequality that coalesce in and around sport. In addition to Harvey, Horne and Safai's (2009) analysis of sport organizations committed to alter-globalization, there is a strong case to be made that, despite the hosting of a global online platform (sportanddev.org) and convening organizations (like the UNOSDP and streetfootballworld), a host of local, sport-based development initiatives take place around the world that predate and/or do not feature prominently within the SDP sector or its institutional structures (Lindsay and Grattan, in press; Nicholls 2010). Documenting and understanding these groups, and making sense of them in comparative analysis to more mainstream SDP activities, is beyond the scope of this text but is an important, ongoing opportunity and challenge for researchers interested in SFD around the world (see Gruneau, in press) and the sociology of sport more broadly (see Wilson 2007). For the purposes of this book, the analyses in the following chapters focus on the political orientations, relations of power and production of knowledge within the comparatively 'mainstream' SDP sector and the implications thereof. To this extent, SDP can be understood to have political momentum and coherence, but an orientation that is particular, not universal, in its approach to development and its understandings of the role of sport on an international scale.

## Overview of the book

The remainder of this book is organized into seven chapters. In Chapter 1, I revisit some foundational theories and studies from the scholarly tradition of sport sociology in order to set out an understanding of sport that rejects essentialisms and focuses on the constitutive effects of political economy and relations of power/knowledge. In particular, I examine the ways in which sport has been understood through Gramscian, Foucauldian and post-colonial theory as well as how sport has been connected to the notion of universal human rights. I argue that the study of sport in SDP can positively and critically draw on all of these perspectives in ways that are complementary and mutually informative to the sociological analysis of SDP.

Chapter 2 is concerned primarily with the history and politics of international development, an understanding of which I argue is required, and should be central, to any sustained, critical understanding of SDP. A brief historical overview of the political economy of unequal development is offered. In turn, I explore the benefits of a commitment to 'equality of condition' as a guiding principle for development and SDP and also explore various strands of development theory (modernization, dependency, neoliberal, post-development, post-colonial) to argue for a theoretically informed study of SDP that learns from, rather than recreates, the study of international development.

In Chapter 3, I begin to employ the theoretical perspectives from Chapters 1 and 2 in analysing data from a research study focused on the experiences of young Canadians who served as SDP interns within an international development programme organized by Commonwealth Games Canada. Drawing on recent research in critical development studies and international social work, I examine why young Canadians may be 'drawn' to SDP, how they approach the task of supporting development through sport and what such encounters say or reveal about the transnational politics of power and privilege. I argue that while interns were often aware of their relative privilege within their 'placement communities', such politics tended to be obscured by the development chore of facilitating neoliberal success for SDP partners.

Chapter 4 builds, in many ways, on the experiences of interns by considering data from interviews with various stakeholders and programme officials working within the SDP sector. Principally, I use these reflections to attend to the question of whether and how the mobilization of sport within SDP differs from traditional approaches to development or the 'orthodoxy' of twentieth century development as modernization. The results suggest that while those working in the field do maintain a critically informed sense of the limitations, if not failures, of traditional approaches to development, the political economy of development and SDP is such that diverging from the dominant paradigm remains a challenge. As a result, I conclude that the politics of contemporary SDP map closely onto the politics of development since the end of the Second World War and are worthy of ongoing scholarly attention.

Chapter 5 shifts from reflections on the challenges of mobilizing SFD to focus primarily on the role of sports mega-events in the field of SDP. Building on the critical mass of literature in the political and sociological study of sports mega-events that draws attention to the cultural significance, but also the massive opportunity costs, of staging the World Cup and Olympic Games, I argue that a mandate of sustainable international development is increasingly ascribed to such events, particularly as they are hosted more often by cities and nations in the Global South. I also explore, through interview data, some of the ways – both positive and negative – in which the massive cultural and economic capital of these events affects those working within the field of SDP, both practically and in relation to their political orientation towards social change.

In Chapter 6, I look specifically at the phenomenon of sporting celebrity and offer a critical analysis of the implications of celebrity athletes as SDP activists and stakeholders. Much has been written recently about the possibilities and limitations of celebrity engagement (sporting or otherwise) within international development and global charity efforts, literature that can inform our understanding of the contributions that celebrity athletes offer to SDP. While international development, and support of organizations within SDP, undoubtedly offers celebrity athletes an opportunity to make a positive contribution, I explore (and question) the depth or sustainability of the social change imagined and supported in and through the 'celebritization' of SFD.

In Chapter 7, I conclude the text with a call for a renewed commitment to critical pedagogy and studies of cultural and political oppression as a basis for ongoing study (and activism) in SDP. I argue for a commitment to solidarity with marginalized people as preferable to the discourse of empowerment that aligns with, and is susceptible to, the hegemony of neoliberal development philosophy. In turn, I suggest that our 'imagination' of SFD should include critical understandings of the politics of development and the various possibilities of the social organization of sport, ideas that can be facilitated by a commitment to ethical and phenomenological understandings of the sporting experience.

Finally, in the analyses that follow, I regularly employ the pronoun 'we' when referring to the activities and political orientations of the SDP sector. I do this, in a manner similar to that employed by critical development scholar Barbara Heron (2007), in order to situate myself within the general momentum supportive of, and 'desiring', the mobilization of sport, sport organizations and physical culture to contribute to egalitarian and sustainable international development. As stated above, I do not suggest that any organization or individual working in SDP is less than committed to positive social change through the opportunities that sport affords, and I wish to situate myself within this commitment and to employ this commitment in the service of critical analysis. At the same, I argue that situating myself as a committed contributor to SDP goes some way towards repelling the argument that critical analysis of development initiatives are akin to support for the status quo of unequal development and global poverty. Rather, following Nustad (2001), I argue that any commitment to critique is a commitment to positive change.

# 1

# Social Theory, the Sociology of Sport and the Study of SDP

## Introduction

Popular descriptions of the SDP sector often refer to 'the power of sport' as a way to conceptualize sport's contributions to international development (see Spaaij 2011). In this discourse, the utility and usefulness of sport for meeting development goals is attached, and simultaneously reduced, to the supposed essential character, organization, experience or nature of sport itself.

For critical scholars of sport, particularly those within the discipline of sports sociology, such invocations of sport are problematic, both in the ways in which they suggest and privilege a particular or universal notion of sport where many occur and the extent to which they suggest that the sporting experience is inherently positive and therefore amenable to and compatible with meeting development goals. I suggest that the notion of 'the power of sport', or that of sport as a universal language and a singular and positive basis for international development, is largely reductive in overlooking and depoliticizing the situated politics of sport and international development, respectively. It is further problematic in its positivist understandings of social activity as it suggests that affirmative benefits of SFD stand as 'proof' of sport's utility in development. The 'power of sport' discourse also tends to suggest a functionalist theoretical orientation (see Coalter 2009; Giulianotti 2004; Spaaij 2010, 2011). Structural-functionalism holds some explanatory power, for it does still yield important insights into the ways in which contemporary sport is organized and interpreted (see Loy and Booth 2004), but nevertheless the functionalist notion of sport in support of international development is limited in its explanatory ability of the process and politics that produce social change (Coalter 2009). From this perspective, 'the power of sport' within SDP is not a truth but a popular discourse subject to interpretation and negotiation (as well as resistance) and, from a research perspective, requiring of critical attention. While there may be a utility of SFD given possibilities it affords to decentre relations of dominance and normativity – for example, in relation to gender and sexuality (Saavedra 2009) – this speaks not to the power of sport itself but to sport as a cultural site at which to deconstruct relations of power.

I am advocating here for post-positivism. Even in the cases where experience suggests that sport did or does offer a convening power towards the meeting of development goals, such experiences, in the tradition of post-positivist critical sociology, are not evidence of 'truth' but rather that which call for understanding and explanation (Scott 1991). Rather than offering a means by which to apply sport to development, the notion of sport as a force for good or a universal experience amidst the challenges of international development becomes the site at which critical investigation, and in some cases deconstruction, is called for. Following Saavedra (2009), the study of SDP rests more on the critical study of relations of power as they are mobilized in and through sport, rather than the mobilization of the inherent power of sport towards development goals. The critical traditions of the sociology of sport are particularly useful in this regard and, in turn, offer an important basis for the substantive analyses of SDP programmes, policies and practices in subsequent chapters.

In this chapter, then, my central argument is as follows: Given the different meanings of sport, the situated politics of development and the social complexities of sport and development, respectively, the idea that practitioners, scholars or activists will ever know with certainty whether, where or how sport is positive or effective for meeting development goals is unrealistic and unreasonable. It is, for all intents and purposes, impossible to confidently assert the transferable conditions under which sport meets development goals or the means by and through which SFD works or not. This does not mean that sport offers nothing to the challenges of development, but rather that the reasonable and responsible goal, particularly of critical research, sport sociology and development studies, is to contextualize and politicize the role and place of sport in struggles for sustainable and equitable development. The role of SFD and the SDP sector is not essential but a constantly moving puzzle and to study sport in its complexities and contradictions calls for the deployment of multiple theories rather than a strict disciplinary adherence (see Horne 2006). To that end, this chapter offers some theoretical insights by which to better understand the SDP sector.

## Hegemony theory and the sociology of sport

Hegemony theory, and the political philosophy of Antonio Gramsci, has been a foundational tool in the sociology of sport, given its utility in illuminating the processes by which dominant ideas are (re)produced and transitioned into the realm of common sense (see Andrews and Loy 1993; Giulianotti 2005; Gruneau 1983; Hargreaves and MacDonald 2000; Rowe 2004, among others). I argue here that hegemony theory is particularly useful for the critical study of SDP because it reminds and illustrates that the social organization of sporting practices and the social and political meanings ascribed to sport are particular and the result of negotiation between actors within relations of power.

The ways in which sport is positioned in support of development, and the ways in which sport is constructed and implemented as part of development initiatives, are not an exemplary result of the power of sport but rather produced through social interactions within a cultural and political context.

In the hegemony framework, power is mobilized and implemented not through dominant ideology, conspiracy or economic determinism, but through socially negotiated processes of domination and consent. While pioneered by Gramsci, Andrews and Loy (1993) noted that Stuart Hall (1985, 1986) made a crucial contribution to the theory by using Gramsci's ideas specifically to overcome the limitations of Louis Althusser's (1969) structural ideology, which had failed to adequately account for the processes by which particular ideologies become rooted in the popular consciousness. The result was a theory significantly more dynamic, both epistemologically and practically, than allowed by previous frameworks, because of its focus on power *in process* within historically contextual material relations. Hegemony therefore, in the cultural studies tradition, offered a reconciliation of the ahistorical determinism of structuralism and the overly romanticized notions of humanism and human agency (Andrews and Loy 1993).

A foundational Gramscian study in the field of sport took place in the early 1980s. In 1983 and 1984, Alan Ingham and Stephen Hardy published two papers focused on the social utility and logic of sport within historical relations of capitalism (Hardy and Ingham 1983; Ingham and Hardy 1984). In these works, Ingham and Hardy took the questions of whether the nineteenth-century playground movement in the United States was either an example of progressive policy reform *or* a new method of social control and argued that it fit neatly into neither of these categories. Rather, they argued, any analysis of sport's emancipatory potential must account for how and why sport, as a cultural form, is repeatedly renewed through processes of negotiation between dominant and subordinate groups. Thus, they understood the playground movement to be the result of cultural interplay between owning-class reform sensibilities and working-class demands for safe opportunities to recreate physically. In turn, Ingham and Hardy argued that the use of this framework called attention to the importance of diachronic analyses of sport's social utility and a focus on the changing social context within, as well as against, capitalism. Here, they put forth that in the United States sport was intimately connected to capitalist logic, illustrated by the shift from the playground model of youth sports based on the protection of child welfare to that of 'anticipatory child labour' or sport as a means of producing future workers (Ingham and Hardy 1984: 96). In their analyses, the capitalist-informed 'pyramid' structure of sporting achievement became institutionalized to the point that concerns for 'public control' over youth recreational practices gave way to 'productive control' over children's sporting labour (Ingham and Hardy 1984: 97), an analysis illuminated by hegemony as a theory of cultural power. It is this tradition of the use of Gramscian hegemony to understand the social and political organization of physical recreation and sport that I argue is useful to the contemporary study of SDP. For scholars of SDP, hegemony helps to investigate the meanings ascribed to SFD and the ways in which these meanings are produced and constrained through negotiations within relations of power.

This does not mean, however, that hegemony, and its application to sport, is theoretically immutable or immune from critique. While hegemony has arguably constituted the dominant mode of inquiry in sport sociology over the past 25 years (an ironic 'hegemony of hegemony', Rowe 2004: 108) the utility and applicability of the hegemony framework for the study of sport has also been consistently revisited. For example, in the 1990s a series of debates took place within the *Sociology of Sport Journal* (*SSJ*) over whether a move to Chicago school anthropology would offer more to the study of sport, a debate that included a host of notable sports scholars including Ingham, Hardy, John MacAloon, John Hargreaves, Alan Tomlinson, William Morgan, Rob Beamish, Rick Gruneau and Robert Sparks.

In this debate, MacAloon (1992) and Morgan (1994, 1997) argued against hegemony as a mode of inquiry because of its limited analytical and explanatory capabilities as compared to critical ethnography. MacAloon (1992) claimed that hegemony both overemphasizes the determining capacities of the social and political modes of production and overlooks the importance of comparative understandings of meanings within cultural practice. From this perspective, hegemony as a tool for understanding international sporting practices lacks an ability to describe because, as a theory of social reproduction, it accounts for effects but not causes of social construction. Furthermore, despite its emphasis on agency and resistance within the dominance/consent relationship, hegemony offers no theoretical account of the specific mechanism by which subordinate groups wrest power from the dominant interests (MacAloon 1992). For Morgan (1994), the meanings of cultural practices, such as sport, are better understood through semiotic theory and ethnographic methodology prior to an analysis of sport's functional linkages to the modes of production. Thus, Morgan (1997) argued, hegemony supporters, in their rush to situate sport within structures of capitalism, too easily ascribe power to dominant groups resulting in the difficulty of using hegemony to perform the theoretical and explanatory tasks – resistance and counterdominance – which are its hallmarks (Morgan 1997).

Supporters of hegemony for the study of sport responded by arguing that any reduction of hegemony to a totalizing abstraction, one that overemphasized economics and failed to describe social reality, was a problem of theoretical application, not of the theory itself (Hargreaves and Tomlinson 1992). Hegemony, they argued, provides a necessary analysis of the ways in which social action is produced and constrained within material power relations, unlike ethnography that is forever trapped by the double hermeneutic of interpreting interpretations (Ingham and Beamish 1997).

These types of debates continue within current social and political theory, particularly around the concept of post-hegemony. The post-hegemony perspective suggests that Gramscian theories are insufficient to explain current cultural politics because the instability of contemporary ideology and identity destabilizes the interplay between domination and consent (see Beasley-Murray 2003). In a recent analysis of hegemony's current viability within cultural studies, Lash (2007: 56) argued that power is now largely post-hegemonic, since postmodern relations of power are constituted less through the negotiated (re)production of ideas and more through the 'logic of invention', where power itself is ontological, part of the making of the real. In this post-structuralist view, culture is not negotiated in the realm of value, as suggested by a Gramscian neo-Marxist legacy, but produced as fact (Lash 2007).

I am amenable to many post-structuralist insights. Yet I defend hegemony here because the post-hegemony framework overlooks a key point. Though few dispute the waning stability of a contemporary ideology, this does not, in and of itself, constitute a definitive argument against hegemony theory. Pessoa (2003), for example, has responded to post-hegemony by arguing that the imposition of dominant ideologies and the processes highlighted by hegemony are not reducible to one another because ideology plays only a part in the process by which the borders of hegemonic discourse are established and (re)established. The materialism of hegemony is constituted discursively, and it is these processes that continue to stand as key sites for critical inquiry. Thus, Johnson (2007) argues that what is needed is a new, and more culturally malleable, understanding of hegemony, which embraces the cultural intersections and complexities of the contemporary, 'or postmodern', moment, not the abandonment of hegemony itself.

I concur that Gramscian hegemony continues to offer an important reminder that sport, even truly global sports like football/soccer, are not benign cultural forms but the product of complex interactions between actors produced and constrained within the cultural and political economy. For example, the global popularity of football is not inherent or inevitable but a post-colonial phenomenon enabled by global capital, migration, media and marketing and corporatization (see Giulianotti 1999a). In turn, hegemony continues to offer a means by which to foreground and contextualize the concreteness – the material conditions – of inequality that define the parameters of sport and physical activity (Bairner 2009) as well as international development, a line of thinking I examine further in Chapter 2. Together, such approaches are still required because the critical ethnography and post-hegemony perspectives outlined above potentially erase such hierarchies and inequalities by a focus on the cultural meaning of sport *a priori*. Potentially overlooked, therefore, is the extent to which the cultural impact of meaning and representation is only intelligible through the 'reality' of material relations (e.g. poverty, ghettoization, war) that organize and reinforce the (inequalities of the) social world (Bailey and Gayle 2003: 91). Furthermore, as I explore in subsequent chapters, mobilizing SFD in SDP regularly assumes and (re)produces dominant ideas of sport's emancipatory potential. Such notions of sport are not apolitical but constituted as commonsense in and through cultural and material hierarchies. While reducing these hierarchies to economics or the modes of production would be problematic, as critics like Morgan (1997) have rightly argued, this need not be the case, particularly given that hegemony theory is concerned with overcoming the economic reductionism of the Marxist base/superstructure meta-narrative (Rigauer 2000).[1]

Retaining a focus on hegemony in this way does not mean that the framework should be used uncritically or be insulated from theoretical criticism and refinement. As Johnson (2007) argues, a responsible and accurate application of hegemony (in this case, to the study of SDP) must take into account how contemporary material hierarchies are constituted in and through an *array* of social and cultural components, beyond merely the economic and class-based, but including also race, gender, sexuality, globalization, neocolonial relations and even seemingly apolitical institutions such as rights-based development. For example, the neoliberal ethic of 'individual choice and personal consumption' that substantiates global economic systems simultaneously informs relations of dominance through transnational interpenetrations with race and gender in the post-colonial (Grewal 2005). Even universal human rights – a framework with an explicit mandate to supersede social and material hierarchies – regularly fail to transcend hegemonic relations since not all (aboriginal people, homeless, suspects in the war on terror) are afforded 'the right to human rights' or the political and economic capital to exercise these rights (see Teeple 2005). Thus, hegemony is only reductive, economically or otherwise, if used in a reductive manner. The utility of hegemony is in its ability to account for the ways in which social processes – including relationships, techniques and knowledge production – within a class society secure the position of dominant groups through the ideological establishment of inequality as 'commonsense' (Giulianotti 2005: 49). As sociologists of sport have examined, sport is precisely produced within these kinds of relationships, which is a crucial theoretical insight given the mobilization of SFD through SDP, ostensibly to redress development inequalities.[2]

In sum, the mobilization of sport needs to be understood within relations of power (as does the notion and practice of development itself). These relations of power are not conspiratorial but do call for explication. Even in the cases where sport has been found to be a positive force for progressive social change or meeting local demands for development (see Fokwang 2009; Kay 2009; Lindsey and Grattan, in press), given the historical and political economy and the place of sport therein, critical scholars should resist the tendency to view the meanings or structures of sport as politically transcendent or mobilized within benign social relations. While hegemony theory constitutes the primary focus of this text, sport also becomes 'bio-political' when produced and constrained within a mandate of empowerment, progress and social change, an insight derived from the Foucauldian tradition of sport studies.

## Foucauldian understandings of power and/in sport

While hegemony theory in the Gramscian tradition remains an important framework for critical studies of sport and physical culture, the work of Michel Foucault has also featured prominently within the sociology of sport. In particular, Foucauldian theorizing has been employed by sports scholars to make sense of the intersections of power/knowledge that privilege and secure bodily practices and regimes of discipline (see Andrews 1993; Cole, Giardina and Andrews 2004; Markula and Pringle 2006; Rail and Harvey 1995, among others). Whereas Gramsci theorized the struggles and negotiations between social and political actors, Foucault's project can be summarized as focused on the production of knowledge within fields of study and how such knowledge 'acts to construct humans as particular objects ... and how humans subsequently become subject to those scientific truths' (Markula and Pringle 2006: 9). Rather than providing a blueprint for political revolution, Foucault offered a methodology for social critique and ethical reflection (Tamboukou and Ball 2002), and an exploration of the tools for political action over prescriptions for change (Markula and Pringle 2006: 18). This makes concepts of bio-politics and governmentality, as well as discourse, important to the study of SDP, particularly given recent critical studies of international development (Asher 2009; Li 2007) that offer important blueprints for marrying Gramsci and Foucault in productive ways.

Bio-power is one of Foucault's lasting contributions to the social sciences. Foucault (1978) illustrated how the emergence of discourses of sexuality in Europe in the nineteenth century constituted a project fundamental to the cultivation of the bourgeois subject. In this analysis, the production of subjectivity was intricately tied to the power to intervene in the knowledge of how one should live (cf. Stoler 1995: 83). Foucault focused on the manner in which power over life was deployed across two poles of society: the disciplining of bodies and the regulation of populations. It was within this framework that he made the historical/genealogical distinction between the sovereign right 'to take life or let live' and the bio-political power 'to make live and let die', establishing a difference between the traditional power that dominated populations or managed bodies through force and the power to confer bio-political change through self-affirmation (Foucault 1978: 241). Such a change could only take place within a society permeated and structured by bio-power, a political technology that 'brought life and its mechanism into the realm of explicit calculations and made knowledge/power an agent of transformation of human life' (Foucault 1978: 143). The traditional, sovereign right to intervene into the management of the population through the threat or use of physical force was replaced by new forms of bio-power that linked knowledge and power to the 'making' of life and lives.

The power/knowledge of sport's utility for meeting goals of international development infuses sport with the bio-political power to change life. Sport becomes linked to biophysical benefits for bodies that participate in physical activity or exercise, social and personal rewards of esteem and teamwork, and even economic spin-offs for communities and populations at large. Sport and play as fundamental human rights within the SDP sector potentially constitute regimes of discipline and regularization that align with the bio-political power to make life and can be understood as a manifestation of sport's positivity or the ability to motivate rather than punish or repress (Cole, Giardina and Andrews 2004). Bio-power connects development to sport because both sport and development are understood to be sites at which life is made, where life is improved, and where the body and the population are made better. As a result of this mobilization, sport – discursively intelligible as socially beneficial and culturally normative – gains legitimacy through bio-power, imbued with the ability to motivate individuals to transform life through sport-based processes of body management.

Foucault's insights into regimes and logic of bio-politics are useful to the study of SDP in at least two ways. First, neoliberalism as a political philosophy and approach to international development remains central, if not hegemonic, in the twenty-first century and in turn is intimately connected to the SDP sector (also see Levermore 2009). The Foucauldian tradition is crucial for illustrating the logic of, and connections between, bio-politics and governmentality – meaning the 'conduct of conduct' – within the neoliberal milieu.[3]

Second, a recurring theme in SDP logic is that of power in its productive sense – often termed 'empowerment' – by which SDP stakeholders often refer to the use of sport to encourage and support positive change in others. Through a Foucauldian lens, such invocations are not inherently repressive, but neither are they merely the benign mobilization or transference of power from one group or person to another. Rather, empowerment is a relation of power/knowledge and intimately tied to the governmental organization of the individual and population via the conduct of conduct. As such, practices of 'empowerment' call for critical analysis of the political economy and social context in which they are championed or even normalized.

Within SDP, therefore, empowerment constitutes a 'discourse' or discursive formation. In the Foucualdian tradition, discourse analysis asks 'how is this possible' more than 'what is here' (Tamboukou and Ball 2002). Discourse is

LIVERPOOL JOHN MOORES UNIVERSITY
LEARNING SERVICES

not a translation between reality and language, but instead it speaks to the practices that shape perceptions of reality (Markula and Pringle 2006: 31). To employ discourse within a research project is not to eschew cultural politics but rather to argue for more complex analyses of power and politics as compared to Marxist ideology, which, for the most part, limited political scrutiny to class struggle (Mills 1997). Discourse encourages explication, and where appropriate deconstruction, of the intelligibility and logic of power/knowledge and social relations rather than attempts at 'revealing' ideological truths concealed by politics. In the case of SDP, sport is never simply a tool of benevolence or emancipation, nor is it always put into practice in the act of colonizing and dominating.

## Gramsci and Foucault: Neo-Marxist discourse

In the previous two sections, I explored the usefulness of theory in the tradition of Gramsci and Foucault for understanding relations of power in sport and, in turn, for critical understandings of the mobilization of SFD within SDP. Such invocations beg for some measure of reconciliation, given the differences in understandings of power between the Gramscian and Foucauldian tradition in the sociology of sport (see Pringle 2005). Specifically, I argue that the two traditions are compatible, particularly in relation to what Torfing (1999: 36) has referred to as the 'essentialist residue' in Gramsci's reworking of Marx and the legacy of hegemony theory in sociology.

According to Torfing (1999: 37), despite his attempts to re-dress Marxist determinism, Gramsci nonetheless understood the economy to be an 'ontological anchorage point' within the constitution of relations of domination and modes of resistance. While succeeding in overcoming class reductionism, Gramsci's consideration of class unities (i.e. dominant vs subordinate) still required a homogenous concept of the economy as an entity governed by its own systems and logic. However, this reliance on an essentialist economy breaks down (particularly considering post-structuralism) if one considers the economy itself to be socially contestable and political. In Torfing's (1999: 37) words 'if the economy was itself political, it would fail to provide an objective grounding for the political' as required by hegemony theory.

Given this limit in classic hegemony theory, Torfing (1999) builds on the contributions of Ernesto Laclau and Chantal Moffe who theorized the economy *as a discursive formation* both constituted by the social and implicated in sociopolitical relations and claims to knowledge. In other words, economic relations constitute 'a terrain for the articulation of discourses of authority and management, technical discourses, discourses of accountancy, discourses of information, etc.' (Torfing 1999: 39).[4] From this critique, the clear avenue for critical inquiry is to discourse, where signification extends without end because of the absence of a universal signified of the economy (Torfing 1999: 40). Discourse, therefore, can be understood as a 'decentred structure' in which regimes of knowledge are constantly negotiated (Torfing 1999: 40).

This is by now a familiar refrain. Hardt and Negri (2000), for example, have theorized contemporary geopolitics in which a centre of power can no longer be clearly identified, let alone ascribed to the stability of the nation state (see Darnell 2010b). For Hardt and Negri (2000), there is no centre and there are no borders, only regimes of truth that are increasingly (bio-)political and implicated in the production of the material conditions of everyday life. Discourse analysis of such politics pushes one to consider how literally every element of the material, including the body itself, is intelligible in and through the decentred negotiation of meaning (see Rose 2007).

I argue that this theorizing works as an updating of Gramsci, rather than a disavowal. Instead of supporting essentialist notions of class character and social identity, hegemonic relations take on a constitutive role, intimately tied to all social identity, including class (Torfing 1999: 42). It also supports a compound standpoint theory in which three seemingly competing interpretations of oppression – cultural, material and discursive – are simultaneously useful yet incomplete, given their inability to account for multiple standpoints of social subjugation (De Lissovoy 2008a). De Lissovoy (2008a: 102) argues that it is not only possible but also optimal to 'combine them as complementary evidences of an overarching social violence' if one is to make connections between their intersections. In other words, hegemony and discourse are mutually conditioned (Torfing 1999: 43), and the meanings produced in and through discourse are social and political, not logical or natural, and constitute the simultaneous conditions of possibility and impossibility in society (Torfing 1999: 44).

Discourse analysis in this tradition is useful for making sense of international development and SDP initiatives, particularly through the logic of neoliberalism. Harvey (2007: 22) describes contemporary neoliberalism as a hegemonic discourse, divergent in its applications but dominant in linking discursive notions of freedom and democracy to the primacy of markets and limited state intervention.[5] Ong (2006: 3) similarly suggests that neoliberalism rests on capitalist logic but increasingly reflects (Foucauldian) regimes of governmentality, based on notions of individual responsibility within the management of the population. That is, whereas neoliberal policies originally focused on the reorganization of the economy (i.e. structural adjustment programmes, discussed in Chapter 2), contemporary, or second-wave, neoliberalism extends to the production of subjects, through the privileging of the (economic) logic of efficiency and the (ethical) logic of self-responsibility (Ong 2006: 11). Neoliberalism also extends into international development given that the democratic limits of globalized capitalism, evidenced by the inability of the market to produce material benefits for all, are regularly reduced to bio-political issues of ineffective conduct amongst marginalized groups (Li 2007: 273).

The discursive weight of neoliberalism is further evident to the extent that it solidifies the sanctity of 'economism' as the most efficient and cost-effective response to international development inequalities (Gasper 2004). For example, the conception, design and implementation of the United Nation's millennium development goals were accompanied by the United Nation's insistence upon institutional reform to promote trade deregulation and support the flow of global capital (Cammack 2006). According to Cammack (2006: 234), it 'is not just that this project is imperialist, but that it represents imperialism in the most advanced form currently conceivable'. I take this 'advanced form' to refer to the extent to which the logic of the boons of capitalism – central to the cultural and political organization of physical recreation and sporting practices historically (see Ingham and Hardy 1984) – is, in the contemporary moment, socially 'productive' in the ways it underpins a range of social and political institutions as commonsense and commonplace. This now includes, at least to an extent, international development and the utility of sport therein. In other words, neoliberalism, as a market-informed basis of social organization, underpins the bio-political organization of contemporary citizenship (Ong 2006: 13) and is discursive in its intelligibility *and* hegemonic in its political recurrence (Li 2007).

I do recognize the concerns raised by scholars like Pringle (2005) about the uncritical combination of Gramscian and Foucauldian, given that hegemony implies direction and purpose within relations between class-based ruling and subordinate groups, whereas a focus on discourse rejects any such duality. I contend, however, that my referencing of the Gramscian tradition, and insistence on questions of cultural materialism in understanding SDP, need not dismiss the utility of discourse analysis or Foucauldian theories of power/ knowledge. Instead, I focus on the ways in and the extent to which hegemonic relations underpin the discursive construction of current understandings of the 'power of sport' within the momentum towards SDP. Such discourses can support relations of dominance (Grewal 2005). This follows other recent analyses (Jacobs 1996; Li 2007; N. Razack 2003) that have successfully employed Gramsci and Foucault in combination in order to produce intimate and nuanced accounts. As Jacobs (1996: 29) argues, 'it is not solely that discursively constituted notions of identity have material effects' but also that the stark material inequalities of the contemporary, and post-colonial, moment should inform critical analyses.

Indeed, international development activities, like those within SDP, are optimal cultural and political sites at which to combine the insights of Gramsci and Foucault (Li 2007: 25) because development is replete with relations of power that are coercive (in Gramscian terms) but also enabling (following Foucault). In her study of development politics in Colombia, Asher (2009) argues that state formation was produced through a discourse of modernization and micro-practices of governmentality (rather than state rule) but that such processes were necessarily produced and constrained by coercive and formative state power. Such results suggest that both Foucault and Gramsci assist in the critical analysis of development to the extent that they both show 'that people accept and spontaneously consent to the modes of domination prevalent in society' (Asher 2009: 93). Or, as Li (2007: 25–6) argues, in the study of development, '[p]owers that are multiple cannot be totalizing and seamless … exposing how power works, unsettling truths so that they could be scrutinized and contested, was as central to the political agenda of Foucault as it was for Gramsci'.

Therefore, despite calls for the abandonment of Gramsci, and the embracing of contemporary power relations as 'post-hegemonic', the Gramscian necessity of connecting theory to material history remains (Bairner 2009: 198).[6] In response, I argue for a neo-Gramscian theory of discourse in which geopolitical relations of dominance (mediated through bio-politics and bio-based economics) produce globalized, institutional understandings of the need to integrate socially marginalized populations into the neoliberal system. Such understandings can be further informed by post-colonial theory.

## Sport, race and the post-colonial

From a global perspective, sport 'is an eminently postcolonial phenomenon' (Bale and Cronin 2003: 4), given that its current forms and popularity are propagated by a historical colonial residue. A host of recent studies have drawn attention to the parallels between contemporary SDP and the historical mobilization of sport within the European colonial project as a means to support or foster social improvement or the education of Others (see Guest 2009; Saavedra 2009). At the least, then, the current mobilization of sport through SDP to meet development goals, or the functionalist notion of sport as a tool of development, is implicated in post-colonial history. This is particularly the case in moments when the universality of sport in SDP is referenced without attendant recognition of the role of colonialism in the construction of sports like football/soccer as globally popular (not to mention the maintenance of football's global popularity through contemporary economic and cultural globalization in ways that might be thought of as neocolonial, see Maguire 2008). As a result, critical analyses of SDP are beholden to reconciling the post-coloniality of sport within the post-colonial politics and spaces of development (see McEwan 2009). At least three connections can be made.

First and foremost, understanding the global popularity of particular sporting forms (like football/soccer but also cricket, and even basketball) to be a product, at least in part, of the history of colonialism leads to the necessity of critical analyses of the ways in which such post-colonial histories shape contemporary relations of power within sport and SDP. While sporting forms like football or cricket have undoubtedly been reclaimed or even reinvented culturally by people and nations within the post-colonial context, the idea that they are empty cultural forms with politically neutral histories (MacAloon 1996) is problematic for the ways in which it underplays the relations of power – the hegemonic formations – in which such reclamations of post-colonial sport take place. Furthermore, historical myopia of sport and colonialism, even in the well-intentioned support of cultural and political agency, depoliticizes the ways in which contemporary development initiatives potentially align with colonial logic or constitute a neocolonizing practice.

This kind of post-colonial theoretical scrutinizing of sport within SDP does not and should not require privileging relativist perspectives on development through 'protecting' cultural forms (like sport) from 'invading' development forces. Contemporary development politics and practices are inevitably more complicated than an invade/resist binary, particularly along post-colonial lines (Asher 2009). Relapsing into a universal/relativist debate is unnecessary in contemporary development studies, given the necessity of change and the globalization of development politics (Gasper 2004). What does remain important, though, is the understanding that sport itself is subject to post-colonial relations of power and that these relations are likely exacerbated, and therefore more important, amidst the transnational politics of SDP.

This leads to the second insight, namely that post-colonial theory is useful not only for understanding how a history of colonialism informs contemporary social and political life but also, following Stoler (2002), for recognizing that the colonies constituted a site at which knowledge of the metropole, and its attendant cultures and subjectivities, was constructed. In Stoler's analysis, the discursive regularities of sexuality spelled out by Foucault (1978) were not produced in Europe alone but rather 'through a more *circuitous* route' (Stoler 2002: 144, emphasis in text) that included relations, particularly with race and racialized bodies, in the colonies. The colonies constituted a testing ground from which tightly bound discourses of sex in Europe *and* in the colonies built upon one another in the production and affirmation of bourgeois subjectivity. Key tenets of contemporary northern culture (i.e. liberalism, nationalism and citizenship) are thus a result, at least in part, of successful social experiments played out in the colonies (Stoler 2002: 147). Such insights encourage us to think of SDP not only as a potential (though never inherent) site of neocolonialism but also, more intimately, as a sector in which sport and its attendant subjectivities are now being (re)created and conceptualized in response to development challenges. In my interviews with interns who served within the SDP sector, their knowledge of sport and its organization and social utility were often challenged within the field of SDP, an experience that aligns with Stoler's post-colonial history.

Finally, then, the post-colonial perspective, particularly as supported by the insights of transnational feminism, draws attention to the connection between sport, race and racism. As Stoler (1995) showed through her reformulation of Foucault, race did not simply result from the colonial context as a means of accounting for and dealing with racial Others; rather, racism was *fundamental* to the affirmation of European, bourgeois subjects, particularly through its interlocking with other markers of difference such as sexuality, gender and class. In turn, sport can be understood as a site at which racialized differences are recognized and marked, and where cultural cues or attributes of sporting competency such as athleticism, character or discipline are reified in racialized terms (see Hylton 2009). As I have argued previously (Darnell, 2010b) social encounters within SDP are complicated by race and the 'colonial continuities' (see Heron 2007) that SDP affords. A post-colonial perspective keeps such critical questions at the fore.

I revisit post-colonial theories of international development in Chapter 2. Here, it is reasonable to summarize that a post-colonial perspective on sport is called for within critical studies of SDP, not only in recognition of the colonial history of global sport itself but also, and perhaps more importantly, as a means of analysing how notions of 'the power of sport' in support of development may serve to depoliticize the relationships between sport and post-colonialism. Such theoretical and practical manoeuvres likely serve to sustain contemporary global hierarchies rather than challenge them in moving towards prosperity and equality for the world's marginalized people.

## Sport and/as human rights

Finally, a theoretical understanding of the connections between sport and human rights is called for. Above, I argued that the political construction and legitimacy of the contemporary SDP sector rests, at least in part, on the notion of sport, and particularly sport participation, as a universal human right. In recent years, a host of researchers have explored the connections between sport and human rights (see Donnelly 2008; Giulianotti 1999b, 2004; Jarvie 2006; Kidd and Donnelly 2000; Kidd and Eberts 1982) and effectively made the case that sport and human rights are not mutually exclusive, in theory or in practice. As Jarvie (2006: 365) argues, '[i]t is not necessary to view the issue of human rights as divorced or separate from the world of sport'. Giulianotti (1999b) put forth a three-point framework for conceptualizing this relationship: (1) Access to sport constitutes a human right in itself, evidenced, at least in part, by Article 1 of the UNESCO international charter proclaiming physical education and sport as fundamental to each person; (2) sport organizations proclaim and promote human rights through fair and respectful competition, seen most notably within the ideals of the Olympic movement; and (3) sport, development and human rights share a historical-political association, both within the context of imperialism where sport served as a vehicle of colonial interests (cf. Baker and Mangan 1987) and as a possible means of emancipation and liberation where such freedoms have been politically and/or socially denied.

It is the latter point that has piqued the interest of SFD activists and scholars. From this perspective, sport and human rights are connected principally because the notions of democracy and liberation central to a human rights framework cannot be achieved without the realization of human rights in sport and physical education (Kidd and Donnelly 2000). Achieving human rights in sport would include both social democracy of sports participation, characterized by access and opportunities for all persons, as well as the freedom *within* sport cultures for persons to participate in diverse ways (Kidd and Donnelly 2000). In this way, advocating for human rights in sports combines a focus on the right to participate with the recognition of the diversity of movement and body cultures around the world (Maguire 2006). In fact, despite evidence that sport has been complicit in the denial of human rights,[7] its potential as a tool to promote and solidify the rights of citizens is often considered too great to dismiss (see Sidoti 1999).

At the same time, human rights and sport are linked because of the opportunity that sport affords to advocate for the realization of universal rights (Kidd and Donnelly 2000), a political logic clearly evident in SDP. Prior to the recent increase in the institutionalization or solidification of the SDP sector, the best-known example of rights advocacy through sport was the boycott of South African sports federations and national teams as a protest against the racist practices and policies that restricted sports participation for the non-White majority under the apartheid regime. Kidd and Donnelly (2000: 138) argue that the ensuing isolation of pro-apartheid sports federations constituted 'powerful symbolic condemnation' that contributed to the fall of the regime. In turn, the end of apartheid offered an opportunity to mobilize sport as a tool for development and therefore was a significant precursor to the emergence of the SDP sector, insofar as it became reasonable and intelligible to argue that marginalized people (such as Black South Africans) possessed an inalienable right to participate in sport and physical activity (Kidd 2008: 374).

With this in mind, one can argue that the notion of human rights underpins the current SDP sector in at least two ways: First, opportunities to be physically active and to participate in sport are considered rights owed to all, and programmes, interventions and activism under the banner of SDP strive to support marginalized persons and communities in the realization of these rights. Second, sport is understood and recognized as a tool for the realization of human rights, primarily through the mobilization of funds, the development of infrastructure and as an entry point and catalyst for education, health promotion and youth development. Qualter Berna (2006: 37) summarizes this dual connection between sport and human rights in SDP in her analysis of sport as a right and a development tool:

> We know sport works. We know its inherent value in addressing the well-being of children and ensuring their happiness. Sport is every child's right to play ... But sport is also a means to an end.

While Qualter Berna's positioning of sport as both a right and a tool towards social democracy and youth development is laudable, it is, at the same time, important to recognize that there are limits to human rights as a politically progressive framework and therefore as the fundamental basis and justification for social change within the organization of sport and the SDP sector. Here, I draw on Teeple's (2005) use of social and political theory to problematize the 'universality' of human rights. While often proclaimed as politically and/or culturally transcendent, human rights are, more accurately, the basis of a civil contract that individualizes citizens, connects personal freedom to ownership and reflects the historical dominance of a capitalist system (Teeple 2005). From this perspective, human rights serve to bestow citizens with rights as possessions but do little to enable or empower citizens to realize or enact these rights. For example, the right to peaceful assembly means little as a right without a concomitant infrastructure to facilitate political congress. Rights cannot be separated from the social relations of dominance that undermine equality and self-determination. However, given the general acceptance of universal human rights within a progressive social framework, rights can, in some cases, be used to obscure power relations that lead to the exploitation of workers, the poor, persons of colour who may be over-determined by their race and other marginalized groups. In the case of the SDP sector, simply recognizing or bestowing rights to sport participation may do little to support persons and communities in the struggle against the broader social and political inequality that prevented their participation in sport in the first place (also see Gruneau, in press).

In addition, the individual 'freedoms' that human rights protect often support the corporate autonomy necessary for international exploitation of marginalized groups within capitalist relations. This suggests that the system of universal human rights serves as part of a 'global enabling framework' of mobile transnational capitalism (Teeple 2005: 19). Sport is far from exempt from such relations. While sport participation is justifiably considered a right owed to all, global sporting forms are also closely 'tied to the opening of new markets and the commodification of cultures' (Maguire 2006: 111). In this sense, enabling mass participation in globally popular sports such as soccer/ football through SDP programmes fails to challenge, and in fact may further facilitate, the continuously unequal flows of global capital that contribute to the 'underdevelopment' of LMICs. In fact, as Kidd (2008: 376) rightly points out, the need to focus on, and advocate for, sport as a human right stems in large part from diminished social welfare policies and structural inequalities characteristic of contemporary neoliberal/neoconservative political regimes. Yet, because of its reliance on universal human rights, the SDP sector rarely addresses these underlying political issues. Similarly, Gruneau (in press) contends that SDP aligns with the expansion of a rights-based culture, more so than with political struggles or resistance against the politics of unequal development.

Democratizing sport or using sport to further a human rights agenda is not easily done. Attempts to address issues of human rights in/through sport have often tended towards neocolonialism through, for example, the continual dismissal of aboriginal sporting cultures and/or the privileging of high-performance sporting systems that exclude mass participation to the benefits of elite athletes and performance maximization (see Donnelly 2008).[8] In sum, positioning sport as a human right does not necessarily offer a stable or progressive political basis for the SDP sector or usurp the power relations that sustain inequality and potentially threaten cultural autonomy. In fact, leaning on sport as a human right, and using sport to advocate for human rights, as the conceptual and practical bases of SDP initiatives potentially can overlook the sociopolitical and ethical complications of 'doing' development, or of SDP practice. Such tensions are worth exploring within the ongoing critical analysis of SFD and SDP.

## Conclusions: Implications for studying SDP

In this chapter, I have explored social theory – particularly in the tradition of the sociology of sport – that has implications for an ongoing, critically informed analysis of SDP. Three points, in particular, can be gleaned from this chapter. First and foremost, the discipline of sport sociology illustrates that the analysis of sport, including its practice and its organization (and also now including SDP), is in substantive ways the study of power. That is, even when sport is understood to foster a productive and positive social experience, such results still beg for analysis and understanding of how they are negotiated, produced and constrained within hierarchical relations.

In turn, and second, the study of sport through the social theories I have advocated here reminds of the limitations – theoretical, representational and empirical – of 'essentialized' sporting forms or experiences. Despite claims of the universality of sport as a basis for SDP, sport is always interpreted and reconciled at both macro- and micro-levels, and therefore holds different meanings in different contexts. Finally, then, for the study of SDP, such theoretically informed perspectives on sport point away from a focus on the application of sport to meeting development goals and towards questions of the politics of development as they are negotiated within SDP. Performing such analyses, I suggest, calls for understandings of the various history and politics of international development in which sport is now implicated through the SDP sector. This history and politics constitute the focus of Chapter 2.

# 2

# International Development Studies and SDP

## Syntheses and opportunities

### Introduction

SDP as a focus of research can benefit from the sociopolitical insights and critical traditions of development studies. From this perspective, overlooking the history of international development and its attendant politics and policies, or attempting to 'reinvent' development theory in the study or practice of SDP, is at the best unnecessary and at worst problematic because it neglects the origins of development inequalities and the contestations regarding how development should be conceptualized and implemented. Furthermore, while approaches to research and practice based on critical theory versus those based on best practices are not mutually exclusive, a focus on practice *at the expense of* power and politics may fail to examine how power and dominance structure the goals, desires, practices and outcomes of international development.

In this chapter, I explore critical issues in development history, power, politics, ideology and ethics, issues then attended to more empirically and substantively in subsequent chapters. I take the politics of development as a basis from which to argue for understandings of development inequalities and 'equality of condition' (Baker *et al.* 2004) as a, if not the, focus for practices of SDP. As Targett and Wolfe (2010) have argued, despite important contributions, a critical mass of SDP research has yet to be achieved, meaning that the 'field' of SDP research remains largely unformulated. This chapter, in response, offers a contribution to staking out a more coherent and politicized field of SDP theory and research by exploring the history and practice of development, and its associated critical analyses, and connecting this scholarship to the current preponderance of SFD.

To do so, the chapter draws on the tradition of critical theory as a way of making sense of social and political operations rather than a strict 'problem-solving' approach. The explication of this distinction is generally attributed to the work of Cox and Sinclair (1996) who argued for the need for critical theory in the study of international relations in order to move beyond the limits of a positivist-based, problem-solving orientation. Cox argued that in the study of social politics and political action, positivism presupposes and tacitly supports a natural, rational state of human actors that underplays subjectivities, histories and the agency of various actors. Instead, Cox showed that relations of social and political power are not inherent, as suggested in a neo-realist approach, but the product of the interplay between individuals and the various institutional forces of the social and political economy. A critical approach is therefore needed to understand how these relations are constituted and their implication for social and political life. Cox's foundational framework is useful in this chapter, and those that follow, for at least five reasons.

First, choosing critical theory over problem solving aligns with the stated goal of this text to construct a better theoretical understanding of the current underpinnings, and the political orientations and limitations, of employing and mobilizing SFD. This book does not set out to solve the development problems of the world through sport and physical activity but to analyse critically how various relations of unequal power and inequality are manifest and how to theorize sport in relation to these inequalities. Second, Cox's approach to theory aligns with the general Gramscian orientation of this text. As Cox illustrated, Gramscian hegemony provides an important basis from which to counter the limits of positivism as discussed in Chapter 1. In turn, and third, Cox's perspective calls for and requires a historicized understanding of social and political phenomena in order to understand the conditions and processes through which relations of power are constructed, a method that I embrace in this analysis. In the previous chapters, I have offered brief historical overviews of sport in the name of the social good and of hegemony in the analysis of sport; in this chapter I offer a brief historical overview of international development so that we may better situate the politics of development in relation to sport-based initiatives. Fourth, then, it is important to recognize the extent to which Cox's framework has been taken up in critical understandings of development and development inequalities. Here, I draw primarily on the work of Payne (2005) who has employed Cox's insights to explore the historical and political underpinnings of development inequalities. Cox's approach offers 'the most appropriate *starting point*' for the critical analysis of the political economy of unequal development (Payne 2005: 19, emphasis in text) because it offers a means through which to understand how and why particular nations, regions, populations and social groups have experienced development so radically differently, particularly since the end of Second World War. This framework moves beyond positivist, neo-realist approaches that might understand such inequalities as nearly ontological and rejects the notion that there 'simply are' people in parts of the world that are 'underdeveloped'. Finally, then, I argue that despite the preferred orientation towards critical theory over a problem-solving approach, we need not abandon the notion of positive change in and through the use and application of critical analyses. To do so, though, requires an understanding of the various ways in which power is exercised in international development, both in the broader political sphere and on the ground or in the field. Given this orientation, the theoretical explication of development in this chapter is purposively both macro and micro in its focus and application. The macro-analysis of SDP, based on historical, theoretical and political perspectives and critiques, aligns with, and is supported by, the microanalysis that primarily examines bodies, encounters and experiences.

In sum, the politics of SFD are evident in that the SDP sector rarely, in my analysis, strives to challenge, resist, destroy and/or rebuild the cultural and political economy of development inequalities (and/or the cultural and political economy of sport), in more equitable ways, nor does it regularly support or advocate for interventions that strive to level the playing field of the political economy (an argument that I examine in more detail in Chapter 4). Rather, the dominant ideology of SDP attempts (with some notable exceptions) to improve the welfare of 'Others' within the structures of merit-based achievement, or liberal egalitarianism (Baker *et al.* 2004), an orientation that in turn supports the current culture of sport and political economy of development. (These are structures and relations in which, it must be said, the staunchest SDP advocates have often enjoyed success and by which they disproportionately benefit.) To contextualize this argument, I offer, in the next section, a brief historical overview of international development and its precepts and practices.

## A short history of development practice and theory

A short history of the dominant political and institutional machinations of international development is called for here for at least three reasons: First, as Wainwright (2008) has argued, the historical politics of development as they were manifest through colonial practices, the state, the internationalization of civil society and the contemporary globalization of economics, can and should be read as a form of power and its operation. Conceptions of international development as 'apolitical' are impossible to justify; the broader politics of development are to be embraced and articulated in any reasonable analysis of its practice. Understanding the history of development therefore supports our understanding of its contemporary operations amid relations of power. This, in turn, dovetails with Biccum's (2010) assertion that theories of a 'new' development politics and practice often elide the historical complexities of development. Such claims to novelty overlook, and even obscure, the continuities and outright continuations between historical colonial practices that worked to assert northern dominance and contemporary development initiatives that arguably do little to upset or challenge these relations of dominance and consent.[1] Third, then, given that the SDP sector tends to be led and championed by stakeholders from the domain of sport, at least more so than the development sector, it is important to recognize that, from the perspective of development studies, sport people are arriving somewhat late to the development game (Black 2010; Kidd 2008).

The genesis of the contemporary era and discourse of international development is often traced to 20th January 1949, when Harry Truman delivered his inaugural address as president of the United States and spoke of the need for economic, social and political improvements in the world's 'underdeveloped areas'.[2] Truman's speech followed shortly after the international agreements at Bretton Woods in 1944 that led to the organization of the International Monetary Fund (IMF), the World Bank and later the General Agreement on Tariffs and Trade (GATT), which became the World Trade Organization (WTO) (see Payne 2005; Therien 1999). The 'Bretton Woods approach' has come to represent an orientation to development based on the importance, if not primacy, of economic liberalization and free trade and to stand in general opposition to the UN development paradigm, which tends to view development primarily as an issue of unequal distribution of resources (Therien 1999). Truman's address contributed to emerging discourses of development particularly by urging the United States and other northern, democratic and 'developed' nations to commit to increasing opportunities for production and prosperity among the world's poor. His address marked a turning point in the social and cultural history of development (Escobar 1995; Esteva 1992; Sachs 1992) and a watershed for the first wave of a global development project, an epoch characterized by three themes of late modern capitalism – decolonization, rationality and development – and influenced by free market economics and positivist social science (Sylvester 1999).

Truman symbolically and practically imbued development with specific meanings, centring capital, science and technology as the foci of a global revolution designed to meet the challenges posed by global poverty, high morbidity due to preventable causes, poor health care and lack of access to education, among others (Escobar 1995). Thus, Truman's speech is often considered the genesis of 'developmentalism', a modernist paradigm that, in its various incarnations, espoused three main perspectives: (1) an essentialist view of the 'developing world' and its members as a homogenous group, (2) an unyielding belief in progress and the modernization of society and (3) the centrality of the nation state as a focal point and lead participant in the development process (Schuurman 2001).[3] International development post-Second World War can thus be understood as an era dominated by modernization theory, underpinned primarily by notions of linear growth and sociopolitical improvement (Nederveen Pieterse 2001). This deeply political, and in some cases, neocolonial movement linked national imaginations of progress with ideologies of economic-based manifest destiny.

However, development interventions led by northern organizations and supported by a developmentalist framework generally failed more often than not to secure sustainable material development for the world's relatively impoverished (Bartoli and Unesco 2000). In fact, the social marginalization of the poor and destitute increased amidst developmentalism and solidified a geopolitical divide of prosperity between those classified as 'developed' and 'underdeveloped' (Escobar 1995). Even the staunchest supporters of the Bretton Woods paradigm were forced to recognize the entrenchment of extreme poverty despite increases in the size of the global economy (Payne 2005). In this way, developmentalism, as both a theoretical approach to conceptualizing development and a practical approach to development initiatives, experienced significant crises, emanating from the critical claims that it was ahistorical and apolitical in regard to global relations of power, that it constructed and sustained a rational scientific approach to development politics, that it contributed to the creation of the very notion of the Third World and its developed, Western opposite and that it merely 'picked up' the traditional colonial discourse of 'stewardship' and re-mobilized it as a neocolonial discourse of 'development' (Nederveen Pieterse 2010: 27–8).

One school of critical thought that responded strongly to the limitations of developmentalist initiatives was dependency theory, or *dependencia*, influenced by Marxist and neo-Marxist theory (some borrowed from the Global North) and championed by scholars from Latin American countries that had experienced developmentalism first-hand. *Dependencia* did not abandon a modernist political ethic but did argue that the marginalization of the Third World owed much to the destructive results of hegemonic capitalism supported by, and through, the developed world (Sylvester 1999). *Dependencia* showed how developmentalism tended to construct the Third World as a cultural caricature, with no claim to history prior to northern penetration (Slater 1993). The most important feature of *dependencia*, however, may have been that it provided evidence of the South 'theorizing back', such as in Latin America where critics argued that the 'evolution' of thought within developmentalist-style modernism included the southern hemisphere and that southern cultures deserved recognition for their role in development processes (cf. Slater 1993; Zea 1970).

The resulting tension between developmentalism as a solution to Third World poverty and *dependencia* as a reply to global economic systems led to an impasse in development practices and the end of the first wave of development (Schuurman 1993). The resulting morass provided an opportunity for new approaches to development, and the second wave of development came to be characterized by Western notions of neoliberalism,[4] advocating decreased state interventions and increased market freedoms within a global economy intended to alleviate rural poverty in developing countries (Slater 2004). Underpinned by the Washington Consensus and the leadership of Ronald Reagan and Margaret Thatcher, supporters of neoliberalism established a hegemony in global institutions like the World Bank and IMF and supported a Washington-led approach to global development and an ahistorical analysis of the poverty and marginalization of particular nations (Payne 2005). The neoliberal wave of development claimed to elevate the poor and relatively powerless to the level of rational actors, free from the constraints of government policy (Sylvester 1999). However, neoliberalism devastated developing economies, due in large part to the failures of economic-based structural adjustment programmes, which became the official policy of the World Bank in the early 1980s and made fiscal and policy requirements, or 'adjustments', a condition of lending (see Rapley 1996; Slater 1993, 2004). Eventually, the fundamental orthodoxy of neoliberalism established through the Washington Consensus was softened under the relatively moderate approaches of the Post-Washington Consensus during the years of Bill Clinton/Tony Blair and amidst internal criticisms of World Bank policy and effectiveness by the likes of economist Joseph Stiglitz (Payne 2005). Still, the Post-Washington Consensus maintained the basic principles of market economics, and as understood in the terms of Gramscian hegemony, incorporated and co-opted the critical challenges posed by neo-Marxism and social movements into neoliberal thinking in order to maintain its position as development orthodoxy.

Arguably, neoliberal development has maintained this hegemonic resiliency, evidenced by, for example, the capitulations of African leaders to the New Partnership for Africa's Development (NEPAD), which formally abandoned the neo-Marxist sensibilities of *dependencia* in favour of African integration within a global economy, primarily as a means of attracting aid and securing debt relief (see Bond 2002; Owusu 2003). In this way, the Bretton Woods model of development through trade liberalization remains dominant, and development approaches based on distributive justice are generally considered to constitute a critical opposition (Payne 2005).[5] At the least, it should be noted that within the political economy of international development, critical responses and social movements since the 1980s largely failed to establish a successful counter-hegemony to neoliberal development philosophy (Payne 2005).

The hegemony of neoliberal development policy and practice has not, however, prevented the emergence of further critical perspectives on development. Most notably, post-development theorists have argued that development practices are based on and (re)produce Eurocentric knowledge and reflect the construction and maintenance of hegemonic power relations and First World authority rather than international benevolence or a commitment to global social justice (see Escobar 1995; Sardar 1999; Tucker 1999, among others). In Tucker's (1999) radical critique, 'development is the process whereby other peoples are dominated and their destinies are shaped according to an essentially northern way of conceiving and perceiving the world'. Post-development scholars have argued that the very term 'development' requires, and in turn (re)produces, knowledge of those who are underdeveloped (Escobar 1995). In turn, development interventions charge communities in developing countries with the nearly impossible task of becoming un-underdeveloped (Esteva 1992).

The post-development perspective sparked debate within contemporary development studies around issues of humanism and cultural autonomy. Supporters of cultural autonomy have argued that development based on universal interpretations of culture breeds imperial knowledge and supports the devastating social, economic and ecological effects of 'global thinking' (Esteva and Prakash 1997). Claiming to know Others – and their cultures – as part of a global village is a modernist concept, which 'is at best only an illusion and at worst the ground for the kinds of destructive and dangerous actions perpetrated by global "think-tanks" like the World Bank' (Esteva and Prakash 1997: 279). From this position, development constitutes a direct threat to cultural autonomy, in particular the rights of local individuals and communities to govern their own social and economic change, and supports, if not imposes, systems of global economics that exacerbate the inequality and marginalization that development interventions claim to redress.

For universal humanists, however, 'only with a universal morality of justice is there a future for humanity' (Schuurman 2001: 14). In this sense, universalism should not be conflated with globalization nor dismissed as economically or culturally imperialist. By attempting to protect cultural differences, universalists argue, relativists problematically essentialize difference; instead, basic material needs can and should be understood as universal characteristics of humanity across cultures (Tomlinson 2001). Tomlinson (2001: 57) therefore advocates 'benign universalism' as a means of situating development in an era of increased globalization, given that universalism possesses an 'attractive inclusivist ethics and politics'.

The relativist/universalist debate is important to SDP research because it contextualizes the social and political terrain of development in which SFD programmes take place. Furthermore, it illustrates a recurring contradiction within development initiatives, namely the tendency for development practitioners to claim 'proprietorship of a universal humanism' that is not available to all (Baaz 2005: 116). This tendency to essentialize the human experience (albeit in a limited fashion), even within a 'progressive' mandate such as development or through ostensibly non-threatening and popular social forms like sport, problematically ignores unequal power relations, both discursive and material, and (re)positions dominant groups at the centre of the experience of being 'human' (see S. Razack 1998). The type of universalist perspective exemplified by Tomlinson (2001) sheds critical light on the ways in which knowledge of culture, and of Self and Other, can be both produced and foreclosed within the practices of development (Baaz 2005).[6]

Where then does such contentious history and theoretical uncertainty leave the study of sport and SDP? On the one hand, it is possible to argue that there is no firm basis for a unified theory of international development that can be lent to sport and positioned as a basis of the SDP sector. To some degree this is true given the intractable politics of development. On the other hand, there are at least four important critical insights that can be drawn out and that are useful and important to constructing a critically informed theoretical framework of development for the study of SDP.

First, the history of international development needs to be reconciled against the political specificities of the contemporary development moment, which is best characterized as: (a) absent of a genuine hegemonic state power, (b) influenced but not dominated by globalization, (c) subject to the shifting nature and importance of nation states and (d) characterized by development as an enduring problem and struggle for all (Payne 2005). All of these factors influence the current mobilization of SFD to the extent that SDP is constitutive of, and constituted by, the broader social and political influences that underpin international development.

Second, then, the binary analyses of development suggested in the debates above (First World vs Third World, North vs South, developmentalism vs post-development, universalism vs relativisim, globalism vs provincialism, modernization vs dependency) do not provide effective frameworks for nuanced and critical understandings of development practices and politics (Nederveen Pieterse 2010). Neither, in turn, is a 'postmodern' approach to development satisfactory, given that it tends to privilege a 'Western' deconstruction of the 'Western' construct of modernism itself (Nederveen Pieterse 2010). Following Nederveen Pieterse (2010), what is called for is a historical/cultural review of the Western development project, one that combines, in a pluralist fashion, analyses of the state, the market and culture, and the relations of power that are constituted and substantiated therein. This is necessary in order to make sense of, and, where needed, to deconstruct development theory and practice, particularly in the cases where such practice is dominated by the relatively powerful, and despite the ongoing initiatives and resistance of those in relatively powerless positions. This is a stage, I suggest, at which the SDP sector currently finds itself. The securing of a unified development theory for SDP is unlikely; therefore a reasonable analysis of political structure, in this case of SDP, must investigate the social, economic and political at the same time and as they overlap (Cox and Sinclair 1996: 137).[7]

Following from these perspectives, and third, the political economy of development, which has tended to stand in as primarily encompassing the material conditions of development and the historical and political ways in which they have come about, can be understood as connected to the *cultural* economy of development in much more intimate ways than previously employed. Following McMichael (2009), the structural/post-structural standoff in development studies, as seen particularly in the material versus discursive analysis of development inequalities, need not continue because the economic relations that underpin development inequalities are *always* practiced culturally. In addition to material well-being, inequality can also be about which ways of life count (McMichael 2009). What this means for SDP practice and research is that the invocation of sport within development and the notion of sport as a universal cultural form or universal language need to be interrogated through the *material* politics and contestations of development. It does not suffice to position sport as a cultural means of redressing development inequalities without critically considering the cultural constructions and meanings of sport itself within and amidst the politics of unequal development.

Fourth, therefore, while we can make theoretical sense of the politics of development in many different ways, I argue for an analysis of SDP that focuses primarily on the intersections of the cultural and political economy of development, by which I mean an analysis of the cultural logic of sport as a response to the structures of politics and economics. As discussed previously, this aligns with the Foucauldian tradition of understanding bio-political regulation as a logic borne of political economy. Such intersections of cultural logic and political economy are best, I argue, for understanding the ways in which sport is mobilized within and amidst development inequalities and for understanding the context of development struggles. With that said, it is important to explore both the materiality and the political logic (and contestation) of development inequality to some degree, and this is where I turn next.

## The political economy of development inequality

In his recent analysis of the mobilization of sport to support development and anti-poverty, Gruneau (in press) argues that little analysis is made in SDP literature of the systemic underpinnings of global poverty. These questions are generally eschewed, he argues, in favour of advocating the expansion of rights, a focus that feeds back onto the question of poverty and its politics by overlooking inequality and structural change. Similarly, I suggest that there is a political residue within current SDP policies and programmes, particularly those led and supported by organizations in the Global North, regarding the historical tension of development's dual mandate (Biccum 2010). The problem highlighted by the critical insights of both Gruneau and Biccum is that the organization of the globally political connects the material advancement of some (primarily in the North) to the poverty of many (primarily in the South) (see Sutcliffe 2007).

There indeed is a significant gap between the material assets of the world's rich and poor, a gap that widened notably between the early nineteenth century and the middle of the twentieth (Berry and Serieux 2007). Many are familiar with some version of the statistical evidence of this. For example, in the early 2000s, the richest 10 per cent of the world's population acquired financial income at a rate of 60 times that of the world's poorest 10 per cent, a global relationship that also largely mirrors the income distribution within the world's most unequal countries (Baker *et al.* 2004). As a result, relatively rich countries are able to spend more on the social needs of citizens and have more secure access to basic necessities like clean drinking water. Such inequality is further constructed along vectors of social and political power. Women continue to earn less money than men in all countries, a fact that tends to be exacerbated in countries with greater inequality levels overall, and inequalities, both inter- and intra-national, continue to come to rest along gender as it interlocks with race, class, ability, sexuality and space (Baker *et al.* 2004).

These forms of inequality are political in the sense that they result from the systems and organizations that people create and implement (and often justify) even in the face of evidence of their ineffectiveness or failure. For example, world poverty is not necessarily a result of a lack of money or resources, but a result of the fact that the distribution of income generated within the world's economy is highly unequal, with the bulk of this unequal distribution occurring internationally, not intra-nationally (Berry and Serieux 2007). When comparing the world's economic growth from 1960–80 to that of 1980–2005, the era of trade liberalization – driven largely by World Bank policies and reforms as part of the Washington and Post-Washington consensuses – did not yield sustained rates of growth for LMICs or significant progress on social indicators like health and education (Weisbrot, Baker and Rosnick 2007). Indeed, the significant economic growth of China and India between 1980 and 2000 largely served to mask the extreme divergence in economic equality within those countries and throughout the world (Berry and Serieux 2007). A result of such inequality in the distribution of income is that it 'seriously undermines the effectiveness of global growth in reducing poverty' (Woodward and Sims 2007: 130).

While recognizing the problematic of reducing development inequality to binaries of North/South or developed/developing, it nevertheless remains useful to consistently remind that people and organizations in relatively rich countries (often situated in the Global North) striving to support the development of people who are relatively poor and living in relatively poor countries (often in the Global South) constitutes a dominant mode of development practice. This should not distract from the fact that relatively rich nations also suffer widening income inequalities intra-nationally, nor should it suggest that the Global North drives all development programmes and policies, including those within the SDP sector. However, I am loath to lose sight in any analysis of SDP of the extent of global inequality and the unequal relations of power and privilege which it constructs and secures, particularly when this international inequality serves as the bedrock for a plethora of SDP programmes supported by the (richer) North and implemented in the (poorer) South.

One result of this is that while development inequalities are inherently political, the ideological construction of SFD initiatives is rarely 'up for grabs'. Conceptualizing, organizing and evaluating the opportunities for development (at the level of the social, economic, political and for individuals or groups) through sport regularly takes precedent over a broader social and political commitment to challenging and redressing inequality. This is an important point of distinction because these perspectives are, as points of both theory and practice, not the same in their respective political orientations. Baker *et al.* (2004) refer to these connected, yet disparate, camps as 'liberal egalitarianism' versus that of 'equality of condition'. Liberal egalitarianism seeks to establish opportunities for persons and populations to succeed, suggesting that the job of policy is to construct the opportunity to compete and that winners and losers will result, justifiably so, from such relations. This differs from equality of condition, which sets out to challenge and eliminate major inequalities regardless of the results of sociopolitical competition. Here, I am arguing that a liberal egalitarianism ethos maintains a hegemonic position within the conceptualizations, orientations and indeed implementations of contemporary SDP programmes and initiatives and parallels the ways in which the economic liberalization model of development maintains an orthodox status over the more radical contestation of unequal distribution (Payne 2005). I base this assertion on several factors, each of which I attend to here and also revisit in subsequent chapters.

First and foremost, connections between liberal egalitarianism, neoliberal development philosophy and the empowerment and activities of individuals have been identified within critical, empirical analyses of SDP. For example, Levermore (2009) has argued that sport appears 'tailor-made' for neoliberal approaches to development, given that it supports a focus on improving physical infrastructure, advancing the social and economic climate for capacity building and investment, and facilitating the involvement of private business and corporations in development practices. Similarly, in her discourse analysis of development policy, Hayhurst (2009: 203) found evidence that 'SDP policy models are wedded to the increasingly neoliberal character of international development'. These findings are consistent with Wilson and Hayhurst's (2009) contention that in the current political and economic climate, sport-based NGOs continue to promulgate market-driven solutions to underserved populations and a capitalist logic in response to development issues. In a similar manner, Gruneau (in press) has argued that the propensity towards SFD aligns with the increased tendency to approach the problems of development inequality by expanding the rights of individuals but not by focusing on structural changes. Such discourses of individual rights as the basis for success, upward mobility and positive development are supportive of a neoliberal approach to development, which views the development challenge primarily as one of facilitating the basis for 'fair' competition. When SDP programmes are implemented in places and states subjected to marginalization and poverty without consideration of the sociopolitical environment, their sustainability is questionable (see Akindes and Kirwin 2009).

Second, there is a post-colonial connection to be made to the hegemony of neoliberal development philosophy, one that suggests that the attractiveness of SDP for responding to development inequalities lies primarily in assuaging guilt for persons in position of privilege. From this perspective, SDP is organized to provide better opportunities to Others in order that they succeed but not to substantively attend to one's own implication in inequality. Following post-colonial analyses of development (explored more below) from the likes of Karagiannis (2004) and Biccum (2010), it is reasonable to argue that neoliberal development philosophy in SDP represents, facilitates and allows 'some' manner of development change, and undoubtedly results in regular instances of individual upward mobility, but does so while eschewing significant and direct challenges to the structures that sustain inequality for vast populations. From this perspective, neoliberalism is best understood as a means of 'inclusion' into the dominant political economy, and/or an invitation to participate and succeed within hierarchical social and political relations, a discourse that is particularly attractive to those in relative positions of privilege, and which they often work to maintain (see Ong 2006).

Third, liberal egalitarianism as a theoretical basis for understanding and redressing inequality is also particularly attuned to sport and dominant sporting narratives of winning and losing and the competitive ethos of neoliberalism. Neoliberal SDP perpetuates and naturalizes the logic that the poor and underprivileged are those who have not 'played the game' of competitive capitalism properly and, in some cases, positions SDP programmes and initiatives as a means by which to literally teach people how to 'play the game' as a metaphor for development within competitive capitalism. Such notions are understandably attractive to successful sports people who come to SDP having, in general terms, 'won' in/through sport and motivated and interpellated to view SDP and sport for good as a way 'to give back' through sport to those less fortunate (see Kidd 2008). What is less discussed in relation to the notion of 'giving back' through sport, though, is that it generally eschews the knowledge – sometimes explicit though more likely implicit or even nagging – that the relatively privileged are implicated in the marginalization of Others and therefore best give back to maintain their ethical subject positions (Heron 2007). As a result, while dependency theory does not fully explain the inequalities of development (Payne 2005), the notion of 'giving back' references an unequal taking at some unidentified political junction. Clearly, the hegemony of such logic is not solely reserved for 'winners'. That is one does not have to be a 'development winner' to understand neoliberalism and/or liberal egalitarianism and to be rewarded for a commitment to aspirational notions of success. Regardless, though, liberal egalitarianism and neoliberal development philosophy constitute but one approach to redressing inequality, one with, in my analysis, three significant deficiencies relative to equality of condition.

First and foremost, liberal egalitarianism does little to attend directly to inequality because it tends to ignore inequality's structural dimensions and, in turn, problematically suggests that people merely have choices to make in determining their relative success (Baker *et al.* 2004). This is clearly limited by the fact that not all choices are available to all people. For example, if sport is used to help motivate or encourage young people to make better health choices about their sexual activity as a means of combating the HIV/AIDS pandemic, such choices are produced and constrained by the availability of health information, access to medical or health professionals, and basic supplies such as condoms or affordable antiretroviral drugs. While the issue of choice in development is not inherently besides the point (see Sen 2000), liberal egalitarianism privileges, if not mythologizes, choice when what is needed is a sober analysis of 'real choices among real options' (Baker *et al.* 2004: 34) for the people and populations living amidst the 'structural context' of unequal development (Payne 2005: 19).

Second, a critical mass of recent research (Baker *et al.* 2004; Judt 2010; McQuaig and Brooks 2010; Wilkinson and Pickett 2009) shows that societies that are relatively more equal are also relatively healthier, happier and more peaceful. Many of the social and economic problems to which development (both international and domestic) attends – poverty, hunger, poor health, insecurity, political violence, displacement – proceed not from a lack of total resources but from the unequal distribution thereof. In fact, contrary to popular notions of the benefits or necessity of competitive capitalism (in SDP and elsewhere), there is even a strong case to be made that pursuing equality of condition can lead to improved and sustainable economic growth (Baker *et al.* 2004). This means that the pursuit of equality is not at odds with economic development but a means by which to improve overall prosperity and economic distribution. At the least, equality of condition is worth pursuing for the extent to which it supports a culture of trust and combats the desperation that proceeds from the constant pursuit and/or protection of individual resources (Judt 2010).

Third, then, equality of condition as a basis of development theorizing offers a positive means by which to pursue social change while remaining cognizant and vigilant of the various relations of power that underpin development and SDP. In other words, actively struggling to support international development through a framework of equality of condition is possible without retreating to the notion of sport as a universal language in order to justify its political palatability. While the notion of sport as a universal language is susceptible to centring particular cultures and social strata as representative of humanity – a process of social and political organization regularly and rightly criticized by post-colonial theory and/or anti-racist feminists (see Mohanty 2003; Razack 1998, among others) – seeking equality can be consistent with support for diversity, difference and a politics of cultural liberation (Baker *et al.* 2004). Therefore, I suggest, it is compatible with the recognition of different sporting cultures and does not require or privilege a notion of universal development or universal sport.[8]

A commitment to equality of condition in SDP would require a shift, primarily in coming to terms with the extent to which inequality in various forms can be sustained in and through sport and physical culture itself. The universalist discourse of sport often used to support its applicability and implementation with regard to development can exacerbate the processes by which citizens, states and organizations 'forget' the politics and the political economy of unequal development. The popularity of sport, the ways in which sport culture can romanticize meritocracy and achievement, and the close ties between sport and spectacle can also result in the politics of development being marginalized or forgotten altogether in SFD. In this way, sport becomes an end in and of itself, not a means of political negotiation (see Redeker 2008). This can be seen when sport and opportunities to play and participate are 'traded' by those in relative positions of power and privilege within development encounters in exchange for gratitude (Lefebvre 2010) and the construction of dominant benevolence (Darnell 2007).

Instead, then, of asking how sport makes the world better or what sport does for people marginalized in and through the structures of unequal development, a critical analysis of the political economy of development asks why people are relatively poor and what sport can do in solidarity with their struggles. Sport cannot be 'applied' effectively to development without first understanding why development inequalities exist. In turn, the larger question for critical scholars and activists interested in sport becomes whether, within this political economy, sport can do more to be an agent of change (see Jarvie 2006). I would argue in the affirmative, but through a renewed focus on development inequality *and* examination of the ways in which sport continues to be organized and mobilized within relations of dominance. In other words, following Greig, Hulme and Turner (2007), a development engagement with inequality needs to be policy based *and* employ a sociological approach conceptualized as more than economic growth. Given the extent to which sport is heavily commodified and susceptible to market logic and the dominant development ethos of competition and growth, this is a significant challenge. Still, sport may offer a cultural alternative to market-based development.

## Culture, development and SDP in the post-colonial

On 8 January 2011, journalist Doug Saunders (2011) wrote in *The Globe and Mail* that recent geopolitical and economic activities between nations conventionally understood to be part of the Global South or the 'post-colonial' world, particularly trade that now by-passes the traditional economic and cultural superpowers like the United States and United Kingdom, offered evidence of the end of 'post-colonialism'. This activity marked new economic and political agency for the world's previously marginalized countries and populations. According to Saunders, these former colonized nations are no longer relegated to marginal or peripheral status. In turn, the notion that the post-colonial regions and people of the world are still beholden to northern dominance is increasingly contestable, particularly as evidenced through the economic success and geopolitical authority of emerging powers like Brazil, China, Russia and India (the so-called BRIC nations). To some degree, analyses of the type put forth by Saunders are indisputable and the centrality of nations like China in the twenty-first century must be acknowledged in any analysis of the contemporary political economy of development. However, for the critical analysis of SDP, I argue that a post-colonial framework still maintains an important, if not requisite, set of theoretical and political insights for at least four reasons.

One, while the dispute has never been completely reconciled over what is specifically and definitively referred to by the term 'post-colonial', it is impossible, if not irresponsible, to ignore that international relations today – which include the relations of inequality to which development initiatives and SDP programmes and organizations respond – are still constructed via vectors of power that have existed since the fifteenth century and the height of colonialism proper (McEwan 2009). In understanding the machinations of global inequality, and in coming to terms with the political implications of SFD and SDP, we do ourselves a disservice to ignore such relations. Two, there is a case to be made that contemporary development initiatives as organized and implemented by global institutions and/or relatively powerful nations stand largely as a continuation of colonialism and a history of Empire, not a shift or break from colonial practices (Biccum 2010). In fact, Biccum argues that development did not begin with Truman's speech in 1949, as the orthodoxy of development scholarship suggests, but instead that it has been reinvented through a series of cultural and political ruptures, which include Truman's speech. These ruptures serve continuously to secure northern dominance, and construct subjectivities that justify northern privilege, through re-engaging northern promises and attempts to 'bestow' development to marginalized people and places. Biccum's thesis raises the importance of a post-colonial framework in order to examine where and how sport has been connected to social improvement and to remind that the events that have precipitated the momentum of SDP may be simply ruptures in the history of sport and development, not inventions (see Kidd 2008; Levermore and Beacom 2009; Saavedra 2009, among others).

Third, while Saunders's analysis suggests that the political realities and organizations of colonization have changed (though not always for the better given that imperial sensibilities, if not the same structural colonization of the nineteenth and twentieth centuries, continue to underpin much of the unequal economics and distributive injustice of the contemporary moment) the *logic* of colonization – what Heron (2007) refers to as development's 'colonial continuities' – continues to permeate development knowledge, practice and subjectivity particularly at a micro-level as subjects are hailed into development service. The critical insights and theories of post-colonial analyses of development are germane and insightful for deconstructing how relations of power/knowledge affect SDP practice and the sociological implications thereof. Finally, then, as McEwan (2009) has illustrated, despite the fact that development studies and post-colonial theory have traditionally constituted combative schools of thought, there are productive synergies between the two, and I suggest that the study of SDP would benefit from post-colonial theory and a decolonizing practice (also see Darnell and Hayhurst 2011; Kay 2009).

To this end, it is important to recognize that for much of the 1990s, development scholars were forced to confront issues of decolonizing knowledge and post-colonial politics (McEwan 2009). Claims to a universal humanism, belief in northern stewardship, faith in linear and scientific progress, and policies of economic imperialism have all been challenged and deconstructed by post-colonial, post-development scholars (see McEwan 2009). McEwan (2009) in particular argues for the importance of six interconnections between post-colonial theorizing and critical development studies. I explore each here in some detail before suggesting some key elements of a post-colonial agenda for SDP research and practice.

First, McEwan argues that within the post-colonial analysis of development, sociological understandings of place and space are important for understanding relations of power. Indeed, 'underpinning many development interventions are the ways in which the South is perceived and represented in the North' (McEwan 2009: 28). Such critical insights hold purchase for the study of SDP. Not only does SDP in practice constitute a site at which colonizing knowledge of the Other can be constructed, or reconstructed (Darnell 2007, 2010b), but equally important is that northern institutions are still in relative positions of authority in relation to global sport and, in turn, in relatively privileged positions within the political and cultural economy of SFD and the SDP sector (see Maguire 2008). As a result, the North comes to be the place – literally and metaphorically – that stands as the developed sporting world, and the place in position to deliver SDP programming, through both sport plus and plus sport approaches.

This leads to McEwan's second connection between post-colonial theory and development, namely that the ways in which the marginality and poverty of the South is constructed and represented has significant implications for development policy and practice. Such representations – such as the ubiquitous visual (re)presentations of poor, Black children in mainstream development discourse or, in SDP, the regular depictions of rural, poor children kicking a football as evidence of the importance and success of SDP interventions – are not false or wrong in and of themselves. However, such simplistic yet powerful representations constantly run the risk of essentializing poverty, or reducing it to the natural plight of the Third World Other, and/or reifying the power and ability of northern institutions to effect or bestow change as a response. As a result, Eurocentrism/Western-centrism needs to be examined and challenged consistently in critical studies of development – McEwan's third connection – for the extent to which development privileges and secures the norms of northern political culture but also for the ways in which development constitutes an opportunity for northern subjects in relative positions of power and privilege to 'learn' the relations of power that substantiate and normalize such privilege. As post-colonial theorists like Stoler (1995) have demonstrated, the spaces and encounters of colonialism were intimately connected to the construction of the northern subject as dominant through race, gender and class. Development discourses and encounters, particularly when supported by universal notions of sport, continue to 'offer' northern subjects a chance to know themselves as dominant yet benevolent, as much as they offer an opportunity to deconstruct relations of power and support equality of condition.

In this sense, development is inextricably connected to relations and machinations of power, as McEwan argues, particularly through the opportunities to construct the agenda of development and to mobilize the responses to development inequalities. While notable exceptions to top-down development, and top-down SDP, do exist, they are always, to at least some extent, affected by relations of power, whether economic, social, political or some combination thereof. The example of the Mathare Youth Sport Association (MYSA) in Nairobi, Kenya is illustrative. Rightly held up as an example of southern agency in development struggles for its work in supporting local youth empowerment and community development in the Mathare slum (see Coalter 2009; Willis 2000), MYSA's success has led to significant financial support from northern charities and corporate benefactors. While few would begrudge MYSA for accepting financial support to continue its work, from a post-colonial perspective, such 'financing' of SDP inevitably shapes the context of power that underpins SDP efforts. While analysis of the impact of northern financing cannot be reduced to a simply anti/pro binary (McEwan 2009), neither should the reliance of southern development efforts on northern funds be dismissed as unimportant or immaterial. Rather, it reminds that mainstream or dominant development constitutes, for all intents and purposes, a 'global industry' constitutive of, and constituted by, neoliberal development policy (McEwan 2009: 29–30). Organizations like the World Bank and IMF are in relative positions of power and authority to determine the context and practice of international development, despite the complexities of global politics and resistance. Similarly, the organization of global sport still rests primarily with dominant organizations like the IOC and FIFA, organizations that have in recent years taken an increased interest in the promotion and practice of SFD.

From this point of view, post-colonial theory lends critical insights into how development and SDP initiatives serve particular economic and political interests but also reminds that the power to oversee the development industry is the political power to define the parameters and orientations of development (see Hayhurst 2009). For example, as I explore further in Chapter 6, the invocation of sports mega-events as part of a broad-based international development agenda should be analysed critically to the extent that it affords organizations like FIFA and the IOC, organizations with dubious records of transparency and ethics (Jennings 1996; Sugden and Tomlinson 2005), inroads into defining the organization and implementation of SFD in the Global South. At the very least, understanding both sport and international development as global industries goes some way towards the critical analysis of how or whether dominant modes of global sport, often based on commercialization and a profit motive, align with the sustainable development agenda regularly espoused in and through SDP.[9]

With these six connections in mind, then, I suggest that it is both possible and important to establish a post-colonial development agenda for the study of SDP. This would have at least four parts: First, issues of top-down versus bottom-up development should be central to post-colonial analyses of SDP (Black 2010). While reduction of any such analyses to binary status is problematic and unnecessary given the ambiguities of development policy and practice (Black 2010), post-colonial theory reminds that the people, organizations and political orientations that underpin any development initiative are illustrative of power in development and call for analysis of the extent to which they privilege stewardship over self-determination. More specifically, amidst recent calls to rethink traditional, top-down development policies that privilege or normalize economic growth, a post-colonial ethos for SDP could champion sport in ways that support alternative development orientations, such as ones that approach economic growth as a by-product, not goal, of development (Woodward and Sims 2007). Such an orientation logically extends to social issues as well. Recognizing the differences in gender performativity around the world and the ways in which SFD is often mobilized to challenge hierarchies of gender (see Saavedra 2009) would call for struggles to support gender-based agency rather than to 'educate' or 'emancipate' marginalized women from the structures of their existence.

Of course, such critical analyses require a measure of self-reflexivity as to why people and organizations in relatively privileged positions are drawn to SDP work in the first place. Second, then, and following Biccum (2010), a post-colonial analysis of SDP needs to attend to the ways in which discourses and policies of development as the benevolent response to inequality simultaneously work to construct subjectivities that normalize, or even tacitly support, the global order of unequal development. This is particularly important, I suggest, given the recent institutionalization of SDP and the fact that it tends to be led by young, sports-minded activists (Kidd 2008) who likely have little significant practical engagement or life experience with anything but the orthodoxy of neoliberal development or the commercialization and globalization of competitive world sport. It is not necessarily a surprise, then, that SDP programmes and policies operate primarily within, and not against, the political parameters of neoliberal philosophy. Nevertheless, sustained critical analysis of the particular political orientations employed in SDP is called for in order to make sense of its contributions and limitations in achieving sustainable and broad development.

In turn, and third, a post-colonial analysis of SDP calls for an understanding of the ways in which social and cultural hierarchies are constructed in and through development. Here the study of race and racism is paramount. Rather than a fact of human life that needs to be negotiated and/or reconciled in encounters between people from groups that are racialized with differential effects, race is better understood as a technology of power within the spaces and discourses of geopolitics, a technology that often, if not regularly, stigmatizes one form of humanity for the benefit of another's development (Arat-Koc 2010: 148). In this way, race, as it interlocks with other social hierarchies, comes to stand as a marker of modernity and development, one that the invocation of SFD does not necessarily challenge and may in fact reify. This is not to suggest colonial conspiracy but rather to recognize the normative power of Whiteness in connection to the colonial project of modernity as it is mobilized *throughout* the Third World and not just *over* the Third World (Arat-Koc 2010). As I have argued elsewhere, the relatively non-threatening politics of sport as a basis for development make such racial politics difficult to extricate (Darnell 2010b), which has implications for SDP as a site for the construction and maintenance of Whiteness as sociopolitical power (Darnell 2007).

Finally, then, clarity is required regarding what it means to invoke and mobilize cultural forms like sport, particularly under the banner of sport's universal status, as the basis for international development. Recently, Taylor (2010: 561) explored the tendencies (and contradictions) of global institutions, like the World Bank, that attempt to reorganize the values and cultural forms of 'post-colonial citizenries' deemed atavistic and irrational and therefore at odds with the apparent rationalities of capitalism and competitive exchange. Such attempts break down when the desire for rational exchange is confronted, if not usurped, by the 'uneven incorporation of production relations within the circuits of capital' (Taylor 2010: 571). This type of critical analysis fundamentally (and beneficially) complicates the analysis of SDP by bringing into question the orientation of sport for facilitating improved development and by suggesting further development tensions. Specifically, if cultural forms (here presumed to include sport) can be deemed to be part of the 'problem' of modernizing development because they are atavistic and irrational, then sport itself is part of the problem of development. Alternatively, rational, modern, universal sports should be used exclusively in SDP. Or perhaps SDP is actually a process of cultural stewardship in and through sport. Or the self-determination of relatively marginalized people is secondary to the discourse of facilitating rational exchange. Or perhaps some combination of all of these is most accurate. Yet, from a critical, post-colonial perspective, none of these positions are acceptable as a basis for sustainable and self-determined development. In sum, the invocation and mobilization of cultural forms, like sport, as central to development processes, is not simply transcendent of, nor subordinate to, global processes but rather constitutive of them (Da Costa 2010). Given, then, that development interventions constitute the ongoing outcome of struggles over meanings and values in social life, and that programmes and policies under the banner of development can be used to institute inequality as much as challenge it (Da Costa 2010), the issue for SDP is not the utility or applicability of SFD but the extent to, or ways in, which sport supports or refutes a political engagement with development. Rather than supporting the application of sport, we need to more fully engage with sport in support of development struggles.

# Development as struggle

The critical deconstruction of international development has often led to destabilization in development studies (Schuurman 1993). The intention of this chapter is not to contribute to such an impasse for the study of SDP but to support the ongoing critical analysis of sport in relation to development inequality. Perhaps no justification for the importance of equality of condition as a basis for development is more significant than the understanding that equality of condition does not have to choose universalism or relativism as a political ethos because it aligns with solidarity and anti-dominance (Baker *et al.* 2004). In this way, equality as a basis of development philosophy and practice responds productively to the criticism that a 'postmodern' approach to development is limited in its utility and applicability (Nederveen Pieterse 2010). It also supports the continuous critical analysis and deconstruction of power in development (Nederveen Pieterse 2010). Equality, therefore, suggests an alternative theory/methodology for supporting SFD, one based not on the 'power' of sport to secure development change but sport as a basis for social and political solidarity with the struggles of the relatively poor and marginalized.

Solidarity with those in struggle links to a commitment to equality of condition in three ways: by supporting a common humanity, by recognizing the overlaps in condition among disparate peoples and by privileging justice, which recognizes and values diversity (Baker *et al.* 2004: 52). It also aligns with contemporary views on development that challenge the notion of top-down initiatives and instead argues for understandings of critical struggles for development, struggles that take place throughout the world on a regular basis. These critical struggles for development can be understood in a double sense: People struggle against their disempowerment within the structural context of inequality, and people regularly contest the ways in which the dominant social reality (in which they are positioned as marginalized if not the clear 'losers') is represented as inevitable and natural (McMichael 2009). In other words, struggles for development need not be considered alternatives to development but examples of development itself (McEwan 2009, drawing on Hickey and Mohan 2005). Such struggles for development already take place when and where there is inequality; it is likely only a colonizing dismissal of agency and cultural worth – dismissals that take place within and between national borders (D. Kapoor 2009b) – that precludes us from taking such struggles seriously. Attention needs to be paid to deconstructing the various machinations of class dominance, Whiteness and universal humanism that lead to a dismissal of culture, as opposed to devising new programmes and policies designed to help poor people.

I am advocating here for an understanding in SDP of development as struggle. Two issues are important: One, progressive theoretical notions of development as struggle understand it less as a paradigm, programme or policy to be implemented and more an ongoing and continuous act of organized resistance. Development becomes the process of articulating concerns, unifying and organizing a presence, and acting against marginalization (D. Kapoor 2009a: 16).[10] Similarly, while development cannot be abandoned in the face of stark inequality, the praxis of development as struggle is one of confronting and destabilizing the cultural and economic forces that construct development struggles as necessary. This type of development aligns with the solidarity model of equality supported here in that it emphasizes action not only in response to objective poverty but also in recognition of northern implication or complicity in development inequalities, both historical and contemporary, in an effort to move beyond ethnocentrism, stewardship and the colonial gaze (McEwan 2009: 288).

Two, support for development as struggle requires coming to terms with the fact that such struggles are ambiguous and non-linear in their politics and actions. Asher (2009) has argued that understanding struggles for sustainable development – in her case within the geography of the Colombian Pacific and at the confluence of ethnic, economic, political and environmental justice – requires consideration of how political economy, social forces and struggles for change interact and shape each other in paradoxical ways. There is rarely a clearly defined 'invade and resist' relationship in struggles for development that pits, for example, corporate and/or state forces against a plainly distinguishable group who resist (Asher 2009). This perspective supports the critical rejoinder of early post-development theory and research that it failed to appreciate the diversity of struggles for development or that it assumed a fixed political orientation (see I. Kapoor 2004). While post-colonial theory remains important for illuminating, for example, how stereotypes and regimes of power/knowledge of the inferior racial Other can dismiss agency or secure the notion of one path to development for marginalized people, the actual struggles for development are regularly complicated by cultural agency and the diversity of interests that construct the development agenda.

This notion of development as struggle as articulated by those like McMichael, D. Kapoor and Asher (among many others) aligns in productive ways with the critiques of SDP by scholars like Coalter (2009). As Coalter (2009: 65) has demonstrated, the contributions or successes of sport in relation to international development are not causal; they are best explained and understood with regard to the *process* of participation. Supporting opportunities to participate in sport or to construct sport in a way that aligns with an individual or community's development are not development ends but rather means. Furthermore, sport may offer the social or cultural hub around which development struggles are articulated and mobilized, furthering the importance of process, not results. The politics of development brought to bear on SDP and attempts to make sense of, if not evaluate, the effectiveness of SFD need to be focused on processes and the agency of people who struggle for self-determination and material well-being through the mobilization of sport.[11]

There is likely a role for external and/or privileged people in SDP if approached this way. Of central importance to development as struggle is not only the ability or knowledge amongst marginalized people to define, determine and achieve their own success but also investment therein and support thereof. As Saunders (2010) illustrated in his recent accounts of migratory populations, the world's poorest people are constantly and consistently active – socially, economically and politically – in the slums or 'arrival cities' of the world. The determining factor in the success of such marginalized people is not simply their resiliency, their motivation or their conduct but the commitment to challenging the 'structural context' that secures their outsider status (literally for many migrants) and the implementation of policies of inclusive citizenship through which they can secure long-term benefits. In Saunders' analysis, this calls for progressive immigration policy that supports people rather than chooses between dispelling and saving them. It also calls for a balanced understanding of people's marginalization with/against their agency in struggling to build a better life. People and organizations connected to sport could become (more) active in supporting these kinds of progressive policies. For the SDP sector, this would require rejecting the seductive binary of progress versus destitution and coming to terms with peoples struggles for development (as well as the structural context that operates against such struggles) as a basis for imagining and implementing sport in ways that support development as struggle.

# Conclusion

To summarize, I have argued in this chapter that sustainable and self-determined development for the world's relatively marginalized, key precepts and goals of the SDP sector, calls for better understandings of the history of development power and politics and the often ambiguous and non-linear struggles of social and political actors to secure their own well-being within this structural context.[12] Thus, while there is always resistance to the structures of unequal development within particular regions, amongst particular groups and led by particular organizations, resistance does not constitute compelling evidence of the absence of hegemonic relations (see Darnell and Hayhurst, in press). The activities and struggles of agents in relatively disempowered positions need constantly to be reconciled against the politically dominant mode of development. Even in the important cases where sport has been linked to achieving positive outcomes in line with an international development mandate (e.g. Burnett 2006; Fokwang 2009; Kay 2009; Lindsey and Grattan, in press) critical development theory calls for an analysis of the structures of inequality, the agency of actors and the processes, not just results, of resistance to inequality and progressive change. Anything less constitutes a disservice to those who struggle for equality of condition and runs the risk of usurping the political contestability of development through recourse to the development outcomes that sport can provide.

The study and practice of SDP therefore requires a critical understanding of, and engagement with, development *politics* in and through sport, as much as development *outcomes* through sport. In turn, this notion of sport in support of a politics of equality of condition potentially feeds back, in progressive ways, into the notion of democratizing sport itself towards social and political equity and sustainability (Donnelly 1993; Kidd 1995). For the purposes of the remainder of this text, then, I take it as foundational that the challenges of international development are the challenges of understanding and redressing global inequality as it manifest through power and politics. These relations of inequality are stark in depth and breadth, hold significant material consequences for people that are relatively marginalized as a result and have historical, social and political underpinnings. In Chapters 3 to 6, I use this perspective as a departure point from which to explore, and critically examine, the deployment of sport-based programming as a response to the challenges of international development.

# 3

# The SDP Intern/Volunteer Experience*

## Introduction

This chapter focuses on the experiences of young Canadians who served abroad as volunteer interns through the International Development through Sport (IDS) programme organized by Commonwealth Games Canada (CGC). Although there are many social and political dimensions and implications of such experiences, in this chapter I am principally interested in understanding the process of 'subjectivation' and the resultant subject positions that are produced and constrained in and through SDP service, particularly for residents of the Global North who come to SDP work from and through relative positions of privilege. In Foucauldian terms, subjectivation refers to 'the multiple ways in which humans get tied to particular identities' (Markula and Pringle 2006: 9) and builds on the tradition formulated by Louis Althusser (2001) in which subjects are constituted as they are hailed – or 'interpellated' – into dominant ideologies (cf. Felluga 2003).[1] Investigating such perspectives afforded an opportunity not only to analyse interns' experiences at a micro-level but also to 'ascend', through theoretical perspectives of sport and development, to the broader political/ethical implications for the SDP sector and processes of knowledge production (Heron 2007).

This type of examination, in this case of the ways in which sport 'pulled' young Canadians to development and SDP and what they learned as a result, is called for given recent development scholarship. Heron (2007) has forcefully argued that the motivations for international development service often draw heavily upon, and reinforce, a northern 'desire' for the development of Others that in turn constructs the Self as saviour. Such processes are produced and constrained within a web of historical, social and political hierarchies of race, gender and class as well as the colonization of spaces. In turn, such service is complicated by the production of subjectivities that arguably do more to facilitate participation *within* the global order of poverty and inequality than to challenge or change it in direct and transformational ways (Biccum 2010).

The chapter proceeds in three subsequent parts. In the next section, I provide a brief overview and summary of critical development research into volunteerism, global citizenship and subjectivities before exploring results of interviews with CGC interns. The chapter concludes with a brief discussion

*Parts of this chapter are adapted from Darnell (2010a, 2010b, 2011b).

of the implications of knowledge production and subjectivation within SDP internships and international volunteering.

## International development and volunteerism

A host of recent literature has investigated the knowledge produced and identities constructed within international development service (see, for example, Epprecht 2004; Heron 2007; N. Razack 2005; Tiessen 2007). This literature has shown the act of serving abroad in foreign spaces and amidst international poverty and inequality to be both deeply transformative and challenging, particularly for young people. International service offers an opportunity for young volunteers to learn about the historical and political dimensions of development inequality and foster critical engagement as global citizens amidst struggles for social justice. At the same time, such experiences can also confirm development volunteers' identities as primarily helpers of 'Others' (Heron 2007) and therefore limit or skew their engagement with broader development politics. These issues are important because claims to northern innocence within development overlook the ways in which northern institutions and organizations are implicated in development inequality and obscure understandings of the interconnectedness, complexities and hierarchies of North/South economics and politics (see Nederveen Pieterse 2010). This critical scholarship has generally positioned the development service experience within two distinct yet complimentary theoretical frameworks: hegemonic relations and the securing of innocence.

### Development service within hegemonic relations

In keeping with the Gramscian theoretical approach employed in this text, it is important to recognize that international development volunteering occurs within, and does not transcend, social hierarchies and relations of power. Even if situated within a framework of universal human rights or a praxis of empowerment, the impact of overseas internships can be undermined by northern expectations, feelings of entitlement and claims to proficiency or capability (Epprecht 2004). There is a tendency in development for the myriad of social, political and material inequalities to which development attends to be reduced to identifying and implementing technical solutions, framed by a northern 'will to improve', that establish boundaries between those capable of, and responsible for, improving through development and those more likely to be in receipt of such processes (Li 2007: 7). In the SDP sector, attempts to improve school-based physical education in LMICs have been compromised by NGOs sending inexperienced volunteers into placement communities 'without notice, let alone a mutually prepared plan for their training and deployment, significantly complicating the work of the already over-burdened teachers' (Kidd 2008: 376). Similarly, research has found evidence in SDP of a misalignment between northern expectations of development goals and values, and local expectations or demands (Guest 2009). Absent of critical self-reflection on the part of northern volunteers, the result of such encounters is that development comes to be structured primarily by the proficiency and authority of the development 'expert' (Kothari 2005).

These analyses problematize the notion of international service as socially and politically benign. N. Razack (2003: 41) argues that international social work is susceptible to socio-spatial relations of dominance, given the increasing permeability of borders resulting from technological advances and capitalist globalization. This is significant for SDP given that the internationalization, globalization and commercialization of sport all facilitate, at least to a degree, its recognition and applicability within international development initiatives (also see Maguire 2008). In turn, presumptions of benevolence in international social work (or the positioning of such encounters as simply cross-cultural learning) that fail to take interlocking power relations into account implicate the discipline in 'professional imperialism' where a presumed 'universal' methodology of social work sustains First World entitlements (N. Razack 2003: 44–5). From this perspective, the use of international social work to gain knowledge and understanding of Others can solidify a 'professional hegemony' in which the universality of social work itself remains unexamined (N. Razack 2005: 101). I suggest that such critical reflections on the universality and applicability of sport – as well as northern-led development – are still rarely taken up in mainstream SDP discourse. At the same time, such critical reflections on universality are only part of the equation. Indeed, as N. Razack found in her research with Canadian international social workers, while recognizing these hegemonic relations rendered the experience difficult for international volunteers, it rarely challenged their sense of innocence within global inequality, disavowals constitutive of a dominant subject position.

## Development service and the maintenance of innocence

In Heron's (2007) research into the experiences of White, Canadian women who had served as international development workers (a sample that included herself), she connected the construction of innocence to the urgency among White, middle-class women to do 'good' work as a means of confirming 'appropriate' notions of femininity and individual responsibility. From this perspective, knowing oneself as a moral person becomes of paramount importance to development volunteers; conversely, if morality is compromised, the sense of self is ruptured or challenged. Canadian women are thus left with the need – or 'desire' – to know themselves as good people, a personal quest for which international development service provides an attractive option (Heron 2007). Development service becomes a moral imperative, fundamentally linked to the maintenance of bourgeois innocence and the unending struggle to 'prevent the potential shattering of moral narratives of self' (Heron 2007: 153–4).[2]

These critical ideas are germane to the study of SDP because they inform and contextualize the reasons why young sportspeople are drawn to SDP work. They also illuminate the broader desire to reform sport in socially progressive ways, through the ostensibly new approaches to benevolent development that SDP facilitates and supports.

In sum, there is always the possibility for international development, the experiences it affords and the struggles to 'educate' northerners of its importance and goals, to produce imperial subjectivities (Biccum 2010: 21). As Biccum's (2010) analyses of northern-led development initiatives suggest, the current organization and proliferation of international development focuses less upon the sustainable reduction of global inequality and more upon the production of subjectivities that support the global order of northern dominance and southern poverty as degeneracy to be reformed. In this way, Biccum raises the idea that development strives to integrate subjects into the machinations of global inequality (in a benevolent way for the relatively privileged and in an aspirational way for the relatively marginalized). Biccum offers an important way to theorize the experiences of people who participate in SDP as volunteers and the knowledge of Self and Other that they accrue as a result.

Still, as in any analysis of subjectivity, it is crucial to recognize that while international development experiences are the site of knowledge production, such knowledge is often tenuous, ironic, ambivalent and contradictory (Heron 2007). For example, liberal encounters with Others – facilitated by programmes like SDP internships – are often built, and rely, upon an ability to 'tolerate' Others but do so in such a way that the entire notion of the Other would be compromised if the encounter truly 'liberalized' them (Brown 2006). At the same time, such notions of tolerance are not reducible to ideology because they are fundamentally, yet often ambiguously, shaped by the very encounters (Brown 2006) that produce and constrain subjectivities. In the following analysis, I embrace this kind of ambiguity.

## CGC and SDP interns

CGC's IDS programme draws support from the Canadian International Development Agency (CIDA) and the Canadian Heritage International Sport Directorate. All 27 former interns of the programme that I interviewed were young (generally under 30), university educated, often in a sport, physical education or kinesiology department, and had demonstrated a measure of expertise with physical culture as athletes, coaches, administrators or purveyors of knowledge. As qualified candidates, CGC had placed them with a sport and/or health partner organization for a minimum of 8 months, and they worked for their placement organization to facilitate the use of sport and play to meet development goals. In the majority of cases, these development goals focused on health promotion, education and youth development in the placement community.[3] While each partner organization was unique, they were all compatible with the general mandate of the CGC programme, which positions the internship as an opportunity for young Canadians to participate in international development by using and mobilizing sport towards the goal of effecting sustainable social change. As CGC states, a major goal of the programme is to 'deliver effective, sustainable, locally responsible, needs-based development through sport initiatives that focus on the pursuit of the Millennium Development Goals in selected countries' (CGC 2008).

During interviews, I asked CGC interns about the positives and negatives (broadly defined) of their time abroad, the reasons that they had been drawn to an SDP internship and the ways in which service had affected them as people. Several thematic consistencies emerged through the analysis. Three are particularly worthy of critical attention and attended to here: the logic of capitalism within SDP, the bio-politics of SDP and the centrality of emotions – particularly guilt and innocence – within SDP internships.

## Sport and the hegemony of capitalist development

First and foremost, interviews with CGC interns illustrated that they tended to be successful sports people (as athletes, coaches, trainers, administrators, volunteers, advocates), that they had enjoyed positive experiences within sport and the organization of physical culture, and that SDP service offered an opportunity to give back or 'pay forward' in and through sport. To this extent, the understanding that sport, to a significant degree, had facilitated their own success within the cultural and political economy in which they lived drew interns to view sport as a means by which to support the success of Others within the development context. That is, many interns understood their own sporting experiences to be reasons why they had been selected for a SDP internship and to be important prerequisites for doing the kind of SFD work that would be required during their placement. Joanne described sport thus:

> So phys. ed. has always been engrained in me as something that I really loved … I've always been involved in sports, since I was small, organized sport or regular sport. So I always found and understood the value of sport and different skills. Like competent as far as sports skills go, so that allowed me to have that knowledge base as far as sports skills. So I guess I brought that and I also brought the attitude of sports is a good thing and sports is beneficial to your health and encourage others to be involved in sports or anything, movement or whatever – Joanne.

To a degree, then, sport was a 'vehicle' towards development, both for drawing young Canadians with sport backgrounds to SDP work and for conceptualizing a basis by which to support change within placement communities. Of course, such understandings of 'sport as a vehicle' beg questions regarding the messages and meanings ascribed by interns to sport and in turn being delivered by sport as a medium of development. In many cases, interns relied on somewhat familiar discourses of sport to describe and make sense of the benefits and messages being delivered through the use of sport in SDP. For example, James linked the utility of sport in youth-centred development programmes to the oft-assumed, or 'classic', benefits of sport – notions attached to sport in Canada dating back to the nineteenth century (Bouchier 1994) – that coalesce around the sense that sport participation builds character in young participants. From this perspective, youth who participate in sport are not only better athletes, and healthier individuals, but they are also better citizens because they learn social relations of responsibility via sport.

> Yeah, sport really was, in this case, a vehicle because all the kids loved playing football. They did. And pretty much they would do anything to play football. It offered a vehicle for pretty much whatever we wanted it to be in this case. So there was certainly, there were all the classic advantages of youth playing sports, the camaraderie, the y'know, the leadership, learning to excel on a field and working within a group for a larger goal, delaying your own personal vested interests. Y'know, all of those classic things were there, through sport as well, but it allowed us to mobilize the community somewhat – James.

There is a host of literature to support (albeit to an extent) the notion of sporting benefits for youth in the way that James describes. Sport among youth has been found to promulgate positive values such as hard work and an orientation to succeed (Ewing *et al.* 2002), support the development of self-confidence and emotional health (Hansen, Larson and Dworkin 2003), and provide an opportunity to learn about fair play and sportsperson-ship (Hedstrom and Gould 2004). Clearly, James's perspectives on sport were influenced by such understandings of sport. However, discursive association between sport participation and character building among youth are not only difficult to 'prove' given the importance and complexities of context (see Coakley and Donnelly 2004; Donnelly 1993) but they often also overlook the tensions and contradictions in sport itself. For example, the same researchers who conclude that sport does indeed facilitate character development often temper their results given that the social context in which sport occurs is of central importance and because of sport's 'utility' for fostering antisocial behaviour and relations of dominance as well.[4]

Given the impossibility then, of claiming any 'truths' about the utility of sport, it is important to situate the construction of interns' perspectives on sport within the broader sociopolitical context. To this end, I suggest that such perspectives were illustrative of the hegemony of capitalist logic, if not always capitalism itself, that continues to underpin cultures and discourses of sport, international development and SDP. Not only does James's reflection illustrate that sport as a vehicle for development was intelligible to interns largely through their recognition of personally positive, sporting experiences, but interns also understood a connection between sport participation and the development of an individualist ethos that aligns with neoliberal citizenship. While positive experiences with, and knowledge of, sport was a powerfully constitutive discourse and knowledge reservoir for interns as they negotiated the context and meanings of sport in SDP, it concomitantly supported notions of citizenship consistent with the dominant mode of social organizing and the political economy in the Global North (see Harvey 2007; Kaplinsky 2005). Sport was thus viewed as an opportunity within development to promote and facilitate the 'inclusion' of marginalized people within (the inequalities of) the contemporary global political economy.

These discursive links between sport and leadership in SDP were further evident to the degree that interns also invoked sport as a means of facilitating and promoting responsible behaviour. The discursive understanding of sport as a development tool stemmed from traditional disciplinary notions of sport as an institution of responsibility and respectability, and relative to opportunity costs, an alternative to deviant behaviour. Drawing on the Foucauldian analysis of sport as a disciplinary technology (see Markula and Pringle 2006; Pronger 2002; Shogan 1999), particular notions of sport and its benefits, in this case related to time management and responsibility, underpinned interns' understandings of the logic of SDP. The following exchange with Florence was illustrative.

SD: And if you don't write (this exam), then your school is pretty much done?

FLORENCE: Right, right. And if you do write it, there's a lot, a lot of pressure because that determines what school you go to basically. And that's why there's, there's no motivation, there's no, it's really... educationally it's a tough world there.

SD: And if they don't go to school, what do they end up doing?

FLORENCE: Mostly what those kids are doing. You hang out with your friends, you do whatever's fun to you.

SD: So then was your programme designed to sort of fill up that time?

FLORENCE: Yep. Give them something positive to do.

The issue for critical analysis here is not the accuracy of these interpretations or whether sport-focused development programmes were effective means of promoting responsibility and leadership. Nor do I suggest that supporting students' educational achievement is less than positive. Rather, what require attention are the politics of the social imagination and the particularities of the subjectivity, understood in and through these processes. It is evident,

I suggest, from these exchanges with CGC interns, that the subject imagined as an SDP partner or participant is intelligible through a requisite lack of leadership and responsibility, and the subject of the SDP intern is one of facilitating responsibility given their previous sporting experiences. That is, the focus on leadership and responsibility – individualized notions of success and achievement – references and solidifies a form of neoliberal citizenship (for both SDP intern and SDP partner, though not in the same way), a citizen for whom sport participation is a formative and/or transformative experience. As Harvey (2007), among others, has argued, there is a link between the privileging and defence of an individualist ethos and the substantiation of increasingly global neoliberal relations that solidify and justify material inequalities. Such ideas are hegemonic within the context of international development in which the variety of possible approaches, and the sovereignty of communities to enact their own development, has been largely co-opted into the neoliberal fold by the 'professionalisation and technicalisation' of the development industry (Kothari 2005: 425). This is the terrain into which sport is now mobilized, and it provides an ideal basis for referencing notions of sport and character development in youth, both historical (Bouchier 1994) and contemporary (see Donnelly *et al.* 2007). For many interns, then, the logic of SDP came to centre on the development of character more than the process of confronting and redressing inequality.[5]

Foucauldian genealogy illustrates how it is possible that interns came to interpret SFD in this way; it is possible if the 'recognizable' benefits of character building through sport are attached, discursively and materially, to development programming. The SDP sector effectively achieves this linking. It is not that the use of sport, supported by CGC and the SDP sector, is misguided but rather that the logic of neoliberalism, and the presumption and construction of a neoliberal sporting subject, is regularly present and rarely questioned. In turn, such logic suggests that the success of the few is available to the many if they would (only) work differently or harder via the lessons and principles that sport affords.

This kind of neoliberal subjectivity and capitalist logic underlying SDP as understood from the point of view of CGC interns is not entirely surprising. Indeed, much of the global efforts to support international development are based on the tenets of economics and come to rest on how to facilitate basic needs and self-determination for the vast sections of the global population who live in absolute poverty (see Gasper 2004). Three important points need to be made, though. One, the experiences of interns suggest, at the least, that the political orientation towards SDP is particular, not universal, in that it imagines and supports the inclusion of marginalized people within the current structures and machinations of competitive capitalism. We significantly limit our understandings of SDP if and when we lose site of the specificities of this political orientation. Second, then, and proceeding from my advocating for equality of condition as a conceptual and political basis for SDP, such commitments to SDP are likely limited in supporting sustainable and egalitarian development. Third, the explication of such logic calls into question the subjects hailed into SDP and the extent to which their own (relatively successful) engagement with capitalism facilitates their support for SDP. Given the post-colonial dimensions of the SDP internship experience, I argue that race and gender, connected to bio-politics, is also important in this regard.

## Race, gender and bio-politics

In the previous section, I explored the capitalist logic connected to sport that underpinned the pull to SDP volunteer work for many CGC interns and the extent to which it underpinned their own subjectivity within SDP initiatives. Clearly, social class was a formative dimension of such regimes of power/knowledge. Here, I argue, that critical scholars would be remiss to reduce the capitalist imperative of SDP, such as it is, to social class at the expense of other social categories and hierarchies. Indeed, the bio-politics of SDP call for attention to the interlocking of class with race and gender and the various encounters within the SDP volunteer experience. This is the case given that hierarchies of race and racism can be understood as a logical conclusion of a bio-political state (Foucault 1997) and that the intersections of race, class and gender with other markers of social respectability are fundamental to the construction of the colonial subject (Stoler 1995). In other words, the bio-politics of SDP are impossible to extricate from social hierarchies, and SDP runs the risk of securing, if not reifying, social relations of dominance if an anti-racist perspective is not brought to bear.

For example, despite the rhetorical absence of 'race' in many interviews with SDP interns, issues of gender, particularly the recognition of the 'disempowered' woman in the development context, were common tropes in the description of the SDP experience and encounter. The recognition of difference was most readily intelligible, and most talked about, through a lens of gender that positioned placement communities as disempowering, lacking opportunities and repressive to women. From an interlocking perspective, such observations have fundamental racialized and classed dynamics. Reflections on the repressed woman in the Global South, always intelligible here in relation to Canadian feminism, exemplified what Mohanty (2003: 170) refers to as 'racialized gender'. James's descriptions, for example, illustrate a perspective on gender, and the role of the SDP intern in working towards feminist causes, that was recognizable in development in racialized terms:

> So yes, that was something that I noted, that there weren't enough, even on a superficial level, there weren't enough physical activity programmes for girls, let alone enough programmes that empowered women. But it's, empowering women was beyond the scope of what I could accomplish there. I mean, one, it wasn't

even really in my mandate though I kind of set my own mandate. It's something I would have liked to have worked on, but it's something that if I'd like to have worked on, I pretty much would have to move there for 5 years and have a more in-depth team and just a better knowledge of the culture – James.

From this perspective, the repression of women was an intelligible cultural aspect of the development context and placement community for CGC interns, and it offered a social and moral platform from which to take up the work of SDP. While James's perspectives on the lack of physical activity opportunities for women, and the conclusions regarding the disempowerment of women, are perhaps accurate, third-wave feminism encourages critical consideration of the ways in which such knowledge is produced and rendered technical. On the one hand, there is little empirical evidence with which to conclude that the intelligibility of the disempowerment of women in development for James was derived from comparison to a system of gender in Canada (one understood to be egalitarian and emancipatory). However, the subject position of stewardship into which interns like James were invited likely militated against their understandings of the agency of women in 'developing countries' to champion their own processes of empowerment. This tension, between local feminist agency and the empowerment of feminism through development and SDP, was a challenging aspect of the SDP intern experience.

Two significant connections can de drawn. First, interpreting the disempowerment of women in placement communities and the subsequent contributions to gender empowerment of sport were undoubtedly complicated by social constructions of race for SDP interns. The 'disempowered woman' was more intelligible and easier to speak of through encounters with people of colour. Second, race was generally avoided during interviews with interns, since it was understood to be inconsistent with liberal notions of racial equality, but the same did not apply to gender in development. Gender was, for interns, a seemingly more objective or benign example of repression and underdevelopment that required only education and perspective in order to enact cultural change. Given the traditional entrenchment of sport as a masculine domain and arena of patriarchal assertions (see Burstyn 1999), Canadian feminists, via SDP, could use the organization of sport as a means to 'educate' the people they encountered, particularly women, about the possibilities for gender equality.

> For me it was almost more of a shock of 'How could you girls not realize that you had the right to play rugby?' Like how could you, but it's funny because coming from (Canadian province), I did not realize it was even more of a man's sport, I had no idea, because in High School, there's men's and women's soccer, there's men's and women's basketball, there's men's and women's rugby and my older sister played, so you just kind of go through the, it's kind of y'know, the guys play and the girls play, there was no question and it wasn't until I moved to (Canadian province) that I started to get 'Ohmigosh, you play rugby?' Like, that's a guy's sport. And that was here even! – Esther.

Esther's descriptions of the politics of racialized gender raise an interesting tension. On the one hand, as a feminist who has challenged gender stereotypes and relations of power within sporting cultures in Canada, she recognized the limits placed on women's participation in and through athletic patriarchy. That is, she did not presume a liberated Canada in gendered terms or at the least she recognized the struggle around the concept and acceptance of women's rugby. Yet, when the context changed from Canada to women playing rugby in the development context, her unit of analysis and perspective also changed, from *struggle* to a lack of *awareness* or *recognition*. This is illustrative of the racial component of transnational gender inequality; within Whiteness, gender equality is achieved through agency, but those expected to aspire to Whiteness are understood to require a gender-based education. Without a focus on interlocking systems and critical reflections on dominance, and enabled by the liberal belief in colour-blindness, this racialized dynamic of 'liberation' and 'education' is easily obfuscated.

What these perspectives illustrate, I argue, is that the commitment to social change constitutive of the bio-politics of SDP holds profound implications for processes of knowledge production and interlocking systems which sustain inequality, both material and discursive. The spatial dynamic of SDP and SDP internships – that internships be conducted to make life better overseas – largely confined gender oppression, at a discursive level for interns, to the development context. (Racialized) gender inequalities were constitutive of underdevelopment and different from interns' sense of self and home. I offer the following lengthy exchange with Serena because it speaks to interlocking systems and the ways in which hierarchies were largely sustained in and through encounters with difference.

> SD: OK. Do you think about any of these ideas or categories differently, talking about race or gender or social class, having gone and seen it and experienced it in a different culture? Now that you've come back to Canada?

> SERENA: Um, no not really.

> SD: Because some people have told me, for example, I'm not trying to put words in your mouth, but some people have told me that they didn't really think about issues of race in these ways until they were sort of the only White person in a Black community or a non-English-speaking community.

> SERENA: Well, yeah, now that I'm back home, I don't think about them.

> SD: But do you think it changed some of the ideas that you had about race or class or gender or the ways you thought about them?

SERENA: I don't think so. I recognized the difficulties that they were having there because of them, but I don't think they translate here, so I don't think about them on a daily basis anymore.

SD: Hmmm. Can you expand on that a little bit? Like what does that mean, not translate here?

SERENA: Um, like the difference in expectations in terms of performance or whatever. I would consider the expectations here to be equal. I mean, maybe that's just my own naïve opinion, so yeah over there, there was a difference in expectation and here I don't feel that way so I don't even acknowledge that there is a difference.

SD: Interesting.

SERENA: Social class, though, I feel different about that now. Um, there was just, you think about the haves and the have-nots over there, and there's such a big difference between the two, but I never really thought of that happening here and now that I've come home I see that that's, that happens everywhere. And it may not be as much of a gap; it may not be as obvious, but it's still there.

The implications of this exchange are important to explore. Following Stoler (1995), even though 'sport' was discursively being 'made' in the circuitous route of knowledge production that the SDP internship afforded, there is little evidence from interviews to suggest that interlocking systems were challenged in and through the SDP experience. In fact, the opposite is more accurate; even though Serena found her perspectives on class to be 'heightened' having experienced the stark poverty of her placement community, the racial dynamic of gender inequality was solidified to the extent that Canada remained a place understood to be relatively free of oppression. In turn, her views of the underdevelopment of her placement community were hardened. Indeed, it is difficult to conceive of bases of international development and SDP, at least in its current or most palatable incarnations, which do not confirm interlocking social hierarchies in the manner described above.

This does not mean, though, that interns did not try to do just that. Amid the tensions discussed in this chapter, interns struggled to position encounters with difference in their placement communities in a way that facilitated their bio-political commitments without implicating them in interlocking relations of dominance. Not surprisingly, though, without a commitment to deconstructing such relations, the 'optimal' – or at least the most useful – position for interns to assume was racial neutrality or attempts to look above or beyond racialized hierarchies. In this way, even if difference was encountered, it could be subsumed in and by a politics of 'equality' that depoliticized difference, facilitated the constitution of the moral self and supported the bio-politics of change in and through sport and SDP. For example, Alexander found that working to improve sport and play opportunities for persons with disabilities was easiest when his position in the racial hierarchy had been effectively smoothed out. Colour-blindness equalled acceptance and supported essentialist, but largely apolitical, solidarities.

SD: Just to go back a second, that experience of sort of forgetting that you were White, was that, that's an interesting one, nobody's told me about that so far, of the interns that I've talked to. Were you expecting that or sort of surprised that that happened?

ALEXANDER: I wasn't expecting it but to be honest with you I took it as a compliment in the context of the conversation. Because they said, 'Oh, he see no colour', and then I realized, 'Oh, shit, I'm the only White guy here for miles' and for me to be as accepted as I was into that community, being the only White people for miles, made me feel pretty good that I was doing the right things that I needed to do in terms of building relationships. I thought, anyway. So whenever you're, like everything I tried in (country), four out of ten of them would work, right? Every initiative I tried, every sponsorship you try and get, four out of ten of them would work, so when you do actually have a success, when you're over there, you need to celebrate it because there aren't going to be that many that are just going to be flowing in. But you need to just take a minute and celebrate that because otherwise you're going to leave feeling like you did nothing, which again I did think some of my colleagues felt like they did in some cases.

Of course, from a critical race perspective, there are limitations in striving for racialized essentialism. If interlocking systems of oppression contribute to the inequality and marginalization to which development and SDP claim to attend, then essentialist arguments of 'we're all the same' (S. Razack 1998: 169) miss the roots of the problem. Yet essentialism largely marked the extent of the SDP intern's anti-inequality toolkit, in both theory and practice. The taboo of racism limited the actualization of a commitment to social change and left interns to invoke a liberal humanist ethic, to which sport was useful politically and discursively, in order to justify and support their interpretations and responses to difference and underdevelopment. The results suggest, then, that CGC interns were not trained, prepared or encouraged to take up the internship in relation to social hierarchies and their position therein. They did, however, recognize that the internship experience held profound personal and emotional significance to them, particularly in relation to the privilege that it highlighted and the guilt it produced. In the next section, I explore these results.

## The emotional experiences of the SDP subject

Recent analyses of development volunteerism have pointed to the importance and relevance of emotion for understanding such experiences. For example, Epprecht (2004: 694) suggests that the strong emotions involved in development work seemingly compel volunteers to 'do something to help'. Similarly, Li (2007: 41) has explored how the contradiction of capitalist ventures within colonial saviour projects – which exploited peasants at the same time as markets were 'freed' – produced a sense of northern guilt to do something, as long as the costs were low. In this way, the importance and significance ascribed to development work is often solidified by the visceral emotions experienced by those who take on its tasks. Such emotions are far from insignificant, culturally and/or politically (see Ahmed 2004).

For CGC interns, 'First World guilt' consistently permeated the SDP volunteer experience. Guilt in this case was not tied necessarily to a sense of implication in the history and politics and marginalization and inequality, but rather to a sense of guilt in recognizing oneself, in effect, as a transnational 'have', a notion solidified by the stark material inequalities laid out in the development context and placement communities. All the interns I spoke with recognized this First World guilt; the differences among interns were in their personal interpretations of guilt and the implications for subjectivity, identity and politics that they ascribed to these feelings. While there were differing interpretations of guilt, in the majority of cases feelings of guilt did not align with, or support the production of, a politicized subject position, one concerned with attending to the relations that support the guilt-producing inequality, but instead constituted a precursor to strategies of White redemption. As Roman (1997) has illustrated, redemption discourses are often produced through the strategy of White identification with the anti-racist struggles of persons of colour as opposed to critical investigation of the privileges of Whiteness within Western liberal multiculturalism. One of the outcomes of these redemption strategies is a continuing commitment to Whiteness and solidification of the discursive intelligibility of White bodies as the entitled racial class (Moddelmog 1999).

For some interns, these feelings of guilt were the direct result of the limits of their achievement in effecting change. In this sense, the helping imperative (Heron 2007) and will to improve (Li 2007) constituted both the political agenda and the discursive terrain of SDP. When these 'technical' goals could not be met, the relative benefits that interns themselves derived from SDP experience stood out in stark terms, producing a sense of guilt in having taken more than given. In addition, however, guilt was produced through recognition on the part of interns that the opportunity to derive benefits from this type of international experience was not afforded to all. They understood the social and spatial privilege afforded them in their SDP programme and placement and experienced guilt in coming to terms with the absence of transnational reciprocity in international development. Loreena's reflections illustrate this compound perspective:

> When you come as a First World person … you think you're going to bring all of this stuff to a new country, but the chances are we're going to take away a whole lot more than we could ever give. And that can come out like, maybe I'm feeling a little bit guilty … not as many (local people) have as many opportunities that we have as First World people to go other places, but you just see so much being in a different culture and people giving you everything – Loreena.

These kinds of results suggest that the SDP experience forced interns to recognize their own privilege, both as relatively affluent Canadians and as transnational citizens afforded a means of mobility and travel. 'First World' was not only a subject position born into but also one experienced through travelling to other countries and living in other cultures. For interns who identified with this type of guilt as part of the SDP internship, there was a sense of inevitability about it, a description of guilt as a *fait accompli* in the transnational development experience. Being the kind of person that would do this work meant being the kind of person who experienced guilt in relation to privilege.

> I think that you'd have to [feel guilt]; you'd have to be fairly insulated to not feel [guilt]. And I felt guilty for my expectation of a certain standard as well. Like 'Oh, I can't believe there's no hot water' and those kind of things. As if that's important! At least I have running water. [But I did] feel guilty about all of the things that I knew I had in boxes at home waiting for me and to know that a few dollars here and there would make a huge difference – Cathy.

Cathy's recount suggests that the guilt of the SDP experience made her question the importance of material goods, both in her placement community and in Canada. For other interns, however, the process of assuaging guilt took place in relation to those persons and communities encountered through the SDP experience. Some interns understood themselves, in effect, to be 'guilty' of being privileged, understood primarily in economic and geographic terms. The experience of living abroad, therefore, combined with doing SDP work, offered an opportunity to explore First World guilt to the fullest and, crucially, to moderate it through processes of knowing, and being accepted by, the relatively disadvantaged, towards an end of White redemption (Roman 1997).

In either case, guilt was constitutive of the subject position of the SDP intern because it was an entry point into the social and geopolitical complications of the development context. Identifying with marginalized Others offered a means to attend to privilege, and address guilt if not assuage it, while leaving the discursive hallmarks of benevolent SDP largely intact. Here it is important to clarify that guilt and privilege were mutually constitutive in SDP. Not only were interns guilt-ridden because they recognized their own privilege, but following Ahmed (2004), their claims to guilt were assertions to confirming privilege. Assuming the subject position of responsibility – a responsibility not for causing inequality as much as for fixing it – is a claim to power or 'trusteeship', as Li (2007) labels it within discourses of development. Guilt invoked a particular sense of responsibility: guilt for being a 'have' and/or for being unable to meet the responsibility of effecting changes. This stands in rather stark opposition to guilt for being implicated in the colonial and economic histories, and contemporary politics, that sustain inequality. In fact, for some interns, the guilt of privilege was unreasonable. They were willing to participate in change, particularly as stewards or catalysts, and to assume an identity of care but not to invoke guilt within a critically reflexive analysis of their own subjectivation.

> I can certainly understand why a lot of people would mention [feeling guilty] and why it comes up, but … there's no reason to feel guilty for the way that we live life over here. We certainly are considerably more affluent here as a culture. As a culture, should our country be doing more? Maybe. I don't know that I'm in a position to judge that. I mean, I do know that Canada contributes significantly and is one of the leaders in promoting development, I mean they sent me over there, I don't know if that counts for much, but … in terms of First World guilt, no, I don't even really believe in that – James.

From this perspective, the SDP volunteer experience can be understood to align with Biccum's (2010) assertion that northern development initiatives serve primarily to secure subjectivities that support northern dominance, both culturally and economically, yet do so in a way that maintains an ethical and benevolent sense of self. While this does not constitute the entire subject position of the SDP volunteer intern, it is worthy of ongoing critical attention.

In turn, and similar to Epprecht's (2004: 269) analysis, guilt was not the only emotional dynamic within the CGC internship experience; compassion and anger were also implicated. That is, emotional encounters in development internships, often in response to extreme poverty, can slide into a desire to assist and an entitlement to assume stewardship (Epprecht 2004: 694). Indeed, for some of the interns I interviewed, their understandings of the shortcomings of their interventions produced a sense of shame, or the inequalities encountered in the development context led to anger. These types of responses tended to serve as both a disavowal of guilt and a response to the structural and subject positions relative to the people and communities encountered in and through the SDP placement.

> I don't think people should feel guilty for what they have, and I think, actually, that Canadian culture is really bad at doing that. It suggests that you grew up with a privileged life and you should be so thankful and almost feel guilty for it, and I don't agree with that. But I really think it's important that you know that other people don't have this life, and that you have this experience. I never felt guilty, I felt angry. I felt really angry, um, because of that lack of

understanding and that lack of, y'know, compassion I guess. It was never guilt for me; it was more that I really, really hated where I came from. I hated it – Melanie.

Melanie went on to describe, at length, that her anger stemmed both from her understanding that few people in Canada (representative in this narrative of where she 'came from') appreciated the impact of their actions on places and people in the Global South. She explained that spending time in her placement community led her to consider this community her family and that she could see more direct links between Canada (or the First World) and the relative inequality of her new family. Her anger also stemmed from what she interpreted as overconsumption and greed in Canada, which stood in stark contrast to the lack of material goods available in her placement community.

Melanie's remarks illustrate the 'pull' on the subject position of the SDP intern. Serving the development process while attempting to preserve First World entitlement or advance their own identity as enablers of change became incredibly difficult, and emotional, within the geopolitical realities and inequalities that interns could not help but recognize. Some interns, such as Melanie, recognized their implication in the system they were trying to redress, but guilt as a way to deal with this would suggest, as Melanie pointed out, a discomfort with privilege. In this regard, anger at the lack of general awareness of the inequalities of the system was useful for establishing and supporting a politics of development and change. Interestingly, recognizing their own implications propelled interns to work harder to enable change through development, an emotionally constituted 'giving back' through SDP.

Finally, there was a clear sense of pleasure in the experiences described by some CGC interns, pleasure in the combination of the selfless act and the exotic culture. As I have suggested elsewhere, there seems to be a pleasure in using sport to 'cross' the development line for the northern subject (Darnell 2007). Farley (1997) has argued that there is pleasure in racist encounters and in the processes and acts of domination and subjection over people of colour. Data collected in this study do not support a conclusion that interns experienced pleasure in dominating, physically or otherwise, the people they encountered as Other. However, being tasked, both by the SDP organization and by discourses of development, with establishing a semblance of order and improvement out of underdevelopment, and doing so through sport while simultaneously negotiating the unexpected within exotic cultures in which they found themselves, was a pleasurable experience for interns. There was a clear sense of enjoyment in the position of stewardship.

> I loved it, I really did love it. I was ready to take a break when my internship was up, I was getting quite exhausted um, of giving so much because I found that, especially when you take ownership of a programme like that, I was going full throttle and I forgot to sort of pull back a little bit so I was ready for it to be over, but I loved the culture and I would go back there in a second – Patricia.

Yeah, yeah, I loved it. Um, I think I mean, the vibe, to experience the vibe of that country was pretty amazing, and I didn't really experience anything negative, like all of the violence is pretty much limited to their own inner gangs and whatnot. The only thing was I remember being irritated by the end, because it's so hard to not stick out, and you're always, always being followed by a flock of people. So that was hard by the end but other than that, yeah, everything was amazing. Everything reached me and just enjoying it. I mean, 8 months is not that long, so it was fun – Danielle.

Pleasure thus stemmed from the successful negotiation of the development context. Giving of oneself, acting as a leader and recognizing one's unique cultural position allowed interns to experience the SDP internship as positive and pleasurable as they carved out a way to be themselves in unfamiliar circumstances. These were deft and complex social negotiations that required CGC interns to reconcile the pleasure and fun of the SDP experience amidst transnational and local hierarchies of race, class and gender. Amanda recounted how she used the sexist expectation that a White woman in her placement community would be seeking a sexual encounter to her advantage as a development tourist.

I did get a lot of men approaching me thinking I'm there to date. But, I'll be totally honest here. Being a woman is advantageous because I made a lot of friends and whether some of them wanted to hook up with me or not, they didn't. So they were my friends and maybe they lost out, but I had a really good time, y'know? And they were willing to like help me out and get settled and drive me around and things, like I never took advantage of it, but things just come to you – Amanda.

The above quotation is an example not only of the interlocking of race, gender and sexuality but perhaps more importantly of the *recognition* of privilege combined with an attempt to disregard or discredit its preferential effects. This combination was recurrent in the experiences of CGC interns. Amanda's description suggests a clear understanding of the benefits of Whiteness but also a concomitant disavowal of *using* Whiteness to one's advantage. In turn, there was pleasure in being in a position to negotiate these power relations, in being the subject who sets the parameters by which race and sexuality are taken up and acted upon. Amanda did not feel guilty, I suggest, because unlike other interns and other elements of the internship experience, she was able to effectively establish her sense of self. In her case, this sense of self took the form of privileged, but not compromised, Whiteness.

Notably absent from most of the preceding exploration of guilt in development service is a sustained analysis of its relation to sport or physical activity. Interviews with interns that focused on notions of guilt did not regularly invoke references to sport; therefore it is difficult to establish how sport aligns with, or diverges from, the politics of guilt as described by interns. At a broad level, I expected that sport could and would have trumped guilt for interns in relation to subject positions, given sport's presumed acceptance and universality, but this was not reflected in the interview data. Sport was useful for interns as an entry point, and in supporting the development ethic of the SDP sector, but it did not level the playing field to a point where privilege was effectively reduced or removed. At the least, the regular recognition and invocation of guilt, as well as anger and pleasure, within SDP service illustrates the political dimensions of development, as they were interpreted and internalized by CGC interns, and suggests, in turn, that such politics are not easily overcome or reconciled even in the cases where sport as a universal and fun activity is the primary focus of development initiatives and interventions.

## Conclusion

In her ethnographic deconstruction of the impact of neoliberal policies throughout the world, Ong (2006) argued that neoliberalism is intimately linked to processes of exception and exclusion. By reducing individuals and populations to their capacity to contribute to the economy (the bio-politics of capitalism) neoliberalism effectively 'excepts' persons from the benefits of citizenship. However, and crucially, Ong (2006: 6) also showed neoliberalism to be a process of inclusion, 'a positive decision to include selected populations and spaces as targets of "calculative choices and value-orientation" associated with neo-liberal reform'. In this way, the reduction of government regulations and social support that constitutes the neoliberal paradigm allows for malleable policies – and bio-political mandates – that subsume individuals and populations into the dominant political apparatus perhaps more frequently than they abject them.

I suggest that Ong's framework holds purchase for making sense of the subjectivities produced within the SDP sector, particularly as it facilitates the travel of young sportspersons to the development context. CGC interns referenced a strong modernization ethic within the SDP sector, characterized by the notion of social and political inclusion. Sport was deemed useful to the extent that it could facilitate the integration – the inclusion – of marginalized persons into globalized relations, relations that interns, at the very least, recognized with relative ease particularly because they themselves had experienced sport and physical culture in positive ways and could draw a line between these experiences and their relative class (as well as race and gender) privilege. In this way, neoliberalism is relevant to the extent that it elucidates the imagination of SDP, if not its policies (though this is often the case as I explore in Chapter 4). Sport was understood to contribute to development through the production and encouragement of motivated, successful, free individuals and communities. This neoliberal ethic of SDP wasn't explicitly reproduced through dominance and consent between CGC interns and SDP participants, but it was hegemonic and discursively intelligible to the extent that it was readily recognized and, in turn, largely considered to be *the* (only) way to get ahead in a globalizing world. This ethic was also compatible with a First World subjectivity that positioned the intern as a steward of development.

The implications of these processes, particularly for the production of subjectivities, are significant. Not only does SDP potentially become caught up in, and reduced to, the processes of producing subjectivities that support the logic of dominance rather than challenge it (Biccum 2010), but the breadth of political orientations to development available to SDP and through the mobilization of sport are reduced in such a way that SDP becomes mostly about reproducing positive sporting experiences for Others. Given that sport and physical culture can secure hierarchies as much as challenge them, the reproduction of relations of power through sport in the service of development calls for ongoing critical attention (see Donnelly *et al.* 2011). Furthermore, when the focus of SDP becomes the delivery of sport in a way that seeks to include Others within capitalist hierarchies, and assuage the Self from the benefits thereof and its associated guilt, then SDP itself becomes a practice of benevolence rather than justice. As Lefebvre (2010) has argued, a recurring if not dominant narrative in SDP service is that of 'exchanging sport for gratitude' from those heretofore excluded from its boons. From a neo-Marxist perspective, such boons are not available to all and attempts to secure them for all that do not also address and challenge the political economy of inequality produce subjectivities that are implicated in, yet largely dismissive of, the relations of power that underpin development inequalities.

# 4

# Development History and Politics*

## Investigating SDP

## Introduction

In the Introduction to this book, I explored some ways in which the current mobilization of SFD aligns with the history of using sport to facilitate the social good. Despite the understanding that sport in support of social progress has a long (and in some cases sordid) history, there nevertheless remains a sense that the SDP sector challenges, re-imagines or departs from the dominant approaches to international development of the past 60 years. As Levermore and Beacom (2009) have argued, SDP can be understood in its current incarnations to constitute a response to the failures of development orthodoxy. Complicating this perspective though is Levermore and Beacom's argument that the current mobilization of SFD is, in very specific ways, tailor-made for the dominant paradigms of development, namely modernization and neoliberalism. In this chapter, I explore whether SDP does indeed offer a new approach to international development.

To approach this question, I draw on a series of interviews ($n = 9$) I conducted with programme officials and managers from SDP organizations. These included representatives from two organizations concerned with SDP advocacy and facilitation, one celebrity athlete foundation, one charitable arm of a professional sports club focused on international development and SDP, one youth sport and coaching development organization and four SDP NGOs working in the Global South and focused on youth education and health. Interview questions focused on policy makers' understandings of the position and role of SFD and its political dimensions and challenges. I draw on the insights collected through the interviews – which are not fully representative of the ongoing changes and increasing diversity of SDP (see Giulianotti 2011) – to draw out some critical insights and reflections as to the political orientation(s) of SDP. These results are not hard and fast, but I suggest that this is largely the point; the results of this chapter serve as a reminder of the various political possibilities of development as

*This chapter draws on ideas and concepts from conference presentations at the 2010 International Sport Sociology Association/RC27, World Sociology Congress, Gothenburg, Sweden and the 2010 Canadian Political Science Association/International Studies Association Conference, Montreal, Canada.

well as the ethical dimensions of development and SDP that result (see Chapter 7). In this way, I follow Hayhurst (2009) in acknowledging the importance of asking *how* development and SDP works as much as *whether* it works.

The chapter proceeds in five subsequent parts. In the next section, I explore the tensions that stem from the goal of reorienting development and practicing it differently, as SDP is now often positioned. I then provide an overview of the structure and orientation of SDP practice and politics as understood from the perspective of SDP stakeholders. Next, I consider the implications of these political orientation(s) of SDP (such as they can be defined or theorized through this data) followed by three themes offered as the basis for an ongoing critical analysis of SDP. Some concluding thoughts are then offered.

## Tensions in approaching development differently

The suggestion that sport offers a new approach to development begs for questions of the political orientation of development that SDP presupposes and imagines. Some recent research studies are useful here. For example, in Crabbe's (2009) analysis of the Positive Futures programme in the United Kingdom (UK), which uses sport-based programmes as a 'hook' for attracting marginalized youth and supporting their education and employability, sport is recognized as an attractive means by which to foster or facilitate the inclusion of the socially and economically dispossessed. In this way, SFD offers a generally acceptable, and largely non-threatening, means of reaching the excluded – particularly youth – in ways that are understood to be different than the host of programmes which to date have not proved unsuccessful in doing so. As Crabbe shows, though, this mode of SDP programming is not universal in its application and popularity but is politically palatable within the ubiquity of contemporary consumer/capitalist culture.

From this perspective, 'alternative' approaches to development in and through SDP are inevitably produced and constrained by the social, economic and political terrain in which SDP programmes regularly operate. SDP finds itself amidst tensions similar to those identified within other sectors of development, social change and philanthropy; the political orientation of activists and NGOs tends to be drawn towards anti-capitalism/anti-corporatism, but they often fail to institutionalize these mandates, given the broader practical limits of such an orientation (Littler 2009). I suggest that this kind of tension is not one that the SDP sector (or SFD scholars for that matter) has fully confronted, but it is visible, if not fundamental, to SDP. It can be seen in the ambivalent relationship between neoliberal, corporatized empowerment models versus a desire for sustainable and even radical social change in and through SDP.

Such tensions in reorienting development policy and practice are therefore not exceptional to SDP but are emblematic of the broader political dimensions of international development itself as well as those of critical development studies. Writing in the development journal *Third World Quarterly*, Frans Schuurman (2009) has argued that development studies as a paradigm or discipline is illustrative of the difficulty of reconciling studies of development policy with or against the critical theoretical analysis of development ideologies and practices. Schuurman's analysis applies both to the study of SDP as a subsection of development studies research and a subsection of sport sociology. He raises the question of whether we should be studying policies that move us closer to best practices of SDP, or even towards findings that can be generalized across various development contexts, or whether we are better to concentrate on conducting critical analyses of development practices, policies, politics and ideologies. How these approaches overlap is also an important line of inquiry.

Crucially, though, Schuurman's analysis also speaks to the tensions within the SDP sector itself. As the data discussed in this chapter demonstrates, the political dimensions of SDP are such that the importance of challenging the dominant development model – that is of using sport as a way to practice development outside of neoliberal or economistic paradigms – continues to be simultaneously produced and constrained by the need to identify and enact specific policies by which to do SFD *effectively* and *within* the standards and logics set out within the current political economy. At its most basic level, SDP constitutes a site of tension as to whether the mobilization of sport for meeting the goals of international development should be constituted as a way to do development differently or a way to do development more efficiently and effectively than has been done in the past. This tension is not irreconcilable, but it is recurrent.

## SDP: Organization, structure and orientation

In this section, I explore whether SDP is 'new' in development terms by providing an overview of the ways in which some SDP initiatives are organized and structured and the challenges of mobilizing SFD that result. I do not adjudicate the truth of such issues as understood by those in the field nor whether these results can be generalized to the entire SDP sector. Rather, I try and make sense of the political implications of the ways in which people in the field understand SDP, particularly when considered against the dominant historical narratives of international development. The analysis is organized into two subsections, sections that necessarily overlap.

## SDP: Organization and structure

First and foremost, it is significant that the SDP sector itself is understood, by the people working within it, to be new. SDP tends to be seen as a burgeoning if still loosely knit network of stakeholders who are interested in supporting development initiatives in and through the opportunities, profile and momentum that sport affords. In this way, and even somewhat aside from the critical analysis of development politics within SDP, the sector can be understood as a new player in (and/or relative latecomer to) development (Black 2010). There are several organizational dynamics that follow from this. One is that the momentum of SFD is understood by SDP stakeholders to suffer at this current stage from a lack of external legitimacy. This leads people working in, or supportive of, SDP to recognize pressure to justify the importance and contributions of SDP.

> I think it's still not accepted as a real serious movement. It still is 'just sport' or 'sport for fun'; it doesn't have the credibility that it deserves yet. So what we're seeking to do is really bring the facts and figures off the table, and that's one of the reasons we've created the association so the researchers and all of the research that is out there can feed into the thematic areas with which we concentrate on, to be an influence of policy work and governmental policy – Jennifer (SDP advocacy organization).

Second, SDP is seen to have emerged through a process whereby various sport stakeholders (organizations, athletes, clubs etc.) embraced the development possibilities of sport more so than one where the traditional development sector took up the opportunities presented by sport. Even though sport can now be understood as part of the emerging fourth pillar of development aid (see Develtere and De Bruyn 2009), much of the championing of the SDP sector has proceeded from the sports community (local, national and global) more so than from the traditional development sector.

Third, while traditional development actors are not at the foreground of SDP organization and promotion, there is increasing involvement of stakeholders from outside the world of sport, particularly corporate sponsors and charitable foundations interested in supporting SDP, or even committed to capitalizing on the novelty and momentum of SFD. The following excerpts are illustrative of these points:

> It's been interesting to see the change of perspective (in our organization). If you ask someone at our headquarters? We're doing sports programmes. We're not doing international development. Ask somebody that works on our national programmes on our national side and ask them what we're doing internationally? It's sports programmes. But if you ask our international team, our core international team … we understand that this is development work – Sally (Youth sport development organization).

> So these big private sector partners are now getting on board with the sport-for-development initiatives. Which is quite a fairly big movement because previously,

there's been very limited, if any, private sector funding in this movement. There have been mainly Western governments involved, and you can name them on one hand – Jennifer (SDP advocacy organization).

These perspectives align with the analysis of SDP interns in Chapter 3, in which the intersections and compatibility of neoliberal development philosophy and class-informed notions of sporting meritocracy combine to position SDP as a means by which to 'give back' (see Darnell 2010a). From this perspective, it is not entirely surprising that stakeholders from sport would constitute the champions of SDP, but it does beg the question of the extent to which traditional sporting cultures, and traditional development politics, are reproduced in and through the discursive and geographical terrain of SDP (see Donnelly *et al.* 2011). It also begs for analysis of the increasing interest in SDP amongst corporations, particularly those connected to sports-related industry, and the opportunity that SDP affords such organizations to construct themselves as socially responsible (and politically non-radical) corporate citizens (see Levermore 2010).

Fourth, while there is recognition of the importance of challenging top-down development, or at the least reconciling the need for a bottom-up orientation alongside top-down approaches within SDP initiatives (Black 2010), SDP is also understood by some working in the field to be primarily a northern-led sector. Again, given the diversity of the activities under the SDP banner, I am not in a position to corroborate or refute the objectivity of such claims, but such perspectives do raise the issue of relations of power that constitute unequal development and in which sport is now implicated through SDP. At the least, it is significant (and largely progressive) that SDP stakeholders recognize northern stewardship in development as an issue germane to SDP (see Giulianotti 2011). While the challenges that this recognition presents are discussed further below, suffice to say here that the recognition of northern stewardship is only a first step towards reconciling the development politics of SDP and that, somewhat more importantly for the purposes of this chapter, the invocation or mobilization of SFD does not necessarily usurp or transcend the effects of a political economy that serves to place northern institutions at the fore of SDP policy and practice (see Hayhurst 2009).

> [Northern stewardship] is an issue because we can travel anywhere in the world, well not anywhere in the world, but particularly in Africa and Latin America and we will see that many of the Sports for Development organizations that have been created and yet are successful have been established by westerners. That's just a fact. But there is a real effort by the movement and by those who have established those NGOs to support the building of capacity for local ownership. It's quite noticeable – Jennifer (SDP advocacy organization).

Fifth, the recognition of northern stewardship and its limitations, particularly amidst the historical failures of traditional development, and resultant attempts to transition away from this type of structure and organizing, mean that SDP is increasingly focused on partnerships between NGOs and funding bodies, on the one hand, and local organizations, on the other.

> I would say that every single sport-for-development organization I've met in the last 4–5 years, they fundamentally rely on the strength of their partnerships, and we're absolutely no different in that. We're only as good as the partnerships that we have in place with the organizations that we're working with. Everything comes from them. If they want us to do something, we respond. We're not deliverers within these countries, we're simply supporting the delivery that they do. And I think every single good sport-for-development organization that I've come in contact with relies on exactly the same types of links – David (Professional sports club).

In this way, similar to findings in research conducted by Giulianotti (2011), SDP programme officials are clearly aware of the general criticism of development programming and aid as a form of northern stewardship or neocolonialism, and they respond through a focus on partnerships. SDP can be understood then to be challenging the historically intelligible paradigm of top-down international development.

At the same time, attention needs to be paid to the ways in which this partnership focus proceeds not only from a critical response to neocolonialism but also from a political economy characterized by scarce resources and, particularly given the financial crisis of 2008, financial limits placed upon the traditional sources of development funding. As one official explained to me, the need for funding continues to lead SDP NGOs back to the Global North because that is where relative financial security is enjoyed and funding is accessible.

> There's tension around managing SDP the right way and not being too presumptuous and respecting the local affiliates and the expertise that they have. But the reality is, without a connection to the North and to the funding that's there, it becomes impossible to operate. So you really do rely on it. I mean that's where the funding is, y'know? There's a lot more decision-making at country level and a lot more collaboration with local governments in making decisions and driving policies, so it is a changing landscape; it's just that it's never going to be completely South–South if you will – William (SDP NGO).

This is difficult political terrain. Such reflections speak to the tension identified by Schuurman (2009) regarding doing development differently versus doing development more effectively. It also speaks to the aporia of development that recognizes its necessity and simultaneous capitulation to global capitalism (Wainwright 2008). In addition, the construction of northern subjectivity is implicated in a political economy of development that requires northern benevolence to support activities that respond to the inequalities that largely proceed from northern dominance (Biccum 2010).

In turn, then, and sixth, within this political economy, and amidst the spectre of neocolonial development and the need for critical self-reflection, the monitoring and evaluation of and in SDP becomes of paramount importance.

> I think one of the biggest challenges [is] it's still really difficult to get hard evidence-based data and studies and analysis that actually demonstrate the impact that sport has. That's something that I think we're going to have to continue to work on. It's something that we'll always be, maybe not battling, but it's something that we'll always be focusing on, in terms of finding out and demonstrating specifically how sport does make a difference and what that difference is in terms of achieving these greater development outcomes – Teresa (SDP NGO).

In an era and terrain of scarcity, proving that money is well spent becomes essential. In fact, interviews with SDP officials revealed a sense of embarrassment or frustration that the monitoring and evaluation of SDP is not robust or effective, a fact that they suggest puts SDP in relative subordination to other sectors or initiatives of international development.

> One thing that I'm really interested in is about effectiveness. Y'know, what we can talk about and say is genuinely effective within the world of sport-for-development, right? I can't really imagine another [sector] of development ... where effectiveness or sustainability is not constantly being researched and tested and probed and analyzed? I don't think there is – David (Professional sports club).

Several implications can be drawn from these reflections. Not only does a neoliberal development terrain require hard numbers and data to 'prove' the effects of SDP, but also securing positive results of SDP likely goes some way towards assuaging accusations of paternalism and stewardship. In this way, the results that 'prove' SDP to be effective have a politically utility, not unlike popular discourses of 'sport as a universal language' or 'sport as a human right' that, in effect, depoliticize the sector and make it more palatable and attractive. This is not conspiratorial in nature, nor should any positive results of SDP initiatives be dismissed out of hand. Still, continued critical analysis is called for regarding ways in which research 'proving' what sport can do for development undermines critical investigations into why development (through sport) is needed in the first place. While some monitoring and evaluation of SDP has been criticized as largely functionalist, if not evangelical in its approach and philosophy (see Coalter 2009), I would, in addition, argue that a scholarly understanding of the pressure to evaluate SDP needs to situate this impulse for proof within development's transnational politics and relations of power. That is, if (as discussed in Chapter 2) the need for development initiatives proceeds from a global political economy that contributes to unequal development on an international scale, then the need to prove that SDP works in response to such inequality should similarly be understood as a product of this political economy. Such results start, I suggest, to provide some insights into the political orientation of SDP, which I explore in more detail in the next section.

## SDP: Political focus and orientation

In many ways, the question at the centre of this chapter – does SDP offer a genuine departure from the traditional approaches to international development? – comes to rest on how SDP stakeholders understand the work that they do in the field of development. In the previous section, I suggested that SDP programme officials keep the criticism and limitations of northern stewardship as a means of development top of mind in the work that they do. At the same time, interview results suggest that the political orientation of SDP – that is, the way in which they imagine and approach making change in the world in and through the mobilization of sport – continues to draw upon and perpetuate the logic of governmentality as the preferred modus operandi of international development (see Li 2007). In this way, the clearly laudable focus on partnerships and sustainability in and through SDP still occurs alongside a political orientation that focuses largely on the conduct of partners, rather than the structures of inequality that constitute the need for development in the first place.

For example, as one SDP NGO official explained:

> We were founded by [athletes] who had friends and teammates die of HIV and AIDS and, wanted to do something about it and also saw that (sport) was a huge powerful force that could be tapped into ... the other key piece was developing a curriculum that was based on fun games and activities that kind of were experiential and would help young people kind of internalize the messages [of HIV/AIDS prevention] a bit more – William (SDP NGO).

I offer this quotation to draw attention to the ways in which this description of SDP programming pulls the political focus of the development struggle (in this case centred around the HIV/AIDS pandemic on the African continent) away from the history and political economy of African poverty, and/or the lack of political will among northern countries and corporations to support the securing of resources needed to combat HIV/AIDS (see Lewis 2005). At the same time, the description pushes the political focus towards the education (or lack thereof) of African children regarding the pandemic and the importance of supporting efforts by which they can 'internalize' messages and presumably modify behaviour. While such education programmes are no doubt useful and important, they stand apart from struggles to challenge the structures by which the people of Africa disproportionately suffer from HIV/AIDS. This is not to suggest that education efforts are mutually exclusive from attempts to redress broader structures of inequality, nor do they exist in a zero-sum power relationship. It is, however, my contention that the focus on the conduct of people is the preferred political orientation within SDP and one that tends to obscure a focus on the broader history and politics of unequal development. Another way in which this can be seen is the development (through sport) of skills that are understood to serve those who suffer from marginalization:

> We address issues of HIV and AIDS because it's very prevalent in all of the areas that we work. We also address issues of gender because it's become an issue within the community ... helping communities to understand and see the value for women to be participating and young girls to be participating in sport and extra-curricular activities. So the needs that we address in a social context come out of the direct result of our sporting interaction within the communities. Lifeskills has always been an integral component of our programme, so we've also worked with concepts of cooperation, teamwork, decision-making, conflict resolution, within the core structure even of our sporting context – Teresa (SDP NGO).

The notion of lifeskills as a focus for SDP has a bio-political dimension in the ways that building reservoirs of skills and capital stands as a productive and positive means of regulating the body as it is socially and politically produced. In the context of international development, such stakes are particularly high. In turn, the logic of governmentality cannot be separated from the preference towards partnerships, given that the focus on the 'conduct of conduct' facilitates a politics of non-interference on the part of northern NGOs. As one North American-based SDP official told me:

> Another success would be that we've really been able to improve our materials and look at our [SDP] training and to really add a lot of support into those and to have a training that people go away with and [then] feel that they can take up [SDP programming] on their own. They don't need us to babysit them all the time. But yet they still feel open enough to communicate with us on a regular basis – Sally (Youth sport development organization).

In this way, partnerships facilitate governmentality but often do so in a way that can be difficult to sustain or reconcile against a critically informed ethos that recognizes the possibilities of neocolonialism. One SDP programme official described to me the ways in which governmentality served to compromise, or at least trouble, the notion of, or commitment to, partnership and local autonomy:

> I'm sure to a certain extent we're still dictating what is going on in some of the communities [in which we operate]. I'm not sure you can necessarily ever eliminate that. But I think as best we can we try to have a collective approach, and I think it shows within some of our programming models and within our volunteer exchange programme; there's a constant and consistent exchange of ideas coming back and forth – William (SDP NGO).

At the least then, balancing the desire for positive change in and through governmentality against the importance of autonomy and indigenous rights speaks to the extent to which SFD constitutes fraught political territory. Still, it is reasonable to suggest that a focus upon the conduct of conduct continues to

LIVERPOOL JOHN MOORES UNIVERSITY
LEARNING SERVICES

offer the most palatable and productive means of imagining, approaching and mobilizing sport towards meeting development goals.

It is worth reiterating that these political understandings of development as understood in and through SDP are not malicious, misguided or wrong; indeed just the opposite is true. These approaches make perfect sense amidst the specific, contemporary challenges of international development, given the constraints of resources that limit the development sector and given the subject positions into which many SDP stakeholders are hailed in and through SDP service (see Chapter 3). What is key for critical analysis is to understand that this logic is a product of the political economy of unequal development. At the least, the political dimensions and implications of SDP need to feature in scholarly understandings of SFD and the SDP sector.

## The political orientation(s) of SDP: Critical analyses

Given some of the current conceptualizations and challenges of mobilizing SFD from the perspective of those working in the field of SDP, it is called for to explore the implications of the results. This is an ongoing project in the study of SDP and not one that can, or should, be considered complete in this chapter or text. Rather, I suggest that a critical scholarship of SDP, focused in this case on the experiences of those working in SDP but also attuned to other data sources, would be well served if approached through three theoretical lenses: bio-politics, social capital and inequality. Each is discussed here.

### The bio-politics of SDP

In lectures at the Collège de France, Foucault (2008) argued that the increasing entrenchment of bio-politics emerged from a particular political economy, one in which the state wielded less and less direct control over citizens and in which the market increasingly took on a measure of irrefutability. The governing of the populace was led, via the political economy, to the market in such a way as to 'uncover' the intelligibility of the truth of governmental practice. Bio-politics and governmentality, as constituted through the production and regulation of bodies and securing of conduct, were therefore an appropriate response to the conundrum of how to structure the exercise of power while still respecting the truths of the market. In Foucauldian terms, this was not constitutive of a social or political conspiracy but rather the 'logic' of social and political organization.

Two implications for the current political organization of SDP proceed from this understanding. One, the application and mobilization of sport to meeting development goals is not, and cannot be, an apolitical activity given that the logic of securing social change, particularly along the axes of the body and subjectivity, proceeds from the particularities of the political economy. As discussed, this political economy in the twenty-first century continues to be one in which the state is regularly and routinely impoverished or disparaged, and/or in which market logic retains a hegemonic status in policy and practice. The universality of sport does not result in SDP being free of these political implications. There is little or no political terrain in which SDP could be mobilized that would transcend the bio-political implications to which Foucault drew attention. Even the most ostensibly supportive, politically non-threatening or seemingly benign understandings of social change in SDP regularly invoke the regulation of bodies and construction of preferred subjectivities in ways that secure a bio-political logic of neoliberalism. The entrenchment of such logic can be seen in the ways in which SDP officials like Julia describe the changes that they aim to secure through SFD.

> Through our programme, we find that investing in 'young people' has a greater and more long-term impact, and I think one of the advantages of being a sport programme and a coaching programme is that people get involved because they want to and because they love to and because they are passionate already about what they do. We're actually developing this whole cadre of really passionate, empowered, informed individuals who are then transferring their knowledge and who are sharing that knowledge and also being advocates on a regular basis for the people that they're working with – Julia (SDP NGO).

This understanding of the importance of investing in people, as opposed to infrastructure or materials, is a crucial one within progressive development struggles (see Sen 2000) and is not to be dismissed out of hand, particularly as it supports a politics of self-determination for the world's marginalized peoples. Yet it remains crucial to attend to the politics of the subjectivities imagined in such descriptive accounts of SDP politics, ones that I suggest are constructed through the positive corporeality of the preferred sporting experience and that have bio-political implications that are both inescapable and particular.

Two, then, despite the tendency to eschew development based on stewardship for development through partnership, it is reasonable to argue that bio-power connects sport to development in SDP in such a way that neoliberal practices are regularly secured, rather than inequalities challenged (Darnell 2010b). That is, the machinations of the contemporary political economy, underpinned by bio-political logic, are hegemonic to the degree that even the most progressive or radical SDP initiatives tend to understand the central chore of SDP as one of securing neoliberal conduct that eschews state support and chooses not to challenge structural or transnational inequality. I am pointing here both to the constitutive political and social elements of the logic of SDP but also to the limits or borders that are enacted around it and that come to mark its political palatability. While SDP stakeholders are clearly committed to avoiding a repeat of the mistakes or failings of traditional development, the hegemony of a competitive political economy regularly serves to secure the neoliberal bio-politics of SDP and its productive capacities as normative.

## Social capital

The bio-political implications of SDP in turn hold purchase for making sense of the conceptualization and application of theories of social capital. This is an important strand of critical analysis given that social capital is increasingly a theoretical tool used to understand the logic of change conceptualized and championed in and through SDP (see Coalter 2008, 2010b; Spaaij 2009, 2011). In general terms, social capital has offered SDP practitioners and scholars an entry point to explore how sport participation facilitates improved social connectivity and resources for persons and populations that participate in sport (or SFD initiatives) in ways that eventually lead to better lives. For example, youth who participate in sport are found to be more likely to participate in community activities outside of sport as adults given the social capital that sport participation facilitates (Perks 2007). When applied to SDP, in theory as well as practice, sport can facilitate social capital in ways that support people's ability to challenge development inequality and secure their own self-determination (see Spaaij 2011). From the most optimistic perspective, increasing sport opportunities and participation increases social capital and leads to improved and sustained development. Such notions of the importance of social capital emerged through the interviews with SDP officials:

> We also do a community development process whereby we help to create and assist with organizing sports structures within the community, linking to existing sports structures, linking on to those. We give individuals and groups training in order to help build capacity for them to um, do more sports administration or to set up more efficient leagues or in terms of coaching and refereeing ... what happens is leaders are trained within the community, and their leaders are past participants from the programmes and they will help younger youth in the community with their lifeskills on and off the field – Teresa (SDP NGO).

Several implications are important to draw out here. First and foremost, what is arguably the preferred notion of social capital in the practice of SDP does not constitute the only way to understand the concept. For example, Coalter (2010b) references Coleman (1998) and Putnam's (2000) use of social capital in understanding social change through SDP – and MYSA in particular – given that these two approaches focus on the relationship and networking aspects of social capital, particularly compared to the broader sociological use of social capital in the tradition of Pierre Bourdieu. As Coalter (2010b: 1377) describes, 'In terms of our concerns with sport-for-development, Coleman and Putnam are the most relevant.' That Coalter makes this assertion and choice is both accurate and logical, given that Coleman and Putnam indeed align more closely with the logic of SDP, but it is precisely this point that makes the Bourdieusian perspective important and illuminating for critical scholars.[1] Bourdieu's notion of social capital offered a means to make sense of and theorize the structural and personal distinctions within the social milieu and to understand how these differences come to be, whereas Coleman's notion of social capital, which Coalter (2010b: 1381) applies to make sense of the development benefits of MYSA, draws attention instead to '"rationally devised material and status incentives" needed to compensate for the weakening of family, community and local government structures'. This suggests that for critical scholars, there may be a tendency to match our understanding of social capital in the *analysis* of SDP to the understandings of social capital such as they are mobilized in the *practice* of SDP. While this may be useful in some cases, it may also limit the imaginative possibilities of critical analysis.

In this way, and second, we can understand the attractiveness of social capital in SDP to derive from the ways in which it proceeds and/or connects to the intelligibility of SDP's bio-politics. Unlike Bourdieu, within the dominant logic of SDP social capital can be compatible with theorizing social engineering of marginalized people, particularly through encouraging a regulated body politic or facilitating social control (see Spaaij 2009). The practice of facilitating improved social capital by and through SDP offers a micro-solution to macro-problems in ways that potentially serve to normalize and/or depoliticize the weakening of the public sphere. That sport is susceptible and compatible with such logic is not surprising, but it needs to be understood for what it is and perhaps more importantly for what it is not. The improvement and mobilization of social capital through sport is not necessarily an approach based on deconstructing relations of dominance and supporting equality of condition. This is because the bio-political social engineering of social capital through SDP does not attend to inequality as much as it professes to help people succeed within an increasingly competitive cultural and political economy. This is fundamentally bio-political in the tradition of Foucault.

The issue I am raising is not whether social capital is important for self-determination but rather how we imagine it being constructed and/or bestowed in and through sport and SDP. The tradition of Bourdieu suggests that social capital is not something to be built or bestowed through international development initiatives as much as it is a theoretical means by which to understand the organization and stratification of society. This theoretical difference is important given recent research that suggests that the issue for successful development is not one of how to intervene in such a way as to produce social capital because even the people in the most dire and desperate situations around the world construct and utilize social capital through effort and agency on a daily basis (Saunders 2010). Rather the issue is how to provide the opportunities or structures in and through which marginalized people can mobilize social capital towards sustainable change. From this perspective, it is reasonable to ask whether a lack of social capital stands as the major development problem to which sport can or should attend through SDP. In turn, is the political economy of unequal development structured in such a way that inequality is produced *yet then rendered an individual failure or lack* to which the facilitation of social capital through sport offers an attractive solution?

Of course, it is not necessary for critical understandings of SDP to argue against the benefits of improved social capital such as they are facilitated in and through SDP. I concur that any production of motivated citizens within 'such difficult economic and cultural circumstances is clearly a major achievement' (Coalter 2010b: 1383). Nevertheless, it is crucial to recognize the specificity of such a political orientation and the resultant limitations. Indeed, Coalter (2010b) does make reference to the limits of social capital, particularly Portes and Landholt's (2000) critical contention that facilitating social capital is likely to yield only limited impact in the absence of state support. To this, I would argue for continued critical scholarship that attends to the issue of whether promoting or championing social capital in SDP potentially constitutes a tacit justification of the antecedents of development inequality and/or the retrenched, neoliberal state.

Third, then, a Bourdieusian approach reminds that social capital is culturally specific, a crucial dimension that we potentially overlook if and when social capital is mechanistically applied or transferred through sport and in support of development. Again, recent research has highlighted the importance of such understandings. As Guest (2009) has illustrated, SDP programmes are susceptible to misalignment between northern notions of the preferred or requisite cultural tools for successful development versus local demands regarding what constitutes the appropriate skills, resources or opportunities for success. While facilitating improved self-esteem to enable self-actualization among poor people is an attractive model, particularly for middle-class stewards in SDP, Guest (2009) found focusing on one's self so openly to be understood as selfish and childish in an Angolan community. This work suggests that social capital is cultural and contextually specific. In response, social capital might be more explanatory rather than offering a stable means by which to theorize the engineering of change in understanding SDP. This does not mean that social capital cannot or should not be invoked in support of struggles towards an equality of condition, but it does call into question the notion that capital can or even should be constructed or engineered through sport for the people who are deemed to be in need of such social resources.

## The politics of inequality

Finally then, it is important to connect the political orientation of SDP to the broader politics of inequality to which development attends, particularly if we understand development to be, fundamentally, a process by which attempts are made to redress inequality (Greig, Hulme and Turner 2007).[2] While changing the development focus from, for example, macroeconomic policy or foreign aid to social or community phenomena like sport offers an important opportunity to rethink or practice development differently, the importance of attending to inequality in development remains paramount. I argue that the data in this chapter, and others, suggests that many SDP initiatives in their current incarnation overlook the question of inequality by subordinating it in relation to projects of modernity and the conduct of citizens. Despite the novelty of SFD, then, SDP needs to be understood, politically and sociologically, as a site in which the politics of inequality are played out and contested.

In addition, rather than a focus solely on sport as a tool to be applied to the myriad of development challenges, attention needs also to be paid to inequality as it is constructed and maintained in and through the organization and culture of sport itself. In a 'state of the union' style address to the North American Society for the Sociology of Sport association in 1994, Bruce Kidd argued for sport scholars to renew their engagement with issues of inequality, including social issues like race, class and gender, but also macro-political issues such as governance, globalization and corporatization. In the nearly 20 years since Kidd's address, the meanings, organization, practice and consumption of sport have shifted, particularly influenced by online technologies and the rapidity of commercialization and globalization of the sporting world, but the importance of a sustained analysis of inequality has not abated. I suggest that SDP is an important new opportunity to review and revise Kidd's focus on inequality.

At the least, scholars of SDP are now faced with the challenge of coming to terms with the ways in which the cultural and political economy, particularly the hegemony of neoliberal development, produces and constrains the political orientations available within SDP. While all SDP stakeholders want for the organization and institutionalization of sport to be in the service of the social good, particularly through its connections to international development and the formalization of SDP, the dominant political economy of development and of sport clearly puts constraints on the extent to which SDP can subscribe to, and mobilize, a radical development politics.

## SDP practice and politics: Three theses

Based on the preceding discussion of the political orientation of SDP, three theses can be put forth regarding the current mobilization of SDP and its political orientation, particularly when considered against the historical trajectory of international development. While these theses are not fully transferable across the spectrum of SDP policy and practice, they do offer a contribution to an ongoing and critically informed analysis of the struggles and implications of organizing and mobilizing SFD.

First and foremost, based on the interviews and other recent critical analyses, it is reasonable to argue that a modernist residue clings to, and influences, current understandings and conceptualizations of SFD within SDP, particularly as it positions SDP as a way to facilitate improvement amongst marginalized persons and populations. Despite the sustained critical perspectives that SDP stakeholders bring to bear on their work and on the sector in general, the tendency to reduce development to a process of improvement, and of securing modernity for those currently denied its benefits, remains an attractive political platform from which to mobilize SFD. As one SDP programmer told me:

> We recognize that sport has the power to make a difference in the basic communication, confidence, self-esteem, empowerment of people, and we want to enable people to access sport and then tack on these additional development goals – Julia (SDP NGO).

The importance of self-esteem or empowerment is not debated here, for these are clearly important and laudable goals. However, the ways in which such conceptualizations of development refer to, and solidify notions of, improving the conduct of persons within development rather than challenging the relations of politics and power that lead to marginalization in the first place suggests a modernization ethos. Such notions of personal empowerment as the building blocks of sustainable development, notions particularly amenable to hegemonic notions of sport as meritocratic and oriented towards the building of character, are not representative of a universal humanism and can in fact stand at odds with the demands of local people struggling towards sustainable development (see Guest 2009).

Such a political orientation towards SDP has social implications as well, particularly in the maintenance of social hierarchies along lines of race, class and gender. As I have explored elsewhere, the Foucauldian notion of bio-power – the productive power to encourage regulation of the body – has implications for race and racism (Darnell 2010b). A bio-political state is one more 'open' to racism as race comes to stand as a marker of modernity (Foucault 1997; Goldberg 1993). From this perspective, modernization as a mandate for SDP closes many of the opportunities for imagination, self-determination and indeed resistance to development inequality at the same time that it opens up spaces, both discursive and geographical, to the justification of social hierarchies as symbols of achieving modernity. Such critiques speak to the importance of sustained analyses of modernization and stewardship in theorizing SFD as well as ongoing critical analyses of whether sport challenges or secures a modernizing politics and ethos.

The second thesis speaks more directly to the focus of this chapter, namely that it remains a challenge within SDP to reconcile critical theoretical understandings of development and ways to do development differently, against the practical challenges of how to implement new approaches and the myriad of conundrums that this constructs. Specifically, attempts to do development differently have led SDP practitioners and champions, particularly from NGOs, to focus purposively on local ownership of development programmes as a means of challenging traditional development hierarchies. This, though, produces a set of new challenges in SDP. As one SDP NGO manager explained, given the focus on partnerships and local empowerment,

> I find a lot less identification to the programmes and to what we do now than before because the programmes are not ours. Precisely what people say is wrong with development; you work for others and the rewards are for others – Henry (SDP NGO).

The initial implication here, and an important one for any policy analyses of SFD, is that doing SDP work within a critical framework is clearly difficult praxis, especially from a managerial perspective. Amidst a political and economic terrain characterized by scarce resources and the importance and mounting pressure of monitoring and evaluation in order to prove the effectiveness of SFD programming, retaining managerial influence of SDP programmes at the same time as yielding control in support of grassroots development that is locally driven is extremely difficult. Even the most sceptical critical scholar needs to take such tensions into account.

Still, there is evidence from the perspective of those working towards development goals through sport-focused NGOs of a disconnect between the goals of (a) the broader international development community, (b) the civil society of SDP, often northern-led organizations, and (c) local programmes and people for whom SDP is designed and intended to be most beneficial.

SD: What will happen in the future for you to be able to say we've met our goals?

SALLY (Youth sport development organization): If the kids in our programme today volunteered to continue to be in our programme tomorrow. I think there's a lot to be said about volunteerism, and in some of these communities that we work with, volunteerism is a very strange term. We advertise that we want volunteers and we'll provide you training, but then they want to know what are they going to get paid? And our programmes don't work that way. We can't. We can't pay all of our community coaches. But if the kids that are in our programmes come back and they want to do it as they get older and volunteer in our sense of the term, that's a positive benefit and that's how we know that the programme has been a success.

This quotation illustrates the intractability and omnipresence of relations of power and politics within sport, development and SDP. If, for example, northern NGOs desire a volunteer culture to support SDP programmes and the meeting of development goals, this should be understood, first and foremost, as a reflection of *their* development priorities and not necessarily of the universality or applicability of volunteerism. This does not mean that such perspectives are inherently misguided or even malignant in their politics but do speak to their palatability within the current political economy. At the very least, such perspectives demand to be recognized for what they are: a political orientation and world view of sport, development and social organization that is largely individualized and competitive as well as hegemonic and therefore continuously contestable.

I also suggest that the above reflection illustrates that in SDP, like development more broadly, every practice is challenging and contestable in managerial but also social and political terms. The goal of SDP NGOs as described above – to support local initiatives and to eschew stewardship in favour of partnership – does not 'solve' the problem of development politics as much as produce new sets of challenges. In other words, the novelty of SFD and the challenging of development orthodoxy through SDP create a new, yet no less contestable, political terrain. Even though sport may be positioned as a new form of development and even though SDP practitioners are working to do development differently, development remains fraught political territory and is best understood as such.

This leads directly to the third thesis that I put forth here, that there is evidence that some SDP practitioners are indeed working directly to protect the development novelty that sport affords, even though this is very difficult to do within the political economy of development and within the pressures to effect and measure, if not prove, sustainable change. That is, for some SDP policy makers, sport is indeed a response to the failure of dominant development orthodoxy as Levermore and Beacom suggest. As was described to me:

> Those people who started local organizations were realizing that the state, the international aid programmes, the football federations, the corporations, they were not fulfilling their role in the society, and that is why they started [SFD] programmes – Sven (SDP advocacy organization).

This counter-hegemonic approach constitutes an ethos of development that I would argue is rarely championed or celebrated through the most visible SDP rhetoric. That is, rarely is the 'power of sport' to support development positioned *against* the activities of governments, institutions or corporations that have failed to support equitable development for decades or even participated directly in exacerbating global inequality. Nor does this political approach to SDP seem likely to stand as an attractive means to invite partners in positions of economic and geopolitical privilege (the same corporations, government, international aid organizations, IFIs) into the SDP fold because it suggests that these organizations are part of the problem of unequal development. However, such a perspective does position SDP as explicitly political work, and understood as such by those in the field, and also suggests that there may be a glimpse of SDP connecting to, or aligning with, sport and radical social movements that seek to challenge the political economy and relations of power that sustain inequality (see Chapter 7). For these reasons, understandings of such an ethos of SDP and its implications are worthy of sustained inquiry in the critical study of SFD and SDP.

## Conclusion

Two broad conclusions can be drawn from this chapter. One, while the SDP sector in its current incarnation may be new, the use of sport for social change is not. More importantly, however, the politics of conceptualizing and implementing development initiatives through SDP are not new. In fact, I suggest that they map quite closely onto the politics of development identified within critical development scholarship over the past several decades. Balancing modernization and stewardship versus self-determination remains a political challenge in SDP.

As a result, and two, the challenges and politics of development preclude the mere application of sport as a solution to or panacea of international development struggles. Sport is not an answer to development, though it may be part of the process of re-imagining and in some cases challenging international development and its political economy.

To a large degree then, while the popular rhetoric of SDP regularly does not hold up to careful scrutiny – to the extent that it champions social change but change limited to the structures and possibilities laid out within dominant cultural and political economy – there is some evidence to suggest a commitment to challenging development amongst those most intimately involved in the day-to-day operation of SDP organizations. This is clearly difficult work as SDP is consistently implicated in, and beholden to, the constraints of the social and political economy. From this perspective, while the invocation of sport for the social good is not new, perhaps more important to recognize for critical scholars is that the political challenges of, and political orientation to, international development are not inherently challenged in and through the deployment of sport. This is not the same as arguing that sport cannot or should not be involved in struggles for sustainable and just development, only that the issue comes to rest on the political orientation and palatability of development, much more so than assessments of the relative 'effectiveness' of sport to meet development goals. The most legitimate novelty of SFD may be in the ways in which it offers a renewed political approach to, and engagement with, the broader challenges of international development. At the least, if we take the argument that nearly all of the suffering endured amidst the world's unequal development is undeserved, yet those who suffer are regularly asked to make up for these gaps in inequality (Gasper 2004), then our attention should be drawn to the need to be careful about, and committed to, the political orientation embraced through the mobilization of SFD. This chapter demonstrates any such commitment to be an ongoing challenge in SDP.

# 5

# Sport, International Development and Mega-events

## Introduction

On 2 October 2009, the IOC awarded the 2016 Summer Olympic Games to Rio de Janeiro, choosing the Brazilian city over northern competitors Madrid, Chicago and Tokyo, and marking the first time the Games had been awarded to a city in South America. The announcement shortly succeeded Brazil's winning, in 2007, the rights to host the 2014 FIFA World Cup, and thus put the country on schedule to host, within 24 months, the world's two highest profile, and arguably most prestigious, sports events. Indeed, one measure of the size and scope of these events is the amount of money budgeted to be spent, with estimates, according to the Rio 2016 Candidature file, of operating costs for the Rio Olympics of US$2.8 billion and a total Olympic budget, including capital investments, of US$11.6 billion. This is in addition to the building of seven new stadiums and the refurbishment of five others for the World Cup at an estimated cost of US$1.1 billion.

The announcement of, and subsequent plans for, these two events in an emerging, southern economy like Brazil is representative of two broader trends within the relationship between sport and international development. The first is the movement of sports mega-events, particularly the Olympics and World Cup but also 'second-order' games like the Commonwealth Games and Pan American Games (see Black 2008) to the Global South. Indeed, with the 2010 FIFA World Cup in South Africa and the 2010 Commonwealth Games in Delhi, India as primary examples, there is an increasing tendency for southern polities to strive for participation in globalization and globalized sport in and through the hosting of sports mega-events. This tendency is clearly now recognized, supported and ultimately enabled by supranational sports organizations like the IOC and FIFA. This in turn leads to the second trend, namely the sociopolitical construction, and essentially the marketing of these events in the Global South as a legitimate and fundamental aspect of development policy and strategy (see Cornelissen 2009). In addition to the generally and traditionally accepted positioning of sports mega-events as a means to build sporting infrastructure and 'legacies' for citizens of host cities and nations, the movement of mega-events to the South has meant that such events are now positioned more broadly as catalysts for social and economic development and part of long-term southern development strategies. For these reasons, any analysis of the contemporary connections between sport and international development needs to consider the role of sports mega-events, the interests of the plethora of organizations and institutions that have a stake in the movement of mega-events to the South and the concomitant connection of such events to development policies and discourses.

In this chapter, I offer a critical and theoretically informed research framework for making sense of the connections between sports mega-events in the Global South and the development agenda, or the promises, for sustainable and equitable development that are increasingly attached to such events. I also examine how these promises connect to the SDP sector. The chapter's central argument is that sports mega-events in the Global South are increasingly organized, marketed and celebrated as legitimate components of a sustainable and equitable development agenda but that such invocations often obscure the ways in which such events are themselves embedded in a political economy of inequality and underdevelopment. To construct this argument, I explore the current social and political economy of sports mega-events and their connections – material and discursive – to international development goals. I then advance three theses regarding the implications of positioning sports mega-events as legitimate development policy.

Throughout the chapter, I consider the intersections of economic, political *and* cultural dimensions given the impossibility of effectively separating them in any critical analysis of sports mega-events (Tomlinson 2005). Furthermore, as Cornelissen (2009) has argued, the study of sports mega-events in development studies has suffered from a lack of engagement with development theory. Thus, I attend to the conceptualizations of development promoted by the state, civil society and popular culture, and the interrelations between the three, in making sense of sports mega-events and SFD.

## The sociopolitical economy of sports mega-events

Much has been written in recent years about the commercialization and global reach of sports mega-events, the reasons why hosting sports mega-events remain attractive to cities and countries, and the ability or likelihood of sports mega-events to deliver on their social and/or economic promises (see Black 2008; Cornelissen 2008; Hall 2006; Horne 2007; Roche 2000; Swart and Bob 2004, among others). While a full review of this literature is beyond the scope of this chapter, I do draw attention here to key elements of the political economy of sports mega-events in order to contextualize their movement to the Global South and their discursive connection to, or construction as, legitimate and sustainable development initiatives. I draw principally on Cornelissen's (2009) argument that sports mega-events in the Global South are used to showcase successful development, particularly for states struggling for legitimacy within competitive globalization, even though the various notions of development espoused through such sports mega-events are rarely problematized within such processes.

First and foremost, then, the development politics of mega-events are evident to the extent that they are explicitly and firmly situated within the broader political and economic sphere. In writing about the Olympic Games, Tomlinson (2005) argues that the primary significance of the Olympic Games is not international sporting competition but rather the connection between the Games and the production and 'profiling' of cities as legitimate spaces within competitive globalization and the expansion of capital and corporate interests into new consumer markets. The organization and hosting of sports mega-events is never a benign act – socially, economically or politically – but always connected to a range of political and economic interests. Particularly since the 'commercial era' of the Olympics, beginning in 1984 with the Summer Games in Los Angeles, it is impossible to separate the Games from corporatization and the pursuit of profit despite the ways in which the Olympics continue to promulgate, if not trade upon, notions of the event in service of tolerance and internationalism (Tomlinson 2005). The result is a dense cultural and political mix of 'sport for profit' and 'sport for good', messages and practices that are ascribed to the Olympics as well as to the FIFA World Cup, which promotes a message of football as a universal language and supports such discourses with the organization and dissemination of Football for Hope (http://www.fifa.com/aboutfifa/worldwideprograms/footballforhope). These meanings are important on a global scale given that sports mega-events require an infrastructure and culture of mass media in order to construct and sustain sporting spectacle (Roche 2006) and therefore have the ability to transmit promotional messages to billions of people (Horne 2007).

This political and cultural economy points towards the fact that while contemporary sports mega-events are products or phenomena of global modernity (Roche 2006), in their current construction and organization they are principally constitutive of, and constituted by, neoliberal policy and philosophy (Hall 2006). This means that sports mega-events are of the same tradition, share many of the same limitations and are open to the same criticisms as neoliberal policy and neoliberal approaches to international development. For example, Gruneau (in press) illustrates how the prestige and wealth ascribed to sports mega-events beginning in the 1980s increased at the same time as economic inequality was exacerbated around the world through anti-Kenyesian economic liberalization, reductions in public spending and the increased mobility of capital. This relationship is not causal; the competition to host sports mega-events did not/does not invariably lead to inequality. However, it is significant that the 'economic scale and significance' of sports mega-events increased as part of the same political economy that privileged deregulation, growth and social policy based on individual rights and did so at the expense of more direct analyses and responses to development inequality (Gruneau, in press: 21).

As a result, sports mega-events now offer states a political instrumentality (Cornelissen 2008) and/or a means of competing for, and establishing, a global identity (Black 2008) that is ostensibly or theoretically open to a range of orientations towards development, but in political and economic practice, and particularly in relation to development, tends to privilege neoliberalism by mobilizing capital and seeking to attract foreign investment. Indeed, it is within the neoliberal political economy that mega-events have thrived (Hall 2006) and in turn come to constitute an important, although I will argue ultimately limited, element of a long-term, sustainable development agenda. This is particularly the case for southern states, traditionally marginalized geopolitically and therefore increasingly desperate to attract foreign money and participate more robustly and effectively within competitive global capitalism. In addition to the political limits identified by Gruneau, whereby sports mega-events for development become more about the improved facilitation of capital and less about redressing inequality, at least three others critical issues can be identified within an analysis of the sociopolitical economy: limited sustainability, chronic overspending and consumption as a form of cultural education/exclusion.

While the hosting of sports mega-events has increasingly become part of broader state-led development policy and goals in southern countries like South Africa (Cornelissen 2009), hosting remains, in many cases, beholden to the goal of an improved domestic sports industry and athletic success, a focus with inherent limitations. The finite number of sports mega-events in the world limits the sustainability of development for cities deemed worthy enough to host. The result is that the development boons of hosting lead to the propensity, if not the necessity, to host again and again in order to maintain a global identity and economic stimulus within competitive capitalism (Black 2008). South Korea provides an interesting contemporary example, whereby the hosting of mega-events (beginning with the 1988 Summer Olympics in Seoul and continuing through the 2002 FIFA World Cup, co-hosted with Japan) has led the country to aggressively pursue subsequent mega-events and commit to producing world-class, high-performance athletes who win medals at a rate beyond that expected by their population size. This is, ostensibly, a form of SFD whereby Korea seeks political and economic benefits as a hosting nation.

On the one hand, this strategy is led and supported by the state, which suggests the possibility of an alternative to neoliberal, market-driven and/or civil society development initiatives. However, such strategies have, in the Korean case, arguably had less to do with shifting from competitive development logic to a social development strategy (as suggested by dominant SDP rhetoric) and more to do with a strategy of mobilizing sport as a means of better participation within competitive globalization with benefits for the state (Kwon 2010). By this logic, being a sports powerhouse through hosting mega-events and/or performing well on the pitch, court or ice at major games is understood to represent, or even directly lead to, success within the globalization of sport and the challenges of development.

Success in hosting sports mega-events is fleeting at best, though, particularly if the media coverage and political instrumentality afforded by the act of hosting cannot be extended beyond the time frame of the games themselves. Successful hosts like Korea therefore find themselves striving to host subsequent events.[1] In turn, given the issue of chronic overspending (discussed below) sports mega-events can become developmental spending handcuffs for the hosting state. Perhaps more importantly from the perspective of critical development studies, if the competitive political economy of international development (and SFD) continues unchallenged, and sports mega-events become an increasingly legitimate means of success within competitive development, then it necessarily structures a world where not all can be successful. In such a model, the success of Korean development *depends on* the underdevelopment of sport elsewhere given that only a small number of mega-events (not to mention Olympic medals and World Cup titles) are available to be won. From this perspective, *dependencia*, underpinned by the Marxist tradition, remains an important critical lens through which to analyse SFD and mega-events because winning the development game – a cultural and political logic particularly palatable in and around sport – is reduced to the importance of 'not losing' at development. Thus, while on the one hand, the active developmental state, such as in Korea, appears beneficial in the face of retreating state participation and amidst neoliberal development, in the case of sports mega-events the developmental state appears to buy into, rather than challenge, competitive globalization, a strategy that requires massive public spending on elite sport and international mega-events at the expense of other development priorities.

This, then, leads to the second development limitation related to the political economy of sports mega-events: chronic overspending. Sports mega-events regularly exceed their budgets and place the hosting state/city in a precarious position whereby they cannot afford *not* to cover extra costs and risk the Games being a failure (Black 2008). The track record and body of research related to spending on sports mega-events suggests that overspending is the normative experience, not the exception. As Horne (2007) shows, overspending on mega-events remains couched in a political ethos whereby supporters consider it to be an 'unknown known' or a recurring tendency but one best left unexplored or unacknowledged. At the least, whether the tendency to overspend is admitted or not, any development strategy based on an economic track record as dubious as that of contemporary sports mega-events appears limited at best.

Furthermore, for peripheral or emerging states, or for LMICs, the stakes associated with hosting are significantly higher both in terms of economic standing and international prestige (Black 2008). Certainly, the popular discourse surrounding the 2010 Commonwealth Games in Delhi positioned the event as an international sociopolitical referendum on the competencies of the Indian economy and state functioning. At issue is that placing such a development burden on something as economically precarious as the hosting of a sports mega-event almost necessarily resigns states in the Global South to overextend in order to achieve, a burden likely passed on to domestic spending or the social safety net. This is particularly likely when the goal of hosting is to perform and assert state prestige and development as the world watches.

In turn, then, a third limitation inherent to the current sociopolitical economy of sports mega-events is that the champions of staging such events regularly trade on the universality of sport amidst the globalization of the political economy but rarely acknowledge the role of sports mega-events in effectively demarcating who is included and/or excluded socially and economically. As Roche (2000: 65) has demonstrated, the 'universality' of mega-events – such as world's fairs or Expos in the nineteenth century and the modern Olympics – employed several 'exclusionary features' that secured racist, sexist and classist ideologies in and through the construction of a presumed collective social progress. Given the intensity of the commercialization of the modern sports mega-events, exclusionary practices continue in a similar fashion. In this regard, the particular and privileged experiences and politics of sports mega-events, by which I refer to the fact that hosting, attending and/or consuming sports mega-events remain an opportunity available to a privileged sociopolitical class, are positioned as a universal sporting experience as if to suggest that the entire world has access to, and indeed does, consume sports mega-events. This is a limit of the universalization discourse at it is constructed at the confluence of sports mega-events and international development; the culturally specific and socially exclusive sporting experience is deemed to be applicable to all and/or comes to stand as evidence of the sporting underdevelopment of marginalized communities, nations or populations. This 'universalist' discourse of sport is one that scholars like Roche (2000) and Peacock (2011) show connects particularly well to the establishment of global sporting governance that the IOC carved out for itself in the twentieth century. This discourse, coupled with the forces of economic and cultural globalization, takes the particular experience of bourgeois consumption of the Olympics and renders it a universal experience and repositions those unable (or unwilling) to consume as 'underdeveloped'. Such markers of underdevelopment then become licence for SFD initiatives, enabled by the movement of mega-events to the South. The Olympics as a form of modernity is imported into a development discourse as a new means of spurring development and justifying the expansion of mega-events to the South and the spending that this requires. Those privileged enough to consume can then employ universal discourses of sport and development as a means of 'educating' themselves about the need for, and role of, sports mega-events in contributing to the 'un-underdevelopment' of Others (Biccum 2010).

With these limits in mind, I suggest that sports mega-events are best conceptualized as a means of, or approach to, development that privileges a philosophy or approach based on more effective and/or more competitive participation within the global economy rather than one that challenges the politically economic order or the structures and institutionalization of inequality. Indeed, following Hall (2006), sports mega-events are quintessentially neoliberal in championing an ethos of global competitiveness and constant economic and political regeneration. What is crucial for the purposes of this chapter is that, based on early analyses of the 2010 FIFA World Cup in particular, simply moving sports mega-events to the Global South does little, if anything, to make such events any more accountable to the public good (see Desai and Vahed 2010). In the next section, I examine more closely the ways in which sports mega-events have been positioned as central to broad, sustainable development in the Global South.

## The development agenda of sports mega-events in the Global South

To this point, I have offered arguments about the limitations of the type of, or orientation towards, development often ascribed to the hosting of sports mega-events, particularly in the Global South. Here it is important to consider that political and institutional forces, as well as relations of power, are also in play and serve to encourage or drive sports mega-events to the Global South. These forces are framed by the notion that sports mega-events can showcase the development of the South, which arguably holds greater weight than the actual contributions of hosting for southern states (Cornelissen 2009). Two forces in particular, then, can be understood to work in self-referential and mutually constitutive ways to drive mega-events to the South: the new, yet historically informed, development agenda espoused by sports mega-event organizations like the IOC and FIFA and the relative desperation of southern states to 'get a piece of the sport mega-events pie globally' (Swart and Bob 2004: 1313).

With respect to the former, it is reasonable to argue that the interest in SDP on the part of the IOC and FIFA works to 'construct' a development agenda in and through the bestowing of the Olympics or World Cup to southern polities. If sports mega-events are understood to constitute an event whereby southern development can be and is showcased, then the awarding of the Games, by powerful supranational organization, or sporting Business International

Non-governmental Organizations (BINGOs) like FIFA (Sugden and Tomlinson 2005) and the IOC, is an active part of the setting of development standards and parameters. Through such processes, southern development through sports mega-events is repositioned as a means by which to recognize and reward appropriate and politically palatable development processes, rather than a means by which to support the struggle for sustainable self-determination and development for the world's poor. The awarding of the Games to the South comes to constitute a development achievement award, more than support for development struggles and local self-determination.

In turn, the development activism taken on by BINGOs like the IOC, through Olympism in Action and its support for Development through Sport, and FIFA through Football for Hope, expectedly aligns with neoliberal development philosophy because to challenge such thinking would undermine the political and institutional primacy and authority of the organizations and their events.

This logic, of course, is not solely constructed by institutions and forces in the Global North, but, as understood in and through Gramscian hegemony, results from the interplay and negotiation between northern and southern interests. The bestowing of the Olympics or World Cup to the South as part of the sociopolitical construction of international development clearly adds a layer of prestige to the hosting of the mega-events from the perspective of the South as well. Despite the track record of overspending, and the opportunity costs that remain incredibly high for marginalized polities, supporting mega-events as a development project becomes attractive, or even a necessary evil, for states wishing to get in the globalization game. This is what Swart and Bob (2004) refer to as the 'seductive discourse' of development for mega-events in the South; development becomes the only way to justify the desire for, and hosting of, mega-events, even though they likely will not or cannot fulfil development promises. The temerity of these promises is played against the notion, supported by the North, that the successful hosting of Games will offer proof of southern development and inclusion within the dominant cabal of global capital's beneficiaries. Following Gramsci, while open to refinement and consistent negotiations, such a relationship of dominance and consent is fundamentally hegemonic and disproportionally beneficial to powerful groups, in this case those within the political economy of globalized sport.

With these ideas in mind, it is reasonable to argue that the development agenda increasingly ascribed to sports mega-events in the Global South is connected to, but markedly different from, the traditional sports mega-event vernacular of 'legacies'. Specifically, whereas the term legacies is often conceptualized primarily in terms of sports development, with a focus on increased sports participation and improved sporting facilities and infrastructure, development here extends the notion to the broad social, political and economic development of a region or country, with sport or the hosting of sports mega-events as its catalyst. Compared to legacies, then, the development agenda ascribed to sports mega-events in the South can be thought of as both broader and deeper in its social and political importance and stakes, and arguably more inclusive of the social, political and health dimensions of development. At the same time, as noted above, such notions of development often trade on the idea of both sport and international development as universal goals and phenomena, which in turn increasingly position the hosting of Games as a means of asserting international prestige and a development agenda within competitive globalization. Again, this is particularly the case for the BRIC economies and other emerging powers in the Global South.

This difference between legacies and development can be understood or theorized through the sociopolitical urgency ascribed to the opportunities that sports mega-events represent for southern stakeholders. As Swart and Bob have demonstrated, the potential to host sports mega-events in South Africa offered a political and economic opportunity for the nation that was constructed and represented as too good to pass up. Similarly, Mourao (2010) found that residents of Porto Alegre, Brazil overwhelmingly supported public expenditures for the hosting of the World Cup in 2014 given the potential for economic and infrastructure development, and despite a general scepticism regarding government competency to deliver on promises like human security. For those living in Porto Alegre, the hosting of the event was understood as one of the best opportunities for the Brazilian people to share in the benefits that regularly accrue through the globalization of capital and sport. There is a level of social, political and economic urgency for southern states in hosting that extends well beyond the legacies of sport facilities and sports participation. It is perhaps an unintended outcome of the linking of sport and sports mega-events to a broader development agenda that this process increases the urgency to leverage the opportunities that sports mega-events afford. Efforts in South Africa, for example, to ascribe a public health or community development agenda to the FIFA World Cup are exemplary of this. While no one would begrudge southern stakeholders for using every opportunity to combat, for example, the devastation of the HIV/AIDS pandemic, such leveraging of the World Cup calls into question the extent to which the desperation of southern states, resulting from the entrenchment of their global subordination within the political economy, contributes to a political environment in which the benefits of hosting sports mega-events are oversold and the opportunity costs of hosting under-examined (Black 2008).

In sum, the sociopolitical economy of sports mega-events, coupled with their increased positioning as catalysts for long-term sustainable development, particularly in the Global South, means that sports mega-events are increasingly important features of the SDP sector. In the next section, I offer three theses to further conceptualize these connections.

# Three theses for understanding sports mega-events in/as development

## Sports mega-events, and their governing bodies, increasingly desire to be involved with international development

Given the compatibility between sports mega-events and neoliberal development philosophy, and the popular rhetoric surrounding SDP and the 'power of sport', ascribing a development agenda to sport generally, and mega-events in particular, is an increasingly attractive proposition for BINGOs like FIFA, the IOC and other transnational or supranational sport organizations. Support for international development positions these organizations as legitimate stakeholders within socially progressive movements. According to those working in the SDP sector, this can be attributed to a desire to allocate funds from sport in support of development in a way that benefits international, elite sport at the same time. As a key international SDP stakeholder/manager explained in interview:

> We have, for example, the IOC promoted to donor status so now they're very much wanting a closer partnership with the world of development or the United Nations. Very much so. So they want the expertise of the world of development to assist them in their programmes. They have their pot of money; they don't know how to spend it. They want to spend it on doing good; they want to reform the image of themselves as a sports organization, to go beyond the games – Jennifer (SDP advocacy organization).

For FIFA and the IOC, the organizations responsible for the biggest sports mega-events in the world, development now constitutes an approach to good global citizenship or, in management vernacular, corporate social responsibility. These organizations can be situated within the CSR for SDP model (Levermore 2010), a fact that should inform the ways in which we make sense of the development implications of hosting of mega-events. For example, in October 2010, FIFA hosted a 3-day workshop in Ghana to showcase the start of a development partnership with adidas. According to FIFA.com:

> The programme is part of the FIFA Partners' Corporate Social Responsibility (CSR) Programme, a collaboration between adidas and FIFA on CSR and implemented through Football for Hope, a movement led by FIFA and streetfootballworld, which uses the power of the game for social development.

Not only do sports mega-events offer the developmental state in the Global South an opportunity to participate within competitive global globalization through hosting, but the organizations that allocate the rights to Games, and benefit from the competition over the right to host, now position themselves as socially responsible development actors. While this does not mean that the hosting of mega-events constitutes the same sociopolitical activity as development itself, it does suggest that the messages of SFD and of the SDP sector are increasingly attractive to sports mega-events stakeholders and arguably substantiate the notion that such events contribute to sustainable development, despite the limitations indentified by critical scholars.

The clear critique of this perspective is that it constitutes little more than the cynical attempt by these supranational sport organizations to manage their brands and divert negative attention, particularly through the media. As Littler (2009: 61) describes, CSR 'offers a form of reputation management in the face of criticism: it offers a damage limitation or risk avoidance strategy'. This is arguably important for the IOC and FIFA whose links to corruption, and an inherent lack of social and economic transparency, veritably cry out for the management of reputation (Jennings 1996; Sugden and Tomlinson 2005). Given that CSR is never something simply performed upon unsuspecting consumers, of sport or otherwise (Littler 2009), and that the discourse of benevolent Olympism has always been resisted and reinterpreted by people around the world (Guest 2009), the effectiveness of such management techniques remains to be seen. Nevertheless, the politics of the visions and implementation of international development championed by supranational sport organizations is worthy of ongoing critical analysis.

## SDP NGOs are increasingly attracted to mega-events

The second thesis to consider in relation to sports mega-events and development in the Global South is that the increased mobility and movement of sports mega-events to the southern hemisphere, coupled with the institutionalization of the SDP sector as a legitimate part of civil society development, results in mega-events becoming increasingly important and attractive to SDP NGOs and other civil society stakeholders working within the sector. A desire to be associated with, if not latch onto, the profile and development opportunities that sports mega-events afford is increasingly important to NGOs working to mobilize SFD. This is evidenced, at the least, in the scramble for funds, access and exposure amongst NGOs within recent sports mega-events, particularly FIFA 2010 in South Africa, and the opportunity that sports mega-events afford NGOs to promote their work and extend its social and political momentum. Both of these 'utilities' of sports mega-events were evident in interviews I conducted with programme officials from SDP NGOs. For example, an NGO manager told me the following:

> We definitely have used and plan to use the World Cup because it's the biggest sports event in the world, maybe the biggest ever. We see it as a stage, a visibility stage, an awareness creating platform of the work that we do in using football for social change – Sven (SDP advocacy organization).

The point here is not the objective effectiveness of football (or sport) for social change (though this remains an important strand of social and political inquiry). Rather I draw attention to the 'spectacularization' of sports mega-events, supported by media, capital and consumption, that becomes attractive to the civil society sector. These actors work constantly and genuinely to justify and promote their work to a broad audience in order to (a) build popular acceptance and support and (b) maintain access to funding from donors and sponsors interested in, and attracted to, high-profile and politically palatable support for international development. In turn, mega-events like the World Cup become increasingly attached to a mediated identity as catalysts of social change, an effect that serves to attract more development stakeholders eager to leverage the promotional opportunities:

> With the World Cup being given to South Africa, I think a lot of people realized that a World Cup in Africa will be about so much more than just the matches that will take place in multi-billion rand stadiums and that it really had a powerful impact on development and reintegration. As a result, we've seen so many new actors in the field, some of them are just actually following the World Cup and coming to South Africa and they'll be leaving in 2011 going to Brazil – Henry (SDP NGO).

The movement of sports mega-events into the regions and countries where the work of development NGOs is most heavily concentrated, and the popular development agenda increasingly connected to these events, means that more and more NGOs strive to connect their initiatives to the social, political and mediated momentum that the events construct and provide. While the promotion of SFD in the Global South is not problematic in and of itself, the processes described above do call for the need for caution and critical analysis. Indeed, the attraction that sports mega-events present to SDP NGOs holds a possibility for the development agenda ascribed to the World Cup and the Olympics to be potentially reduced to a single stop on an international tour of SFD. While sports mega-events may draw important attention to social issues such as HIV/AIDS in South Africa or income inequality in Brazil, the rush to be part of the development agenda of sports mega-events as they move around the world suggests, at the least, a limited commitment to long-term and sustainable development.

Furthermore, it is difficult to imagine that the attractiveness of sports mega-events to NGOs and the connections that ensue would not have an impact on the political orientation of SDP NGOs themselves. As Littler (2009: 56) has articulated, NGOs generally tend to support, at least ideologically, an anti-corporate politics, 'but they are frequently afraid of developing their practice to that conclusion for political reasons'. From this perspective, the desire to be associated with sports mega-events and their development agenda likely reduces the ability or likelihood of SDP NGOs to question or criticize the political orientation of the events themselves, which, as discussed above, are generally understood as constituted by and constitutive of corporatization and neoliberalism. Again, results from interviews I conducted with SDP programme officials are illustrative here, particularly the perspective of this SDP official working with football programmes in Africa:

> Even people who sat, historically, on the other side of the debate and said 'I believe that sport has yet to be justified as a valid tool for achieving social change and development, however you want to call it, however you want to define it', when something like the World Cup comes along, all of a sudden that debate is still kind of being had, but everyone is like, 'Ok, should we talk about this later?' – David (Professional sports club).

The opportunities for development that is led by civil society, and the promotion of international development efforts that sports mega-events offer, likely mean that the SDP NGOs that hitch themselves to the development opportunities of sports mega-events also put themselves in a position whereby they, at the least, refrain from critical analysis of the possibilities and limitations of SDP (Gruneau, in press). They may even (have to) conform to the corporate logic by which contemporary sports mega-events operate and thrive. As a result, the political orientation of SDP NGO policy and practice, particularly in relation to the hosting of sports mega-events in the Global South, is worthy of ongoing critical analysis.

## There are competing discourses of development related to sports mega-events

The third thesis that I put forth regarding international development and sports mega-events in the Global South is that there are competing discourses between the notions of development and SDP put forth by supranational sport organizations like the IOC and FIFA versus the actual development politics and effects of hosting mega-events like the Olympics and World Cup. In other words, the ways in which the IOC and FIFA construct a development agenda for sport – and position themselves as international development stakeholders – do not necessarily align with the political and economic machinations of actually hosting the Games, even though the two are seemingly conflated within the rhetoric and justifications of hosting mega-events in the Global South.

For example, and as I have explored elsewhere (Darnell, in press), the IOC has gone to lengths to solidify its commitment to SFD by partnering with the United Nations. In 2009, the General Assembly of the United Nations granted observer status to the IOC, so that the IOC may now take the floor at the General Assembly and participate in consultations, though it holds no formal voting. The IOC, in turn, has also participated in two United Nations–IOC Forums, the first of which, in May 2010, resulted in the publication of 19 recommendations 'on how to maximise the impact of various activities in the field of development through sport'. Several of these recommendations connect sport to development in ways that potentially challenge modernization, top-down or neoliberal development and position the IOC as a progressive stakeholder. For example, Recommendation #2 encouraged the IOC to build better relationships with government authorities to leverage the opportunity that sport affords to achieve development goals, a departure from neoliberal development policy that tends to eschew state interference and potentially recognizes calls for the sport/development relationship to be put more squarely on the public policy agenda (Kidd 2008). Recommendation #4 also called for a stronger relationship between the IOC and the United Nations in order to move towards 'the mainstreaming and embedding of sport within UN programmes for humanitarian development', which suggests a commitment to the broader international development agenda and for SDP to attend more directly to the politics and challenges of development, as opposed to the mere application of sport to tackle social issues (Coalter 2010a).[2]

Similarly, FIFA's flagship development programme, Football for Hope, suggests a political orientation to international development – and the role of sport and sports mega-events within development – that builds on the limits of neoliberal development. The programme, in collaboration with self-described 'social profit organization' streetfootballworld, lends its support to non-profit and socially oriented programmes in five substantive areas: health promotion, peacebuilding, education and children's rights, anti-discrimination and social integration, and the environment. Football for Hope proceeds from a philosophy and modus operandi that seeks 'to maximize the potential of football by making a concrete contribution to sustainable development' and does so by attempting to centre social development programmes based on football within the efforts of five development pillars: public sector, private sector, civil society, multilateral institutions and the world of football.[3] While the concept of global football as an equal stakeholder or contributor to international development is perhaps debateable, the conceptualization and partner-based approach put forth by Football for Hope does potentially support a sustainable development praxis. Football for Hope also focuses its efforts on supporting local organizations, which is a significantly different approach and orientation than organizing and implementing 'top-down' SDP programmes (Black 2010). In addition, Football for Hope is notable as a SDP organization that can be considered truly international or global in that it supports programmes in Europe, North America and Australia as well as the stereotypical 'development laboratories' of Africa and Central and South America, a fact which ostensibly challenges the modernist notion of development as the stewardship of the South by the North.[4]

These examples of the orientations towards SFD of the IOC and FIFA do ostensibly recognize the limits of modernist, neoliberal development. At the same time, as discussed above, neoliberal development philosophy remains hegemonic in relation to the hosting of sports mega-events (Hall 2006; Gruneau, in press). This suggests, on the one hand, further corroboration of the SDP as CSR thesis, as development commitments may offer sports mega-events and their organizing bodies a chance to construct a positive image. It also suggests that the political construction and mobilization of SDP in and around mega-events, and the promulgation of SFD by the IOC and FIFA, need to be considered in connection to, but different from, the social, political and economic processes of actually *hosting* the Games. Little is understood, in other words, and even less evidence available, of the connection between the international development philosophies and commitments of the IOC and FIFA and the activities and processes that lead to the staging of the Olympics or World Cup. How does, for example, the Olympics as an event, particularly one often paid for with state support, actually create 'a climate for peace' or move beyond the competitive nature of elite sport? Does the construction of 20 Football for Hope centres within South Africa as a benefit of hosting the 2010 World Cup offset the incredible public spending and opportunity costs accrued by the people of South Africa? Does it constitute a legitimate form of sustainable development? As it is currently organized and implemented, it is difficult to imagine or conceive of the highly commercialized, spectacularized and elite sporting competitions of the 30 days of the World Cup or of an Olympic fortnight contributing to such goals in meaningful or radical ways. What this suggests, then, is that the international development agenda of these mega-events is less connected to the hosting of the Games themselves, which still constitute primarily a neoliberal project, and more to the external advocating for sport and SDP that the IOC and FIFA take on. Given then, that the neoliberal development agenda of sports mega-events and the softer, social development orientation of SDP are arguably conflated amidst the rhetoric of the benefits of hosting, critical analysts of sport and international development should pay close attention to the different orientations of development connected to, and mobilized through, sports mega-events and their organizations.

## The development possibilities and limitations of sports mega-events

To this point, this chapter has primarily examined the political orientation and implications of connecting sports mega-events to international development, particularly in the Global South. The preceding analyses, I argue, suggest the need for a critical sociology that considers both the development possibilities and limitations of sports mega-events. In this section, I consider the implications of these perspectives.

First and foremost, the perspectives of those working in the field of SDP do suggest that the spectacle of sports mega-events, particularly as they are animated within the globalization of sport and the intensifying global media apparatus and culture, potentially lends important attention to development issues and struggles, both within the Global South and in connection to sport and sporting culture. That is, the sheer popularity of sports mega-events, intensified by media coverage, and the fact that huge audiences consume the games, means that when connected to a broader development agenda, mega-events can help to bring such issues to the fore. Mega-events serve to articulate development issues within the collective consciousness of a global sporting community and the broader culture who may pay attention to sports mega-events more so than they would other sports events. For example, the regular promotion of Football for Hope on sideline signage during the 2010 World Cup in South Africa likely raised an awareness of the efforts of the organization, if not the increasingly institutionalized connections between sport and development initiatives. As well, for SDP NGOs who struggle to mobilize funds, and who operate within relative anonymity outside of sport spectacles, the opportunity for promotion that sports mega-events afford should not be dismissed. That is, the opportunity for development 'education' that mega-events proffer is clearly an important possibility, though it does beg for continued analysis of the messages, meanings and political orientations disseminated and interpreted and the social and political actions that result.

Similarly, it is reasonable to argue that the SDP sector, coupled with the hyper profile and attention paid to sports mega-events, has propelled the organizers of such events, particularly BINGOs like the IOC and FIFA, to embrace, adopt and mobilize a SFD agenda in new ways and to significant degrees. The spotlight shone on sports mega-events as the world's premier sporting spectacles is arguably part of the same politically economic processes that encourage, if not demand, that sporting BINGOs act in a progressive manner in order to establish and maintain their global sporting authority and brand image as socially responsible. Clearly, some of the lessons of the limits of traditional development can be seen in the IOC–UN recommendations and FIFA's Football for Hope policies, as discussed in this chapter.

A similar process occurs, I would argue, at the level of the emerging or LMIC state, whereby the sheer intensity and scope of the hosting of sports mega-events, coupled with the broadening of the SFD agenda beyond the level of mere legacy, encourages states to do more than just host sports events, but to at least attempt to leverage the opportunities that such events afford into sustainable development projects and processes. Such opportunities to raise awareness should not be dismissed out of hand. Still, whether considering BINGOs or states, the 'encouragement' towards development that might result from the profile and prestige of sports mega-events does not preclude, but in fact explicitly begs for, analysis of the political orientation and implementation of development policies and practice.

Of course, in keeping with the critical praxis at the core of this book, there are also significant limitations to the relationship between sports mega-events and international development. Principally, there are the limits of universality as a basis of sport and development, respectively. Significant work remains, particularly in places like South Africa, India and Brazil, to decouple and then reconcile the recurrent and even dominant narrative of sport as a tool for social good against the actual hosting of a sports mega-event, particularly because the connecting of sports mega-events to a broader development agenda conflates the two. That is, popular rhetoric about the universal nature of Olympic sport, or the incredible popularity of football around the world, lends itself to popular constructions of sports mega-events as celebrations of this common humanity, rather than political and economic decisions about how best to organize the social and material world. In turn, the particular attractiveness of a universal humanist discourse in and through sports mega-events aligns with similar notions or philosophies of development that often overlook how the social and economic inequalities that development is concerned with disproportionally advantage some over Others along lines of race, class, gender and geography (McEwan 2009). The invocation of sports mega-events as key components of development policy and strategy in the Global South runs the risk of positioning elite commercial sport, and its myriad stakeholders, as the stewards of development, or even trading on sporting nationalisms, as reified through spectacle, to flatten the politics of development and construct singular or dominant development narratives.

Indeed, as this chapter has argued, there is a strong case to be made that the political economy that contributes to the institutionalization and maintenance of global inequalities is the same political economy that allows sports mega-events to thrive and to be increasingly fawned and fought over by polities including those in the Global South. This suggests the continuing need for analysis of the extent to which the IOC and FIFA invoke or even trade upon universalist or populist discourses of sport and development to secure their relatively privileged positions as the simultaneous stewards and beneficiaries of international, competitive, elite sport and now SFD. If the processes and policies connecting development to sports mega-events are more concerned with the rehabilitation of the neoliberal political economy, the inclusion of new neoliberal states and the charitable aspirations of northern sporting institutions, then its sustainable development prospects, particularly for addressing inequality, are clearly limited.

Finally, then, the limitations of sports mega-events for development can be conceptualized along the lines of the limits of neoliberal policy, in a manner similar to the critique laid out by Gruneau (in press). While the neoliberal environment that encourages the expansion and prestige of sports mega-events secures a political economy that does little to challenge inequality, it also secures a political economy based principally on economic growth. As a result, the material limitations of expanding sports mega-events around the world, and particularly to the South, are called into question. At issue is the understanding that the constant or infinite growth of the world's emerging economies is incompatible, if not diametrically opposed, to the achievement of sustainable development, particularly in relation to the environment, climate and natural resources (de Ciochetto 2010). This does not mean that the residents of the

Global South are less than entitled to the boons of development enjoyed by those in the North, but rather that the neoliberal development agenda, with its focus on competition and the movement of global capital, is specifically based on the notion of relative competitive advantage whereby equality is eschewed in the name of success relative to competitors. Such philosophies of, or approaches to, development are likely unsustainable and pose an ongoing challenge to the invocation of sports mega-events as catalysts of sustainable international development.

## Conclusion

In this chapter, I have argued that issues of the competitive global political economy and the hegemony of neoliberal development philosophy are called to the fore when sports mega-events are positioned and understood as drivers of development. I have also drawn attention to the ways in which sports mega-events effect the efforts of various actors in the field of SDP, such as NGOs, who are drawn to the attention of SFD that mega-events create, if not always sustain. The cautions that I raise stem, at least in part, from the argument that in the current cultural and political economy, '[m]ega-events in sport are staged for corporate profit, personal aggrandizement and for state driven national pride' (Sugden and Tomlinson 2005: 43).

At the same time, the limits for sustainable international development that I have identified do not inevitably proceed from sports mega-events, particularly given that the move to the Global South and increasing institutional connections to international development may, at least to a degree, represent a new era in the organization, and social and political significance and impact, of sports mega-events. In other words, perhaps the institutionalization of SDP offers or presents an opportunity to reform the meanings and hosting practices of mega-events (see Kidd and Dichter 2011). Similarly, the linking of sport to international development may offer a means by which to re-conceptualize the role and contributions of sports mega-events to the broader social good. Such opportunities would clearly be in line with FIFA's goals through Football for Hope and the IOC's historical presentation of themselves as not only the stewards of international sport but also contributors to global solidarity and peace (Peacock 2011). At the same time, given that resistance to the Olympic Games as an event or social phenomenon rarely challenges the construction and organization of elite, competitive or 'prolympic' sport itself (Heine 2010), it may be the case that what is called for in reforming sports mega-events for development is not only a critical analysis of and resistance to the institutions and political economy of such events but also resistance to the hierarchical, competitive politics that are often hegemonic and mobilized in and through the use of SFD and the SDP sector.

# 6

# International Development
# and Sporting Celebrity

## Introduction

In June 2010, the Sport Information Resource Centre (2010) issued a press release detailing a fund-raising event in support of SDP NGO Right to Play. According to the statement, the event, a golf tournament held at the Silvertip Golf Course in Canmore, Alberta, Canada, featured title sponsorship from electronics manufacturer Samsung as well as support more generally from 'corporate Canada'. In addition, the tournament featured a host of Canadian Olympic and Paralympic athletes, many of whom had won medals at the recently completed Winter Olympics in Vancouver. Dubbed the 'Red Ball Celebrity Golf Classic', the event featured a charity giveaway in which the winner received 'a weekend back-country helicopter fly-in trip to the spectacular Mt Assiniboine Lodge, which is operated by the family of Olympic silver medallist Sara Renner' and also included a silent auction as part of a gala evening. The event was hosted by sports broadcaster Mark Connolly of the Canadian Broadcasting Corporation (CBC) with all proceeds from the event benefiting Right to Play, described in the press release as an organization 'supported by an international team of more than 300 Olympic, Paralympic and professional athletes from more than 40 countries ... empowering children and communities to look after themselves and each other'. As further evidence of Right to Play's efforts, the release made reference to the fact that Canadian Jon Montgomery, fresh off his gold-medal win in the skeleton in Vancouver, would be leaving immediately after the event to travel to 'a Right To Play field location in Uganda where he will visit two schools and one refugee camp'.

A central theme of the event, evidenced in part by the name ascribed to the tournament itself – the Red Ball Celebrity Golf Classic – was the central position of high-profile or even celebrity athletes as part of its attraction and strategy for mobilizing awareness, support and capital for Right to Play and their aid and development programmes and initiatives. As such, it set out the role of Canadian athletes in using their sport-based public profile to support international development. The press release quoted Canadian Olympic Medallist Becky Scott:

> As Canadians we often take for granted how fortunate we are to have access to sport which plays such a critical role in our personal and social development.

This incredible gathering of Canadian role models will be used to celebrate their remarkable achievements in sport this year, while raising crucial awareness and funds in support of our Sport For Development and Peace projects in the most disadvantaged areas of the world. We look forward to once again celebrating the Red Ball Movement in Canmore.

Scott's quotation and the Red Ball Celebrity Golf Classic in general are one example of the ways in which well-known athletes, whose exploits are reported and oftentimes celebrated through media and corporate communications, increasingly connect and contribute to international development initiatives and SDP. The event also served as evidence of sport connected to development through acts of corporate sponsorship (in this case Samsung), the cultural consumption of celebrities by audiences via media, the purchase of products with a mandate to support development and the act of consumers giving to charities that are constructed and supported by famous sportspeople. In this chapter, I examine the phenomenon of corporatized sporting celebrity in international development focusing on the ways in, and the extent to, which celebrity athletes are active in international development and the sociopolitical implications thereof. The focus of the chapter is a critical consideration of how celebrity athletes, and the 'celebritization' of sport more broadly, are now connected to development initiatives. I examine what this connection means for (a) understandings of development, including SDP, (b) the likelihood that SDP can or will deliver sustainable change and (c) the ways in which these processes effect the construction and consumption of development as well as that of athletic celebrity in general. The chapter draws on recent critical analyses of celebrity development, and celebrities *in* development, particularly the ways in which the phenomenon of celebrities taking interest and action in development issues and initiatives connects to the 'sexification' of international development (Cameron and Haanstra 2008) and a propensity towards marketized international philanthropy (Nickel and Eikenberry 2009). I also draw on the sociology of sport literature that has demonstrated athletic celebrity to be more than a neutral or benign by-product of an advanced media and consumer culture and, more accurately, a product of connected media and corporate sectors that identify athletes' marketable components and commodify their images in service of audience building and product endorsement (Darnell and Sparks 2005; Gilchrist 2005). I argue that while mobilizing (sporting) celebrity towards development positively increases the attention paid to development issues – particularly struggles in the Global South as understood from the perspective of northerners – this progress is also limited by the ways athletic celebrity secures the political economy of inequality and justifies attempts to 'give back' to those less fortunate in ways that are potentially narcissistic and/or paternalistic.

The chapter proceeds in three subsequent parts. In the next section, I offer an overview of recent literature in the social sciences concerned with celebrities, in relation to development, philanthropy and internationalism as well as sport and sport culture. This is intended to extract some of the key theoretical and analytical debates in this literature, most pointedly the extent to which the celebritization of development contributes to or detracts from the ability or likelihood of achieving sustainable change. This is followed by analyses of the process of celebrity participation within SDP from the perspectives of those in the SDP field. The final results section offers a critical reading of media coverage of a particularly socially active celebrity athlete – two-time National Basketball Association Most Valuable Player Steve Nash of the Phoenix Suns – as a way of exploring the centrality and indispensability of media within celebrity culture and of drawing out a host of critical issues and implications regarding the celebritization of sport, development and SDP. The chapter concludes with some critical reflections, particularly regarding consumption, and the importance of ongoing research into the multifaceted and complex relationship between celebrity, sport, media, aid and development.

## Celebrity, development, sport: Possibilities and pitfalls

Recent years have seen increased scholarly attention paid to the relationship between celebrities and development as well as to the associated global media coverage of development issues and the activities of corporations in supporting or 'sponsoring' development efforts. For example, the endeavours of global rock star Bono to fight debt and poverty on the African continent, actress Angelina Jolie's work to combat world hunger and support child adoption, and the efforts by actors George Clooney and Don Cheadle to raise awareness of and mobilize a response to the conflict in Darfur have all been exemplary of this move towards the 'celebritization' of development. In addition, the Product (RED) campaign, supported by the likes of Bono, has engaged companies with world-recognized brands (like American Express, Gap and Armani among others) to dedicate a percentage of profits from RED-branded products to The Global Fund to Fight AIDS, Tuberculosis and Malaria. Similarly, the ONE campaign (known as such in North American and as Make Poverty History in the United Kingdom) has employed a host of celebrity activists to mobilize efforts in the North in order to combat poverty in other parts of the world.

Celebrity-led efforts such as these have become important sites for analysis by critical scholars. While some of these analyses have argued that media-supported celebrity involvement in development, diplomacy and internationalism more generally does an important service in building awareness, mobilizing funds and securing change within a relatively stagnant political system (see Cooper 2007, 2008), others have argued that celebrities in development primarily serve to depoliticize or oversimplify development (Dieter and Kumar 2008) and/or recreate, if not maintain, the most traditional colonial narratives of saving distant others (Magubane 2008).

Before analysing this debate in some depth, clarification of the term 'celebrity' is called for. American cultural analyst Daniel Boorstin (1961) is generally credited with the foundational analysis of celebrities, developed in his 1961 text *The Image: A Guide to Pseudo-events in America*, in which he coined the oft-cited notion that the celebrity is one who is 'known for being well-known'. While this analysis still holds purchase to an extent, it is important to recognize that the radical changes within the media and cultural economy since the 1960s have had an impact on the culture of celebrity and the scholarly analysis thereof. For the purposes of this chapter, therefore, I follow the more recent work by Graeme Turner (2004: 8) within cultural studies and his assertion that the contemporary celebrity is best understood as a public figure who takes on a celebritized persona through media representations that move beyond coverage of his/her public role (i.e. actor, hockey player, singer) to include his/her private life as well. A result of such processes is that the promotion of individual stars (i.e. authors, actors, athletes) through press reports, marketing and advertising regularly takes precedent in the media and popular culture over and above what is ostensibly the primary work that celebrities do (i.e. writing books, making films, playing sports) (Turner 2004: 36–7). This point is relevant to the study of celebrity athletes in development, given, as I argue below, that their work in development has become newsworthy in and of itself, beyond just their performances of the ice, field or court.

Two further points from Turner's analysis are worthy of attention here. First, contemporary celebrity is both produced and exists at the nexus of a dense process of cultural and capital production and consumption. It is a mistake, or at least an oversimplification, to assert that celebrities are solely a media product or that only the corporations who hire celebrities to endorse products are responsible for the entrenchment of celebrity culture. In practice, these forces are undoubtedly influential, but so too are the strategies and desires of celebrities themselves – notably for this chapter, including their desires to be good citizens and support international development – as well as the interpretative and consumptive practices of audiences, many of which are underpinned by their own desire to consume responsibly and/or effect change through consumptive practices (Littler 2009). The activities of both celebrities and consumers are further supported and influenced by (shifting) media technologies that affect the flows of information and capital required to make someone a celebrity. The strategic connection of issues of international development to this media–celebrity nexus has likely only served to make it more complex, and I strive to embrace this complexity in this chapter by considering celebrity in its material, ideological and discursive forms.

Second, Turner, drawing on literature from the sociology of sport (particularly the works of Andrews and Jackson 2001; Giles 2000; Whannel 2002), makes the case that while celebrity athletes share much in common with celebrities from other professional fields, they are also uniquely constructed and have characteristics and implications that stand alone, at least to a degree. For example, celebrity athletes arguably still connect to a notion of meritocratic achievement in the sense that they can, through their athletic performances, 'prove' their ascendance or excellence. Furthermore, athletes are laid bare to audiences in a way that actors who often perform in character are not, and celebrity sportspeople continue to have a connection to nationalism and patriotism not expected of, or afforded to, other celebrities. Similarly, the celebrity athlete seems ready-made for cross promotion in that their athletic persona can (and often does) extend beyond sport while the same does not necessarily hold for celebrities who cannot or do not perform athletically (Turner 2004, drawing on Klein 2001).

Of course, as Gilchrist (2005) has argued, the relationship between the performance and the representation of a star athlete is not straightforward, nor automatic and, particularly when connected to a community or nation, can produce tensions between the meanings of high-profile athletes as legitimate heroes or merely ephemeral 'stars'. Neither, it should be stated, is the consumption of celebrity athletes by audiences a linear or universal process but always based on cultural positions and relations of power (Andrews and Jackson 2001: 5), a point to which I return below. Crucial for this chapter, therefore, is the understanding that the (global) celebrity athlete is firmly embedded in the (global) political economy as both product (a sellable brand) and process (a link in the endorsement/advertising chain) (Gilchrist 2005: 28). This confluence, I suggest, increasingly affords celebrity athletes access and agency in relation to international development as they are materially privileged but also come to represent important cultural and political arbiters. In this respect, the celebrity athlete should be understood as constitutive of, and constituted by, the elective affinities between news reporting, advertising and endorsing within the broader vortex of media production (Darnell and Sparks 2005). In turn, when connected to issues and activities of international development, the celebrity athlete represents more than a mere response to the political economy of development inequality but a part (and a product) of the same globalized, economic and mediated processes that underpin the challenges of international development itself.

Indeed, it is from this perspective that much of the recent critical analysis of the celebritization of development has proceeded. In the broadest sense, the criticism of celebrities in development, and celebrities within activist politics, suggests that the attention paid to celebrities renders the politics of development superficial and facilitates the popularization or mobilization of policies that are often ill-conceived but legitimized nonetheless in and through celebrity endorsement (West 2007). The nuance required to make sense of the incredible complexity, both material and political, of the challenges and struggles of international development is likely lost when celebrities, supported by media and corporate fanfare, become the centre of the discussion on development issues and purport to have solutions to development (Dieter and Kumar 2008). Cameron and Haanstra (2008) have argued that these processes are part of the recent construction of 'development made sexy', signifying both the popularization of development through celebrity culture and also interest in development that is literally based upon the sexual appeal of celebrities and global stars that tends to usurp the politics of development itself.

A question, then, is what affect does celebrity culture, and do celebrities themselves, have on development processes? At the least, the claim can be made that celebrities are poorly positioned, as non-elected officials, to mobilize change and may in fact undermine processes of governance by circumventing such processes (Dieter and Kumar 2008). Similarly, but from a more discursive position, regardless of the various ways that consumers interpret them, the fact that celebrities are the product and centre of media attention may serve to position famous people like Bono as the focus of development initiatives, a process that Magubane (2008) refers to as 'Applied Hegelianism', owing to its construction of the (northern) Self through the (southern) Other. Similarly, trying to effect change through consumption, such as through the purchase of fair trade products, does not necessarily attend directly to the question of what constitutes fair practices and therefore is open to criticisms of consumer navel-gazing or attempts to secure northern innocence (see Littler 2009). From this perspective, campaigns like Product (RED) have been criticized for mobilizing celebrities and corporations to take on a responsibility to attend to development issues but primarily in a manner that trades on cultural notions of hip consumption in the name of 'solving the problem of "distant others"' (Pontey, Richey and Baab 2009: 301). These distant Others are rarely named or known, and their social and political history and context is rarely explained. Indeed, as Fain (2008) has illustrated, Product ONE's use of celebrities to raise awareness of global poverty tends to construct northern saviours, reinforce individual consumption and objectify the absent poor. At the least, questions of social justice and relations of power that sustain inequality and underpin development initiatives tend to fade when the (sexual) appeal of the celebrity is made central to the development mandate (Cameron and Haanstra 2008).

In sum, there is a strong post-colonial and post-development analysis to be made regarding the celebritization of SFD, particularly in its construction of racialized hierarchies, a process that I have explored in some detail elsewhere (Darnell 2007). There are two other points of critical analysis that need to be made as they relate directly to the analysis offered in this chapter.

First, while a general sense holds that it is important to raise awareness about international development issues via the media, *in practice* the media/celebrity culture of development has actually been shown to have some negative effects upon the processes and programmes that attempt to make a positive contribution or change to development inequality. As Cottle and Nolan (2007) have argued, contemporary NGOs increasingly compete for a 'brand' identity in and through media coverage of their work and in support of the development issues to which they attend. To this end, NGOs increasingly expend significant resources seeking celebrity and publicity, and avoiding media-based scandals, in ways that often overshadow if not undermine local development efforts and participation and generally undercut the ethics of international humanitarianism that NGOs ostensibly champion. As a result, development and humanitarian NGOs can be viewed as embedded within a 'media logic' by which these organizations require media coverage of their work to attract resources but employ 'communication strategies which practically detract from their principal remit of humanitarian provision and symbolically fragment the historically founded ethic of universal humanitarianism' (Cottle and Nolan 2007: 863–4). Media coverage of development and the operation of development initiatives and practices (including SDP) within a media culture are not inherently positive and are worthy of critical analysis.

Second, there are material limits to the marketization of philanthropy that seeks market and consumptive-based solutions to development inequalities, an ethos in which celebrities are increasingly central figures by way of their connection to product-based charity. Nickel and Eikenberry (2009), in particular, argue that marketized philanthropy, based on the twin cultural engines of consumption and celebrity, encourages First World citizens to buy their way to guilt-free transnational equality and depoliticizes the relationship between the market, distributive justice and the general well-being of humans around the world. Philanthropy through consumption and/or celebrity requires conformity to the market in order to raise funds, but it does so in ways that push the focus first and foremost to the consumption of products or stars and not to ending poverty or building international solidarity. In a somewhat polemical form, Nickel and Eikenberry (2009: 981) assert that 'celebrity philanthropy is an uncritical celebration of celebrities and their production of an elite society that can only be philanthropic by virtue of its ability to distance itself from poverty'. From this perspective, the argument that market-driven solutions to development issues are, at the least, better than no action at all does not hold. On the contrary, the privileging and entrenching of market relationships through marketized development may actually contribute to and exacerbate development inequality by normalizing a political economy of northern resource extraction and overconsumption versus southern underdevelopment. From this perspective, initiatives like Product (RED) may feed a notion of cosmopolitan consumption underpinned by international altruism in ways that do little to challenge privilege and imperial benevolence. When combined with Cottle and Nolan's work, these critiques illustrate that it may in fact be possible to worsen the struggles against development inequalities by invoking celebrities and their supporting media/marketing apparatus.

Of course, it is important to note that some scholars and analysts are more sympathetic to the role and contribution of celebrities and celebrity culture within the struggles for international development, and such arguments are not without merit. Cooper (2007), in particular, has argued that given the increasingly fractured nature of media and politics, and the incredible complexity of the challenges of globalization, celebrities actually serve as important surrogates or conduits by which to hold the public's attention and raise awareness of important issues, many of which connect to development. 'Celebrities possess some clear presentational advantages especially in the form of branding and popular appeal', and it is the analysis of this effect, according to Cooper, that has proved superficial, not the efforts of celebrities themselves (Cooper 2007: 17). In response, what is needed is not the dismissal of celebrity activism, or celebrity *diplomacy* as Cooper prefers, but a more nuanced understanding of what celebrities can or cannot do in development or what we, as citizens and consumers, should or should not expect them to do, within the shifting terrain of global governance and policy (Cooper 2008). Cooper's arguments are important here to the extent that they remind not to simplify, generalize or conflate the implications of different celebrities (such as pop stars like Bono versus 'celebrity' economists like Jeffrey Sachs) or to assume an understanding of the motivations of, or strategies employed by, celebrities and celebrity athletes in service of international issues and development.

This, in fact, leads to the final theoretical issue for outlining the role of celebrities and celebrity athletes in development, namely that of consumption, both cultural and material. In this way, I refer both to the consumption of celebrities by audiences and also the recent trend towards material consumption itself as a basis for change and/or response to inequality (see Littler 2009). It is important to address consumption in some regard here if only because of the wildly different perspectives espoused by scholars and critics in recent years. On the one hand, 'celebrity from below' – the construction and maintenance of celebrities and celebrity culture through modes of consumption – does exist and is an important feature of our cultural and political economy, and one not to be dismissed out of hand (Turner 2004). Indeed, the consumption of celebrity can be enriching, if not fundamental, to the constitution of the contemporary subject and is therefore influential in identity politics. The consumption of celebrity can also constitute a response to the social conditions in which people find themselves (Turner 2004), a point that holds important implications from a neo-Marxist perspective. Similarly, while the notion of shopping for social change does produce a series of tensions, not the least of which is the tendency for the question of moral action to be reduced to a moral proscription of political correctness, there do remain opportunities for change in and through participation, material and discursive, in the cultural economy (Littler 2009). For example, the popularity and profile of Steve Nash and the work of his foundation may, in addition to raising funds, offer an important cultural repository for fans, consumers and/or citizens to connect to development and act on an impetus of change in relation to development inequalities. Such opportunities are undoubtedly important.

At the same time, the politics and implications of these consumptive processes are not easily reconciled within cultural studies, and several analysts have argued that material and cultural consumption *as it is currently practiced* does little to make the world a better place. As part of his recent diatribe against the illusory nature of contemporary Western culture, journalist and critic Chris Hedges argued that the ubiquity of celebrities results in a culture based on anxiety and insecurity in which citizens are never fully actualized but trapped in comparing themselves against the standards of the celebrities they consume. Sport is implicated here insofar as celebrity athletes are promoted and paid so that, through the exploits of celebrities, consumers may know themselves better. This consumptive relationship, when taken to its extreme, constitutes or renders celebrities (whose every peccadillo is reported and broadcast) 'cultural slaves' in that their remuneration stands as exchange for consumers' negotiations of their personal failures (see Klosterman 2009: 71). The result of such a relationship, according to critics like Hedges (2009), is the proliferation of 'junk politics' or the analysis of the consumptive individual's moral failings at the expense of deeper scrutiny regarding the structural or institutional dimensions of social justice. From this perspective, the politics of international development for the northern citizen are increasingly (only) interpreted in terms of consumption (whether to, or not, and by how much) as a way to make the world better. In turn, as Hedges argues, as material conditions and political processes deteriorate, both domestically and internationally (evidenced through the 2008 financial meltdown, the proliferation of intense political partisanship, wars seemingly without end), the more consumers seek refuge within the illusory culture of celebrity, which ultimately supports a downward spiral towards eternal consumption and away from a political engagement with social change.

This process connects to sport and development not only because athletes like Nash are now celebritized as development activists but more importantly because the invocation of sport and sporting celebrities has the possibility, owing to its mass popularity and commercialization, to subsume politics, where sport comes to be considered a political end as opposed to an integral part of broader political processes (see Redeker 2008). When placed within the momentum towards SDP, the celebrity athlete can draw the attention towards sport and celebrity and not towards – or even actively away from – international development. In an illusory culture, sport comes to be a goal to be achieved (sport as *evidence* of development) as opposed to a social institution in the service of politicized development struggles.

For critics like Hedges then, the focus on celebrity culture, and the consumption thereof, is fundamentally destructive. Such insights are important, but from the perspective of neo-Marxist theory, it is problematic to claim that the celebrity phenomenon experienced by cultural actors renders them dupes. There is a limit to theorizing the celebrity consumption experience as a one-way failure or as an authentic or creative lack on the part of the consumer. Not only does this perspective do a disservice to the agency or complexity of cultural consumption but it also stands in marked distinction from social analyses of sports media and advertising audiences which shows people understanding what they are consuming, even if they are not in a political or cultural position to act on these understandings with complete freedom (see Wilson and Sparks 1999). So while critics of popular culture like Hedges, and to a lesser extent Chuck Klosterman,[1] likely overstate the ideological power of the celebrity and understate the interpretative agency of the audience, they do make an important contribution in illustrating that the celebrity is connected to a broader cultural dynamic. What requires attention, therefore, is how the celebrity philanthropic icon, and the celebrity athlete who 'gives back' through development activism, is produced through a complex social relationship underpinned by (a) the connections between sport and international development, (b) the construction of celebrity athletes, (c) the celebrity as philanthropic, conscientious activist and (d) the media economy.

While I do not dismiss the importance of consumption in these relationships, I do here focus on the particularities of the social and political economy that produce athletic celebrity in the service of development and use this analysis to raise a series of critical, consumptive cautions. In so doing, I follow Turner's (2004) assertion that the cultural and political account of celebrity culture needs to recognize its role in reproducing individual capitalism as well as the ways in which consumers of celebrity construct identities within the broader structures in which they find themselves. In other words, any analysis of attempts to secure change through consumption cannot be reduced to the impulses of individuals, but neither can the actions of individuals be understood outside of the political economy that produces the need and desire for different social and material relations (Littler 2009).


## Sporting celebrity in SDP: Insights from the field

Interviews with those working in the field of SDP yielded five themes regarding the role of celebrity athletes.


### Drawing attention to development

The role of the celebrity athlete in development can be conceptualized as one whereby celebrities principally serve to bring awareness to key development issues, awareness that is useful in turn for those in the field seeking to build social and political momentum and mobilize funds towards effecting change. From this perspective, it is clearly the case that sport constitutes and offers a relatively novel approach to international development, one that requires some measure of justification and validation. The cultural profile, if not authority, of the celebrity athlete is useful in this regard. A primary means of development work that the celebrity athlete provides is the celebritization of development itself, meaning increased interest in the topic, and concomitant attention drawn to the importance of development inequalities and attempts to redress them. From this perspective, sport becomes less a tool for development practice (although it certainly is still approached as such) and more useful in establishing the importance and need for development and change.

> [Sport is] still more of, as I say, a raising awareness and advocacy tool. There's the Goodwill Ambassadors which are appointed by the various UN agencies, the famous athletes that I think get the messages across, but as a programmatic tool within the development work of the agencies – Jennifer (SDP advocacy organization).

While this relationship of raising development awareness through celebrities and mobilizing celebrity media coverage and relationships towards development work is not unique to sport or SDP, it is important to note that the role of the celebrity athlete is particular in securing and justifying the place of sport within development. If SFD and SDP is not yet accepted within the broader development community and not yet recognized internationally, the celebrity athlete brings a measure of justification and significance to the sector. Particularly from the perspective of NGOs, the utility of celebrity athletes within their work is positive; it affords a higher profile and greater visibility, contributes to securing a reputation and maintains the momentum of the organization.

> Being involved with famous footballers has ... only served to increase the visibility and the image that we get. Um, and I mean obviously having people like David Beckham come and say 'I really appreciate the type of work that this project does' is something that really boosts our reputation um, and y'know, well we'll be having a big footballer come out and deliver a course for us in June, and it generally serves to just increase the visibility and the reputation of the project – Julia (SDP NGO).

At the same time, the utility of athletic celebrity in development is not restricted to mobilizing sport itself in development, but it is also evident in the ways that celebrity athletes are concerned with development more broadly and use the opportunities afforded them to support more traditional development issues and initiatives. As the director of a celebrity athlete foundation described in an interview, the tendency is for celebrity athletes to focus on sport in the service of development, whereas the opportunity also exists for celebrity athletes to contribute to development more broadly and in ways that do not necessarily mobilize or focus on sport.

> A lot of your typical athlete foundations ... focus on improving sports programmes in at-risk communities and I think that's typical of athletes; they'll use their charities to build basketball courts or have basketball leagues those kind of things. And that was one thing that made us say, OK, we don't really need to do that, other people are handling that – Helen (Celebrity athlete foundation).

In either case – employing athletic celebrity specifically to mobilize sport and sport programmes in development or using the opportunities of sporting celebrity to meet development goals in a more traditional manner – it is important to note that for NGOs working in SDP, celebrity athletes in development appear to be principally representative of sport – and its cultural and media profile – more so, in some cases, than celebrity entities in and of themselves. That is, celebrity athletes are useful to the extent that they represent the utility and importance of sport itself in contributing to development. The advanced media culture of sport – particularly when commercial sport and celebrity athletes are involved – also makes it easier for those working in the field to mobilize and justify the use of sport towards development ends. This phenomenon constitutes the celebrity exceptionalism of athletes of the kind Turner (2004) describes; Bono is rarely presented as an advocate on behalf of music, but David Beckham comes, or at least is asked, to represent and justify the benefits that sport can contribute to the challenges of international development.

> I think when people hear the word sport, you talk to government and mention the word 'sport' they see the bright lights and the famous people, and it's maybe a much more attractive medium even though it's going to only be used for development or its going to be used to bring a message to a community within a context. I think they still see the bright lights (of sport), and ... that allows them to be a little bit more open in certain contexts to sport as a tool for development instead of some of the more traditional means – Teresa (SDP NGO).

It is reasonable to suggest, then, that this utility of the celebrity athlete stems, at least in part, from the extent to which the SDP sector is embedded in a media culture in ways similar to those described by Cottle and Nolan (2007). Particularly in the cases where celebrity athletes themselves are the face of development organizations (i.e. charitable foundations) or serve as spokespersons for development causes, the profile afforded them in and through their sporting performances, supported by the sport/media relationship, serves them well in mobilizing attention and securing a positive reputation. The celebrity athlete's intimate relationship with media is key here; the better the relationship, the better the results for charitable work.

> We never have a problem getting coverage for [our programmes], and whether that's because [celebrity athlete] is behind a camera 82 nights a year just for his

job or whether it's because he's a good guy and he has a reputation as someone who's respectful to the press that helps us. But I think just generally his visibility of course would help any endeavour, and the fact that it's positive visibility helps his charity – Helen (Celebrity athlete foundation).

The celebrity athlete can serve development in two explicit ways: mobilizing awareness, in and through the sport/media complex, of the importance of particular development issues (awareness that can be constructed both within SFD and without) and also, from a more practical or pragmatic perspective, serving the NGOs and charitable foundations that work for change in SDP or development more broadly. The same representative of a celebrity athlete charitable foundation explained both of these phenomena to me:

['Celebrity athlete' has] been able to start dialogues [about development issues] among professional athletes, the corporate world, and the media … I'm not saying that he tries to be provocative all the time, but he does ask people to think and formulate their own opinions on things. Um, and I think that's a role that celebrity can be playing.

In my previous job with a non-profit, you'd knock on somebody's door and they had no idea who you were. [Now] you call somebody from the 'Celebrity Athlete' Foundation and people typically answer the phone – Helen (Celebrity athlete foundation).

For those working towards development goals, particularly within the increasingly competitive field of international non-profit organizations and NGOs, the social and political cachet and distinction that the celebrity athlete affords is clearly of benefit. So too, does the celebrity athlete generally come to stand in for that which sport has to offer – materially, socially and politically – to development. As a representative of broader sport culture, celebrity athletes represent, and even actively model, the successes possible in and through contemporary sport, particularly at its intersections with media, capital and celebrity (discussed further in the next section). In this sense, the celebrity athlete becomes a type of billboard for what sport can do and transmits a message that is important and attractive to those working in development and SDP, particularly as they strive to build political capital within development and institutionalize SDP.

With these points in mind, at least three critical cautions are worth making. One, through a dependency lens, the celebrity athlete represents what is possible through sport but not what is possible *for all* through sport. The fame, media coverage and material benefits afforded the celebrity athlete are fundamentally exceptional; as a result, any notions of the celebrity athlete as representational of the development possibilities of sport are limited at best. Second, the practical fact that the celebrity athlete does lend a certain credence to development issues, or to the work of SDP NGOs, does little to reconcile the limits of celebrity authority when it comes to the importance, and political dimensions, of development issues in the first place. The point here is not that the efforts of SDP NGOs or sport-based charitable foundations are ignoble, only that the credentials of the celebrity athlete to act as arbiter of such work are at best limited or even spurious. Even though they generally perform well on the court or field (although, as tennis player Anna Kournikova infamously proved, even this is not always required for contemporary athletic celebrity) given that celebrity athletes are produced and constructed through media/marketing processes, they therefore stand as representatives of the disproportionate benefits, both material and political, accrued to some over others. Put differently, (why) should citizens or organizations concerned with development inequalities concern themselves with what celebrity athletes have to say on such matters when they are able to say something at all principally because of the ways in which their images have been produced amidst the inequitable structures of the cultural and political economy? Similar to my argument of sports mega-events, it is more accurate to think of the celebrity athlete as a product of the same political economy that sustains development inequality; invoking them then as important stakeholders (if not experts) in the redressing of inequalities is at the least ironic, if not flawed.

In turn then, and third, the act of the celebrity athletes raising the importance of development issues, or 'opening doors' politically as described by those in the SDP field, runs the risk of centring the celebrity athlete himself/herself within development issues, a form of Hegelianism of the kind argued by Magubane (2008). While the balance of such processes is difficult to determine (i.e. do the benefits of the awareness of development issues raised by celebrities outweigh the detriments of securing the focus upon the celebrity himself/herself?) any discourses which attempt to redress inequality by focusing primarily on those in relative positions of privilege and authority may do little to challenge the relations of power that sustain inequality.

## Raising capital

Following from the insights and critical analysis in the previous section, it is not surprising that the celebrity athlete was also recognized by those working in the field of SDP as having a particular utility regarding the opportunity to mobilize economic capital towards meeting development goals. While the authority or contribution to development of the celebrity athlete derives to a significant degree from his or her media constructed persona, closely related to this is the fact that celebrity athletes are both comparatively wealthy and enjoy access to further wealth in and through the corporatized underpinnings of celebrity culture. Celebrity athletes are therefore in a unique position to make a financial contribution to redressing development inequalities and uniquely suited to support SDP programmes. These contributions can take place through partnerships with government or with civil actors like NGOs, as the following quotations exemplify:

['Celebrity athlete'] from Brazil, he's a fairly well-known athlete ... he's trying to get all the Brazilian athletes to contribute to a fund, which then helps development in Brazil. They have worked with the Ministry of Works ... so rather than implementing sport-for-development programmes themselves as famous athletes, which many of them do anyway, it's rather pooling their resources which are fairly substantial to then be able to work with the government, to then be able to meet the development agendas of the governments – Jennifer (SDP advocacy organization).

We didn't start as a youth development through sport organization. It really [started] through our partnership with the ('Celebrity athlete' foundation) when we became the first NGO in the world to benefit from his financial support. That was quite big for us, to have the number one in the world support us, and that then led pretty naturally to us starting sports programmes in the sense that after he was on board, we had ['Corporation'] on board, which is his main sponsor, and various other stakeholders that are in that field of sports and development through sport – Henry (SDP NGO).

At issue here are not the objective benefits of mobilizing capital, as this is undoubtedly needed in the many cases where governments or civil actors strive to meet development goals, including in and through sport. As a result, few would criticize celebrity athletes simply for giving money to charities or development efforts or working to raise funds. Similarly, few would find SDP officials wanting for accepting such funds in the face of formidable development challenges. What is called for, though, is an analysis of the movement of such capital within the broader politics of development and the limits of marketized philanthropy as articulated by critics like Nickel and Eikenberry (2009). With regard to market logic, the injection of capital raised by celebrity athletes back into the programmes of social change through sport does little to challenge the structures by which celebrity athletes became disproportionately wealthy in the first place. In fact, the case can be made that the underwriting of development projects and NGOs by celebrity athletes constructs a hierarchical development industry in which the deliverance of basic social needs comes to rely on northern benevolence. Such programmes are questionable in relation to the sustainability of their practices and efforts, well meaning as they may be. In turn, the broader politics of development are potentially reinforced along lines of benefactors and recipients, lines that continue to run along axes of North/South, White/racialized as they intersect with capital and wealth. This is the significance of the limits of market and celebrity-based philanthropy; at the moment when the structures of inequality are most in need of critical analysis and/or resistance they are potentially secured through a process of raising and distributing funds. Relying on celebrity athletes to underwrite development may limit the chances of achieving future sustainable development that does not require celebrities and their access to money.

## Sport organizations and philanthropy

Given that the analysis of sporting celebrity in this chapter includes the analysis of media and corporations (since the celebrity philanthropist and the broader celebrity culture are produced and sustained by corporate and media flows, both cultural and material) it is also germane to analyse the interest in development of professional sports organizations and clubs. Indeed, perspectives of professional sports were captured in interviews both from the interview with a professional sports club that supports international development efforts through its charity work and from the point of view of an SDP NGO that derives funding from one of the world's richest and highest profile professional sport leagues.

Both organizations shared the perspective that the work to be accomplished in and through the funding of development – in this case the funding of SDP programmes specifically – needs to be done locally, through partnership with local individuals, organizations and communities. In this sense, the funding of SDP programmes by northern professional sports does not necessarily result in northern NGOs setting the research agenda or asserting undue authority or control over local efforts in the South. Even though the desire to support social change in and through sport leads northern sport organizations to 'look South' for the best place to spend their money, the political orientation of this charity is clearly progressive to the extent that partnerships and local agency are recognized, if not paramount.

> We're an award-winning [pro sport club] here and the charitable foundation of this club is without a doubt one of the strongest in the [northern country], so it's quite natural that we would broaden our scope to take in something more of a global element. However, I would say that in actual fact, every single sport-for-development organization I've met in the last 4–5 years, they fundamentally rely on the strength of their partnerships, and we're absolutely no different in that – David (Professional sports club).

Athletic celebrity figures in this process. The backing that NGOs receive from the charitable endeavours of northern professional sport is solidified by the star athletic power that professional sport can lend to development. In turn, the professional sports leagues themselves benefit by attaching their sport, their stars and their strategic endeavours, to development efforts and the work of NGOs.

> We're quite fortunate because we're the [northern pro sports league's] charity. They provided some of the initial funding to get [SDP NGO] on its feet and has been providing significant core backing to our programme in the last couple of years and also providing access to certain personalities and figures. Essentially

the [northern pro sports league] came to us and said, 'OK look, we're trying to support the [bid for major sports event] and [celebrity athlete] is our new ambassador and we'd love to promote the work that you do by bringing him into your programme and also highlight the work that we're doing with you through him' – Julia (SDP NGO).

It should come as little surprise that professional sports, fortified with the celebrity presence of famous athletes, would enter into support of international development projects with some measure of return expected on their contribution. The point here is that such practices are similarly open to the criticisms of celebrity and corporate-led development discussed elsewhere in this chapter. The charity-based model of development funding is clearly limited in terms of sustainability, particularly given the ongoing instability of international markets. The positioning of international development as a charity wing of northern professional sports by which they attempt to secure their own strategic goals may undermine the long-term stability of such programmes. The establishment of development initiatives based on northern funding may, in turn, secure the relations of northern dominance that underpin development inequalities rather than challenge or deconstruct them. And finally, given the popularity of northern professional sport, and the regular criticism of its culture and operations as elitist and overpaid, the contributions to development initiatives may constitute attempts at the 'greenwashing' of northern sports – and the rehabilitation of professional sports in general – more so than attempts to improve the lots of people in the South. From this perspective, celebrity athletes/professional sports as a basis for SDP and international development initiatives is open to the same criticisms of development education more broadly; its political orientation suggests a strategy of maintaining notions of northern dominance through benevolence/southern degeneracy rather than reconstructing the system by which such dichotomies are constructed and maintained (Biccum 2010).

Notably, the limits of the corporatization of SDP can also be seen in the reflections of civil society actors working in the field. When the corporate interests that underpin much of the organization of dominant, contemporary sport culture take up a place of prominence, both representational and material, within SDP and development initiatives, their interests can be difficult to extricate from the goals or mandate of SDP NGOs. At the least, clashes are possible, even likely, as the following quotation explains:

There's a bit of challenge with funders like [multinational corporation], there's the inclination that there will be quite a bit of branding. I think that's one of the big challenges because we don't want to use our programme to sell someone else's product. And yet we do have an obligation to our funders to provide the reports and the impact and the photos. So it's sort of the challenge of mitigating the expectations of both the funders and of the people that we work with because if we're driving around in a [sponsor's] branded vehicle, people are going to come to us every 5 minutes saying, can you give us kit? And that's not really what we're about – Julia (SDP NGO).

This description points to the difficulty, in practice, of separating sport and athletic celebrity from the consumer culture for the purposes of a more egalitarian, benevolent and community-focused approach to SFD. The political and economic capital that these sports organizations and celebrity athletes have accrued, and which subsequently positions them as contributors to development initiatives, are produced within the same political economy that eventually asks them to 'give back'. Yet checking corporate impulses because the topic or context has turned to southern development proves difficult or even unlikely for northern professional sport. At the least, for a multinational corporation working as a sponsor of an SDP NGO to question the political economy by which they construct and maintain their brand – as might be called for within the ethics of development – is, to an extent, for them to question the capital and expertise which puts them in the position to contribute in the first place. Asking such sponsors to militate against their own corporate and branding goals is akin to asking them to question the organization and hierarchies of global, corporate sport culture at large.

## Role modelling

Not surprisingly, those working in the field of SDP also spoke to the importance of well-known athletes, including but not limited to celebrities or international stars, as role models within development initiatives, particularly when the focus of development programming comes to rest upon underserved youth. In this way, successful athletes are not only in a position to act as catalysts for change through their activist work but the success of high-profile athletes is also attractive and useful to those working with youth as a way to encourage youth involvement in SDP programmes and pass on the key messages of individual action. This is hoped, in turn, to secure the social change underpinning development initiatives.

> Basically we were founded by professional soccer players who saw that soccer was a huge powerful force that could be tapped into, and engaging the role models was kind of key to that ... it's a way to create that direct connection with [local] role models. Um, and then there's the international role models as well. Even just simple messages from the superstars we've found just kind of help get the messages home and get people excited and interested in the programme – William (SDP NGO).

Such processes are important and apparently effective within the cultural and political terrain of SDP and the challenges of mobilizing change, particularly among youth. That is, sports are meaningful for many (though not all) young people and when mobilized as a means of transferring a message as a basis of change, role modelling is key. Indeed, role models in SFD may offer young people some form of 'proof' that change is possible and relations of power can be challenged, as in Meier and Saavedra's (2009) analysis of Zambian boxer Esther Phiri and the sporting competencies of women. As the above quotation attests, celebrity athletes are attractive from the point of view of many SDP NGOs. Rather than having to 'construct' role models, the celebrity athlete, by virtue of his/her position at the confluence of capital, media and athletic success comes nearly 'ready-made' to serve as a conduit for such messages. The case of Phiri in particular suggests that such meanings can and do transfer to youth in positive ways depending on the fit.

Still, like much in the current practice of SDP, the political orientation of such processes is open to criticism, particularly the extent to which the mobilization of role models in this way challenges and/or secures neoliberal philosophies underpinned by bio-political solutions to inequality based on a physical self-actualization. The role modelling effect in SDP is difficult to extricate from the processes of commercialization and corporatization or the twin engines of consumption and celebrity that secure marketized philanthropy (Nickel and Eikenberry 2009). Indeed, Meier and Saavedra (2009: 1170) point to such difficulties by suggesting that 'with a celebrity role model the success must receive robust media attention to promote the destination as desirable and the route there as charted and feasible' and that '[r]ealistic, detailed stories' are preferred as a result. While good advice, this is clearly easier said than done for SDP NGOs that operate within a set of material and political constraints. Establishing such 'realistic' and 'detailed' stories that can subsequently be reasonably positioned as opportunities available to the majority of underserved youth requires challenging the dominant, pyramidal structure of sport (in which few, and certainly not all, can win) and challenging the limited access to material and political benefits within capitalism (in which, again, not all can win). Such efforts, however, rarely accompany initiatives that are based principally on the motivational power of celebrity role models. Absent of such efforts (which are undoubtedly often beyond the scope of the average SDP NGO given their purview and limited resources), rather than challenging the political economy that produces and constrains the poverty and lack of education available to many of the world's children and youth, the role modelling approach and effect appears likely to align with and justify a bio-politics of individual consumption and conduct. Such politics can be understood to proceed from the particularities of the political economy of contemporary development inequality and celebrity culture itself. As a result, the role modelling of the celebrity athlete (himself/herself part of a celebrity culture) as evidence of the benefits of elite sport and the promises of SDP potentially reinforces individualized consumption in/through capitalist exchange (Turner 2004). The resulting likelihood of long-term, sustainable change is therefore questionable.

## Celebrity athletes and the politics of change

At the least then, the theory, critiques and data in this chapter point to the ways in which even the invocation of athletic celebrity and the work of celebrity athletes in international development are beholden to the politics of development and social change. The experiences of those working in the development field as it intersects with sport and athletic celebrity suggest that SDP officials, while recognizing the opportunities that the cultures of celebrity and sport afford, also negotiate the political possibilities and limits of their work. The work of celebrity athletes to raise awareness of development issues, to mobilize resources and/or to support the use of SFD still occurs within a particular political economy and is therefore beholden to its possibilities and limitations, and places celebrity athletes and their stakeholders/supporters in a position whereby they recognize that they must navigate the political terrain of development. The following quotation is illustrative:

> We [went to] the White House two weekends ago and met with President Obama about [an initiative] and talked to them about helping us to get the [pro sports league] involved. And one of the things that we've said to the [pro sports league] is hey, not only is this something that can help in every one of your franchise cities, this would be the first time that a professional sports league anywhere in the world was involved [in an initiative like this]. And I think that that's something that athletes can do and celebrity can do, to say hey, these are where our resources are going. We're thinking individuals and we're part of a big business conglomerate, and that's part of sport, right? Sport is a big part of the world's capital market right now. [So the question is] how do you use that influence, that sphere of influence? Where are you going to direct it? – Helen (Celebrity athlete foundation).

There is, from such a point of view, a sense of responsibility regarding the ways in which the celebrity athlete recognizes the resources available at his/her disposal and situates this in explicitly political terms. In the case of corporate, media-driven professional sport, there is a political dimension and even a responsibility to the privilege accrued by the celebrity athlete. While the political orientation of how, when and where to wield that influence in order to contribute to sustainable development and make the world better (if not necessarily more equitable) is contestable, the recognition on the part of celebrities, including athletes, of their political authority and resultant opportunities to act is regularly taken up in SDP. Such motives should not be overlooked.

## Conclusion: Critical considerations

On 29 July 2009, the following ran in *The Vancouver Sun* newspaper:

> Nash gets back to his (grass)roots. Local hero hits the pitch for charity, and will bring his Suns to town in October BY IAN WALKER

Professional athlete. Two-time National Basketball Association MVP. Movie producer. Professional soccer team owner. Professional soccer league owner. Philanthropist. All around great guy.

Steve Nash didn't get to where he is by listening to most people. Good thing. The Phoenix Suns guard may never have played hoops past high school if he had.

So it was fitting a few years back when the Victoria native opted to deep-six the Steve Nash Foundation's Charity Classic basketball game – brought to you only upon the terms dictated by the NBA – in favour of a more grassroots approach to charitable sporting endeavours.

This coverage of Nash and his fund-raising Showdown in Downtown football match in Vancouver, with proceeds benefiting the Steve Nash Foundation and its international development efforts, encapsulate many of the issues of athletic celebrity, corporatization, the media and development explored in this chapter. First and foremost, the connections of athletic celebrity to development extend beyond raising awareness and funds for development aid and initiatives but also incorporate and influence the media construction of celebrity athletes themselves. Athletes who support development are generally viewed and constructed as better people and celebritized through media coverage beyond their exploits on the court and including their (charitable) activities off of it. Celebrity athletes supporting development are not undeserving of such positive media attention, but this process does suggest or illustrate the extent to which development and/or SDP efforts, such as raising money for a charitable foundation, is increasingly reliant upon the media culture and its intimate relations to the construction of elite sport and star athletes. Most pointedly, if sport-based development charity and social change is dependent on the media culture and media coverage, then it raises questions about the sustainability of such efforts, the competition for coverage among SDP organizations and even the media's ability to direct the charity industry, given the need for foundations to appeal to media in order to achieve their goals.

It is also significant that the work of celebrities in contemporary development tends towards the charity and role modelling approaches. I would argue that this softer approach is more culturally attractive and politically palatable to athletes like Nash who are undoubtedly well versed and successful in the political art of fund-raising and image management. The fact remains that it is a different political orientation to mobilize celebrity to raise funds than to work for change through human rights, claims to social justice or a politics of equity, to offer but three examples. It is also arguably different than the political orientation to social change through sport in the tradition of athletic activism, such as the famous black power salutes delivered by Tommy Smith and John Carlos at the 1968 Olympics (Zirin 2008). This does not mean that celebrity athletes like Nash are inherently devoid of political engagement or that they avoid controversy[2] (though the competition for positive media coverage likely militates against courting political controversy at least to some degree), but it does suggest that when produced and constrained within the dominant political economy of international development – particularly as it is 'made sexy' by the presence and attractiveness of celebrities – the discourse of charity is more attractive and palatable than that of resistance or struggle.

In turn, it is also reasonable to question who constitutes the focus of such cultural and political activity. In the celebritization of SDP, athlete charitable activity arguably becomes the focus more so than the world's nameless poor. If the point of celebrity athletes in SDP is to raise awareness of development, but such awareness rarely extends beyond the celebrity athlete himself/herself, then has anything significant been achieved in securing sustainable development changes? These tensions illustrate that a type of corporate, media culture surrounds and imbues charity and development in SDP much as we have come to understand it within the broader sports/media complex. The tools are the same here – promotion, marketing, celebrity – even if the goals are to raise money for charity and development rather than for profit. The political challenge, though, as Nickel and Eikenberry (2009) show, is to challenge the corporate competitive system that remains a contributing factor to poverty and inequality. The work of celebrity athletes in SDP may not challenge the political economy of unequal development as radically as possible or required or even hoped.

In sum, there are two sets of implications of the sport/celebrity/development nexus that call for ongoing critical analysis. First, it is clear that celebrity athletes are successful in, and valued for, drawing on their media image and the media/celebrity/sport nexus, to mobilize awareness and money for development programmes and charitable foundations. In turn, few would begrudge the SDP NGOs and celebrity athletes for trading on such opportunities to raise money for charity, particularly in political spaces and climates where public funding for critical health and education is lacking. There are, however, structural limits to this approach to social change and development. Not only is celebrity and corporate-based philanthropy not a radical and sustained challenge to structures of inequality, both international and domestic, but marketized philanthropy may secure such structures (Nickel and Eikenberry 2009). There is little evidence to suggest a move towards development as struggle in and through the celebrity/sport/development nexus.

Two, there are discursive limitations to such politics and policies. It appears to be politically unpalatable for celebrities, and celebrity athletes, to challenge inequality within a development framework in any explicit way. As a result, they tend to mobilize support for development but not to overtly politicize this process. The Steve Nash Foundation is a good example of this. Nash is arguably one of North America's most politically oriented, engaged and productive celebrity athletes. If the Steve Nash Foundation does not or cannot forward a politicization of SFD, or if Nash has decided that it is better not to, then it will take a major change in the cultural economy and discursive terrain to encourage celebrity athletes to do so (see Darnell 2009). Ongoing critical attention and investigations into such processes are called for.

# 7

# Conclusion

## Critical praxis and pedagogy in SDP

### Introduction

With the preceding analyses in mind, this final chapter offers a series of critical conclusions about how and where SDP can position itself, sociopolitically and in terms of both research and practice. The goal of the chapter is to 'operationalize' Nustad's (2001) assertion that critical (and post-) development studies offer a positive contribution to development initiatives (including, in this case, those within SDP). I focus on key questions of power that are at the core of the development context and mandate as well as central to the study of development inequality and responses to it.

In general terms, an ethical and politically engaged way forward towards sustainable development in and through SDP is to challenge, and eventually abandon, the notion of sport's political transcendence in relation to international development and to embrace instead a carefully crafted, though explicit, political vision for SDP. Such a vision can and should underpin the way we do SDP research, the way we work with students interested in SDP and the ways in which we prepare ourselves, and others, to act as global citizens within initiatives focused on sport and physical activity. I argue that while the global interest in sport, and faith in its universality, continues to be offered as a key to its development *utility*, the accessibility that sport affords is better conceptualized as an entry point for confronting and addressing the politics and power relations inherent in international development struggles and volunteer service.

The chapter proceeds in four parts. Next, I draw on recent work in the study of development and SDP to offer an ethical framework for mobilizing SFD. This leads, in turn, to a discussion of a critical praxis for SDP, one that is attuned and committed to histories and politics of inequality and relations of power within development and sport. I then offer some connections between the discipline of critical pedagogy and the field of SDP as a way to conceptualize and actualize an ongoing commitment to a sustained, critical understanding of both the promises and perils of SFD. I conclude with some final thoughts and future questions for SDP research and practice. Through these foci, I position this chapter for an audience that includes both those working in the field of SDP as practitioners and/or researchers, and for those who concentrate primarily on work in the classroom. It is my hope that the theoretical and political insights offered here may be of use to students or volunteers who are taking to the field of SDP, those who work with or for SDP NGOs or other organizations, or anyone who looks to sport as a way towards building a more just and egalitarian world that challenges social and material hierarchies of power and privilege.

## SDP and the ethics of development

In the Introduction to this text, I made reference to Gasper's (2004) conceptualization of the ethics of development that proceed through three stages: ethical questions about development policies and the experiences they afford, ethical examinations of the core concepts and theories employed to understand those experiences and actions, and the ethics of development practice. As stated previously, I also follow Gasper in focusing attention of this text primarily on the first two stages, though they undoubtedly influence the third stage, which itself is of essential importance to critical development studies. Here, I follow Gasper's analyses further by looking at the concepts and values that underpin development work and the ethical implications for SDP that result.

As the preceding chapters have argued, there is evidence of a modernist, capitalist logic in contemporary SDP both in the philosophy of competitive, merit-based achievement and the palatability, if not privileging, of neoliberal approaches to development as they are mobilized through sport. These understandings of how sport contributes to development echo Gasper's contention that mainstream development theory in the twentieth century tended to privilege efficiency and effectiveness over other development values and conceptualizations. In this way, twentieth-century development can be understood as constitutive of and constituted by 'economism' or an economic logic of social change positioned as the basis for development policy, practice and interventions. Economism in Gasper's (2004) terms has several dimensions: that the economy constitutes a separate and relatively insulated sphere of social and political life, that this economic sphere is primary within the social order, that people are primarily economic men (sic), that most or all of life should be valued and managed in and through economic calculation, that the complexities of social development can be measured in economic terms such as gross domestic product and that the economy should be managed without interference. Economism for Gasper (2004: 81) does not equal, and is not reducible to, pro-market fundamentalism, but it does refer to 'the hypertrophy and overreliance on narrow economic ideas' which, once accepted or engrained, are hard to dislodge in and from public life. In this way, the ethical dimensions of economism arise from the ways in which it privileges competitive rationality at the expense of other modalities and the ways in which it may secure and normalize the privilege of the successful few by perpetuating the notion that they earned their success through a benign system of merit rather than within structures of inequality. In turn, economism potentially overlooks alternative values of development and tends to downplay or depoliticize the extent to which citizens from around the world are connected in and through development issues and are implicated in development inequalities (Gasper 2004).

Two points follow from such insights when trying to make sense of the ethics of development in relation to SDP. One, economism underpins much of the logic of SDP to the extent that the convergence of sport, capitalism and the political economy of development creates a social and political terrain in which sport is understood to offer a rational and inexpensive means to development. While such approaches to development are not inherently wrong or misguided, and the analysis of the relative benefits/limitations of such approaches to development through sport ongoing, it does remind of the importance of an ethical analysis of the particular political orientations employed through SDP. Throughout this text, I have argued that neoliberal development philosophy permeates SDP in a plethora of ways. Even in the cases where analyses of SDP's politics diverge from such conclusions (see Lindsay and Grattan, in press), Gasper's ethics of economism remind scholars and practitioners of SDP to be attuned to the ethical dimensions of any development philosophy. This is especially important, I would argue, for point number two that reminds that one of the strengths of sport as a means of supporting development is the opportunity it affords to practice development differently (see Levermore and Beacom 2009). Within development based on economism, the issue of development and its complexities and challenges often comes to rest on what can be afforded (or not) rather than the formulation of alternative values or approaches. In response, I submit that an ethical chore of SDP is to continually maintain space for different values of development that extend beyond the neoliberal economism of development. This may mean, first and foremost, tempering our belief that the rational and utilitarian application of sport leads to significant changes within a development framework and instead positioning sport as an important cultural experience in and of itself that offers an opportunity to engage with the history and politics of development inequality.

Such ideas necessarily complicate the otherwise useful distinction between sport plus (development) and (development) plus sport. On the one hand, plus sport still maintains important ethical implications to the extent that it suggests that the focus of SDP should be on development issues and struggles, and sport in the service thereof, as opposed to the mere application of sport in the hope of sustainable change. On the other hand, resisting economism as a, if not the, organizing value or principle of development and SDP may require coming to terms with sport as a cultural expression, one that is consistently (if not inextricably) politicized and negotiated socially, and therefore not easily 'applied' to the meeting of development goals. Indeed, this might mean refocusing SDP away from development and back on to sport itself, and towards a sport plus orientation, but one designed explicitly to offer a means of engaging with and challenging the structures and politics of development inequality (see Harvey, Horne and Safai 2009). Reconciling the relative strengths and weaknesses of the two perspectives remains an important ethical chore in SDP research.

At the least, critical studies of SDP call for ongoing attention paid to the ways in which the popularity and attractiveness of sport – actual or presumed – may in fact render sport particularly prone to philosophies and processes of economism, regulation and inclusion characteristic of contemporary geopolitical relations of integrated, globalized capitalism. The ethical mobilization of SFD, therefore, will require critical reflection upon the actual effects (both positive and negative) that sport has for meeting development goals and attention paid both to the possibilities and the limitations of sport in effecting social change. Critical ethnographies, like those conducted by Li (2007) and Ong (2006), provide evidence of the impact of neoliberal development and the ways in which it promotes sociopolitical regulation at the expense of self-determination. In turn, these studies illustrate the importance of continual ethical decision-making regarding the impact of sport in SDP. If SFD is principally a tool to regulate behaviour, then I suggest that it fails to meet its ethical responsibilities to support equality of condition and development as a process of self-determination (Sen 2000). In response, a critical praxis of SDP is called for.


## A new praxis for SDP

The concept of praxis is an important one in the social sciences for the ways that it affords researchers and theorists a means by which to articulate the mobility or applicability of critical analyses. In this way, praxis represents the process of theory becoming practice (Lather 1991) or a way to conceptualize 'reflective action that intervenes in a social context' (De Lissovoy 2008b: 129). Previously (Darnell 2006), I outlined a framework for researching SDP that drew specifically on the notion of praxis as a means of linking theory and research to the 'real world' (see Hall 1986). Here, I revisit this praxis framework and consider it against the analyses in the preceding chapters of this book. It is important to note that in the philosophical spirit of a praxis orientation, the goal here is not to offer 'solutions' to the limitations of SDP, such as they have been outlined in the preceding analyses, but to offer a vision for how to conduct SDP, in research, theory and practice, in more ethical and politically engaged ways.

In developing this praxis framework (Darnell 2006), I have argued that three areas of sociological theory are particularly useful and applicable for making theory practical: post-colonial, third-wave (or transnational) feminist and post-structuralist. First, when drawing on the perspectives of post-colonial theory, it becomes clear that the notion of disinterested or politically transcendent knowledge is itself political and therefore impossible to substantiate (see Smith 1999). That is, the 'knowledge' or claims to truth that emanated from the colonial encounter were never benign; rather, such knowledge often constituted epistemic violence, the ramifications of which endure despite well-intentioned desires for a purely post- or anti-colonial world. Claims to knowledge in development and SDP, therefore, require a focus on historical and contemporary accountability and responsibility, as much as, if not more than, social or material progress. SDP within the post-colonial, including the transnational encounters that this affords, is more complex than facilitating participation; it requires recognition of the material and discursive hierarchies that colonialism solidified. Research and practice in SDP that begins from this perspective will look quite different from charitable acts. It will actively seek to oppose the colonial continuities that privilege Whiteness, secure the 'natural' dominance of the Global North and propagate a First World subject position based on benevolent inclusion.

In turn, SDP can benefit from the third-wave feminist contestation of presumed social solidarities. As Mohanty (2003) illustrates, dialogue based on the recognition and celebration of sociocultural *difference* offers more to the promotion of social justice because it rejects essentialisms that serve to secure dominance. This does not mean that camaraderie need necessarily be discarded, only that the struggles for equitable and sustainable development to which SDP programs respond are socially and culturally contextual and specific. For SDP researchers and practitioners, this perspective brings the limits of universal human rights as a basis for sport and development into sharp relief. Again, as Teeple (2005) has argued, human rights are not truly universal because they do not afford all persons the means necessary to realize their rights in practice. Combining this perspective with a transnational approach, it becomes clearer still that the presumption of universal rights can overlook, and even normalize, the tendency to seek universal, essentialist forms of social change that only operate *within* hierarchies, not against them.

Recognizing difference in this way draws upon the insights of post-structuralism, the third element of the praxis framework that I outline here. The universalist/relativist debate in development studies – one that pits a desire to rely upon and privilege the universal experiences of humanity (such as the organization and culture of sport) against a rejection of the objective standards to which development refers – becomes less important in an approach to praxis informed by post-structuralism. The critical issue for SDP is not whether development should or should not happen, and/or the ways in which sport should be mobilized to these ends, because both of these approaches presume a social stability that has been rigorously challenged by post-structural theory (see Haraway 1991; Lather 1991). Rather, an ethical praxis embraces ambivalence in recognizing that essentializing difference is as problematic as privileging similarities (Grewal and Kaplan 1994). The issue is not whether or not SFD programmes should happen but rather the social imagination that such initiatives support. Through the lens of post-structuralism, searching for, and establishing, a stable social and political basis for action becomes secondary to embracing the ongoing irreconcilability of the ethical challenges as they have been outlined in this text. Similarly, context and political vision become increasingly important as both researchers and practitioners are left to consistently and critically reflect upon the goals and desires of the SDP sector and the limits of SFD.

In sum, I argue that a praxis orientation should start from the understanding that traditional power relations underpinning the contemporary global political apparatus have become decentralized such that geopolitical hierarchies are increasingly intelligible and yet simultaneously less questioned for their histories, circumstances and politics (see Hardt and Negri 2000). These relations of 'Empire' have the ability to reduce international development to a process of attending to the symptoms of globalized inequality and rarely to its cause. Through this text, I have strived to illustrate that the compatibility of dominant sporting culture with the bio-political regulation of the socially constructed body serves – strategically or not – to align the SDP sector with these apolitical trends in approaches to development. I argue in response that a critical praxis in and for SDP will seek to challenge and deconstruct global hierarchies, as opposed to finding and supporting evermore creative ways of motivating people to survive within discursively material inter- and transnational inequalities.

I do recognize the enormous challenge of this praxis within SDP, particularly given that material inequalities – the lacks of goods, infrastructure, opportunities and resources – continue to be rightly recognized as symbols of the need for development and SDP and as the impetus for mobilizing sport towards meeting development goals. The praxis framework that I am outlining here need not dismiss the importance of recognizing inequality or responding to it. The issue rather is the ways, both discursive and material, in which these lacks are taken up and rendered intelligible and the actions that they promote under the banner of SDP. It is crucial both to differentiate material injustice from colonial continuities *and* to make explicit the links between them because even redressing material inequality – particularly in the short term or within the dominant capitalist paradigm – does not necessarily address relations of power in a substantive way. It is possible (and problematic) for material inequalities to be taken up in the service of colonial continuities, whereby Foucauldian subjects who know themselves as sophisticated and benevolent trade on their privilege in an effort to re-dress the effects of marginalization in and from which they benefit. Just like anti-racism goes beyond claims of colour-blindness and challenges racial hierarchies, in this praxis-based approach that I have described, research and practice in SDP should question the implications of claims to innocence and consider SDP as a sector committed to challenging oppression.

Fortunately for those interested in such a praxis, there are theoretical models in place that offer important insights. While several abound, here I draw on the work of Noah De Lissovoy (2008b) and his conceptualization of the politics and praxis of the *terran*. De Lissovoy uses *terran* as a term to theorize, describe and attempt to balance the need for a global solidarity within struggles of inequality and against the limits of a presumed solidarity, particularly as it is increasingly celebrated within globalization and new communication technologies (see Hardt and Negri 2004). In this way, a *terran* identity encapsulates the 'essential globality of any effective oppositional class as well as the situatedness of human struggle within specific geographies' (De Lissovoy 2008b: 149). A praxis of SDP must be, therefore, historically and geographically informed both with regard to development inequality and to the social and political dimensions of sport. This is necessary in order to address and resist the tendency of sport's popularity to flatten the politics of international development in the ways that Li (2007), Ferguson (1994) and others have described in development more broadly. In all cases, the inequality and marginalization that marks the 'need' for an institutional and international sector of SDP has deep political antecedents and implications. Absent of such reflections upon these antecedents within SDP though, the 'lacks' that are characteristic of 'underdevelopment', and serve to solidify and justify the need for SDP in the first place, are susceptible to reduction to the limitations or misconduct of marginalized people. Thus, from an ethical perspective, serving in the SDP sector requires awareness of the geopolitical relations that contribute to, and sustain, the very need for international development and the concomitant desire to mobilize sport as a tool to address inequality. Claims to historical and political innocence in and through SDP are ethically irresponsible.

The *terran* also offers a means by which to conceptualize and positively acknowledge the international dimensions of sport as formative to SDP, and support the momentum of SDP in contributing to international development, but to do so in a way that remains vigilant in rejecting essentialisms (of cultures, ethnicities or physicality) and situating the inequality to which sport attends through SDP within historical context. It may even be possible to bring SDP into alignment with social movements that reject top-down models of regulation and stewardship and instead stand as the product of situated learning in the context of collective action and communication (De Lissovoy 2008b: 143). Arguably, it is here that sport and SDP have the most to offer. Not only is sport increasingly recognized as a social or cultural node or hub around which such political organizing and resistance occurs (see Harvey, Horne and Safai 2009), but the undeniable popularity of global sport like football/soccer may also offer a means by which local movements that challenge inequality can connect transnationally in a manner akin to Hardt and Negri's (2004) conception of *multitude*. Of course, to avoid the essentialist solidarities to which De Lissovoy draws critical attention, such transnational connections will have to recognize the cultural specificities of both sport and social struggle, but surely this is increasingly possible, particularly in an age of new media connectivity (see Wilson 2007). Such a praxis would also align with the argument that development initiatives should strive to support the self-determination and struggles for sustainable self-sufficiency of marginalized people more so than attempting to 'motivate' or 'educate' them towards proper conduct (see Saunders 2010; Sen 2000). Such a praxis would be recognizable 'when local struggles start to see themselves in others elsewhere' (De Lissovoy 2008b: 152).

In fact, I contend this may be where the presumed universality, popularity and relatively benign politics of sport – such as they are – are most applicable. In the cases, for example, where migrants struggle for social, cultural and economic sufficiency amidst market hierarchies, retreating state support and xenophobia (see Saunders 2010), perhaps sport offers a means by which to facilitate peaceful geographic migration and socio-economic integration or to support those marginalized along lines of race and class into legitimate cultural and political citizenship. Sport, in this way, might offer a means by which to begin to come to terms with the political antecedents of development inequalities in a manner similar to Giulianotti's (2004) advocacy of 'sentimental education'. Again, vigilance would be required to protect the transformative orientation of such endeavours and avoid simplistic – if not colonizing – claims of understanding the Other, but possibilities clearly abound to mobilize sport towards explorations and understandings of people's struggle for self-determination within the terms of the cultural and political economy and in resistance to them. As De Lissovoy makes clear, the praxis of the terran is concerned with both the incorporation of people into the global workforce as a form of domination (in a manner similar to that described by Ong 2006) *and* with their expulsion from economic and social citizenship. With such a praxis in mind, and a commitment made to challenging inequality and dominance, sport and SDP can be amended to support progressive development politics, particularly if supported by critical pedagogy.

## Towards a critical pedagogy of SDP

To this point in the chapter, I have argued for the importance of ethical considerations of development within SDP and for a critical praxis oriented towards mobilizing SFD in ways that challenges the conditions of global inequality. Both of these imperatives can be supported, I suggest, by a sustained critical engagement with the politics, policies and vision of SDP, an engagement productively conceptualized through the lens of critical pedagogy. Two reasons substantiate the importance and appropriateness of this connection. First, given that the ethos of critical pedagogy demands that it be accessible and open to a wide audience (Kincheloe 2007) and given that sport constitutes an entry point, invitation or non-threatening means into international development and its myriad challenges and inequalities, SDP informed by critical pedagogy may constitute an important and unique means by which to engage in critical conversations about international development. Such conversations may be mutually beneficial to both those in relatively privileged positions who wish to support change and to those who are considered the 'targets' or 'partners' of SDP initiatives. Amidst calls for critical pedagogy to be repositioned as a way to engage with marginalized voices – particularly that of persons marginalized along the intersections of race, class and gender (see Kincheloe 2007) – critical pedagogy seems well suited to challenge the subjugated knowledge and social and political hierarchies that have been highlighted in critical scholarship into SDP (see Darnell 2007; Guest 2009; Nicholls 2009).

Second, current approaches to critical pedagogy are consistent with challenging hegemonic knowledge and relations of power. Throughout much of this text, I have employed a hegemony framework to make sense of the ideas, politics and structures that enjoy a status of 'commonsense' in SDP. I have done so in order to show that the capitalist norms or discourses that underpin much of SDP thinking and action are not universal in conception or application and that, in many cases, SDP as a sector concerned with sustainable development would be well served to think through and beyond these hegemonic ideas. It is in this sense that a critical pedagogy of SDP may be most called for. According to Weiner (2007: 69), the chore of critical pedagogy is to 'break the hegemony of realism which suggests that the future will turn out more or less the same as the present'. Realism here can refer both to the ways in which development inequalities are often de-historicized, depoliticized or taken for granted as well as the rather staid manner in which sport is positioned in relation to meeting development goals. In this sense, critical pedagogy encourages SDP stakeholders to consider that sport will/can be radically different in the future of SDP and that notions of development (i.e. why it is necessary, how we approach it, what we do about development inequality) will/can be different as well. Clearly, this kind of re-imagining will take pedagogical and political commitment and effort, along at least three vectors.

## Material inequalities and social hierarchies

A critical pedagogy of SDP will need to conceptualize, contextualize and challenge the material inequalities that underpin development and are inextricably linked to the SDP sector. By this I mean that critical pedagogies of SDP will remind advocates of the sector that the need or impetus to mobilize SFD does not proceed, at least initially, from the universality of sport but rather from the inequalities and hierarchies, both material and social, which constitute the context of international development. While this point may seem banal to a large degree (*of course* there are marginalized people to which development initiatives, including SDP, attend) it is nonetheless fundamental to the extent that it reminds that this inequality is a result of historical, social and political organization *and* that the mobilizing of sport in response is equally socially and politically implicated and contestable. Such a measure of critical self-reflection is crucial, I argue, particularly given the number of SDP initiatives organized and funded in the Global North and implemented in the South, which run the risk of pathologizing southern poverty as degenerate (Biccum 2010) and solidifying northern responses as benevolent (Heron 2007). Instead, if critical attention is drawn to the reasons why development is needed around the world, then sport can be conceptualized in ways that challenge these relations of inequality.

In turn, the centrality of social hierarchies is key to a critical pedagogy of SDP, particularly for people who wish to work as advocates or volunteers for sport-based development initiatives. As I suggested in my analysis of the experiences of CGC interns (see Chapter 3 and Darnell 2010b) the development context in which SDP programmes operate is inextricably linked to social hierarchies particularly along lines of race, class and gender as well as sexuality and ability, all of which are complicated by the material inequalities of development. The culturally universal dimensions of sport do not overcome such hierarchies. Rather, a critical pedagogy of anti-racism and its intersections particularly concerned with the material and discursive power of Whiteness is called for (see Darnell 2007). Not all actors and stakeholders within SDP enjoy the same relations of authority and privilege. In turn, sport offers an opportunity to enter the political terrain and spaces of development but to do so in ways that challenge relations of power rather than rely on the universality, popularity or 'power' of sport to usurp these structures.

## The politics and meanings of sport

A second feature of a critical pedagogy of global social change is a commitment to solidarity, which recognizes material and social hierarchies, as opposed to universalist discourses that attempt to overcome or depoliticise them. For example, De Lissovoy (2008b: 146–7) argues for 'oppositional solidarity' given that there is no stable 'abstract unity' outside of the actual experiences of oppression, through which to organize struggles for social change. When applied to SDP initiatives that seek social change through sport, these insights suggest that the universality of sport, even as it is intelligible through the immense popularity of watching and playing sport, does not serve as a stable basis of SDP if it presumes a solidarity that is removed from the actual experiences of poverty, inequality and oppression. When situated in the context of international development, sport does not necessarily bring us all together because of the fact that development inequalities are not universal. In turn, positioning and mobilizing sport as a tool towards rights-based development, an ostensibly progressive step, does not address or overcome social inequality in any essential way. Instead, I suggest that sport may be best understood as a means by which to engage in the process of negotiating and constructing solidarity amidst development inequalities. As D. Kapoor (2009b) has suggested, development starts with understanding not only local needs but also the histories and politics of local struggles. What can bring us together through sport is a commitment to challenging the politics of inequality, but this commitment must be the starting point, like D. Kapoor (2009b) suggests, rather than starting from a universal language or meaning of sport.

Furthermore, as scholars of sport have demonstrated, sport is neither inherently good nor bad but a cultural form produced and constrained within the social milieu and susceptible to the relations of power that propagate inequality in the society at large. It is always possible, despite good intentions, for sport to be taken up in SDP in socially regressive or negative ways, such as normalizing violent competition, solidifying racial and gender hierarchies, or further solidifying the exclusion of non-participants. What is needed, therefore, is not the refined *application* of SFD but a *re-imagining* of SFD that challenges relations of dominance. I concur with Maguire (2006) in arguing that the dominant sporting status quo – characterized by competition, continuous improvement, achievement orientation and the solidification of social hierarchies – begs for critical evaluation against the vision of social change that SDP espouses. As a result, there may be an opportunity, in addition to a responsibility, to re-imagine sport as a practice that recognizes dominance and offers a tool to resist it, a project already laid out by critical philosophers of the sporting experience.

For example, according to Shogan (2007: 119) 'this new sport ethics encourages noticing, questioning and refusing when necessary the norms and demands of sport'. The context of international development may actually offer an important and unique opportunity to interrogate and question sport in this way. That is, instead of deploying traditional, competitive sporting practices (i.e. football/soccer) as a means to model, inspire and empower achievement in development, a process that may re-inscribe and reproduce traditional norms of dominance and discipline, new forms of sports like football, or new sporting forms altogether, could literally be invented. Theoretically, these new sporting forms could use opportunities for teamwork to privilege social equity and social spaces for all. SDP is not limited or beholden to traditional sport; SDP offers a significant opportunity to re-imagine sport. Sport can offer a means of supporting and facilitating self-determination as opposed to reinforcing and

LIVERPOOL JOHN MOORES UNIVERSITY
LEARNING SERVICES

normalizing an ethos of achievement that underpins the logic of capitalism and reduces its inequities to a matter of individual failings.

## 'Re-imagining' development through SDP

Finally, according to Weiner (2007: 75), critical pedagogy is needed given that 'the official discourse of schooling attempts to fix the meaning of being a teacher as well as end the discussion of what constitutes an educated person'. In this type of traditional praxis that Weiner describes and critiques, the gamut of possibilities of approaching social change is effectively reduced to a politics of conformity particularly along lines of subjectivity and notions of what constitutes the 'preferred subject'. I would argue that similar tensions are evident in much of contemporary SDP policies and programming where the vast range of possible understandings of development are regularly reduced to neoliberal notions of individualized citizenship and the logic of competitive capitalism (see Hartman and Kwauk 2011). As a result, a critical pedagogy committed to development as the process of supporting self-determination, both within the political economy and amidst social hierarchies, is needed, more so than the promotion of SDP as a means of 'educating' marginalized people into the operations and machinations of capitalist development. Especially where sport obfuscates the particularities of development inequality, or where poverty is rendered intelligible as degeneracy rather than the effects of oppression and dominance (Biccum 2010; De Lissovoy 2008b), SDP should challenge such notions, not reproduce or tacitly accept them.

Again, I would suggest that critical scholars and teachers – of both development and sport – are well positioned to support this type of critical pedagogy of SDP by advocating and supporting a move beyond evaluative and prescriptive analyses of the role of sport in meeting development goals and towards profoundly more imaginative explorations of what sport offers to development and how it should be organized and deployed to meeting such goals. Such a shift will likely require moving beyond positivist interpretations of SDP data that tend to focus on how the application of sport leads to particular development outcomes and that can be 'generalized' across cultures and geographies. Instead, SDP will be asked to come to terms with the impossibility of securing universal answers to questions of justice, power and praxis (Kincheloe 2007: 16). This shift will also, crucially, require pedagogies of non-control that recognize the primary task of education and activism (through sport) as more than the transfer of knowledge from an expert to a subordinate, compatible with functionalist notions of sport in support of development. Instead, this shift will be characterized by re-positioning sport in order to facilitate the actions of students/learners as authentic subjects with agency amidst the historical specificity of inequality (De Lissovoy 2008b: 9, drawing on Paulo Friere). From this perspective, the appropriateness of SDP and the effectiveness of sport to support the achievement of sustainable development goals is not a truth to be discovered but an opportunity to be embraced within an unfolding terrain of the political and social possibilities of social change (De Lissovoy 2008b: 10).

If all that I am describing here seems ambiguous, poorly connected to SDP policy and rhetoric, or even difficult to imagine in relation to the actual implementation of SDP programmes and initiatives, I would argue that this is largely the point. Exactly what is needed in SDP is a move *away* from questions of 'what works' and 'what doesn't' and a contemporaneous move *towards* understanding the historical and social experiences of sport and development as they are formed and performed within SDP. This may suggest the need for a phenomenological approach to SDP, one concerned less with 'generalizable', objective knowledge and more with insights into, and reflections upon, the complexities and diversities of the sporting experience (Kerry and Armour 2000). In the tradition of Husserl, the phenomenologist is asked to re-examine presuppositions and assumptions through the juxtaposition of examples, as opposed to generalizations that are ostensibly supported through empiricism (Kerry and Armour 2000). From this perspective, SDP's twin hegemonies of sporting meritocracy and the free choices provided by neoliberal development philosophy are ripe for re-examination in and through the experiences that occur within the field of SDP. Indeed, it may be the case that we need to suspend and challenge our understandings of, and beliefs in, sport (and development) in order to truly employ and mobilize sport in ways that diverge from traditional development and athletic orthodoxy.

For example, I would caution that the idea that SDP advocates like Johan Koss are 'living testimonials' to SFD (see Kidd 2008) or that there is an 'intuitive certainty' (Kruse 2006; cited in Coalter 2010b) of the contributions of the SDP sector largely resign us to the status quo marked by unequal development and achievement-based sport in the name of upward mobility. Particularly in relation to SDP research and methodology, a phenomenology of SDP would begin to open up more possibilities to implement SDP differently through approaches to monitoring and evaluation that are not restricted to the terms laid out by the dominant cultural and political economy (see Crabbe 2009).

Furthermore, phenomenology holds potential for SDP for the ways in which it draws attention to the body. As I have suggested throughout this text, SDP logic regularly invokes the notion of the active, regulated, disciplined and successful body. As Ahmed (2006: 552) describes, 'Phenomenology helps us explore how bodies are shaped by histories, which they perform in their comportment, their posture, and their gestures.' In this sense, SDP research would be well served to focus on embodied experiences and to strive to make sense of these experiences as they are constructed amidst the history and politics of unequal development. Phenomenology, in this way, opens up possibilities for rethinking – 'a queer phenomenology would function as a disorientation device' (Ahmed 2006: 566) – in order to challenge our notions of what sport and development are and to reorient ourselves to how these politics are often literally 'played out' in and through SDP programmes.

In sum, such a phenomenological approach to understanding SDP, informed by Husserl, might ask us – as researchers, practitioners, students, champions and/or organizers of SDP – to let go of the knowledge, skills and expertise that we (think we) hold and begin to practice anew towards sustainable development. Similarly, in the tradition of Heidegger, we might think about the extent to which the SDP sector rests not just on the popularity or universality of sport but also on the organization of sport and its development mandate to make the world a better place, a mandate that is always already understood. To employ a sporting metaphor, this phenomenology of SDP would be like learning to dribble a basketball with one's left hand or kick a football/soccer ball with one's left foot after a lifetime of playing with the right. The chore of SDP is not the successful application of SFD but the learning and questioning of the organization and mobilization of sport in support of the cultural, social and geographic specificities of development struggles. This will be difficult but ultimately rewarding. For, as any good athlete knows, being able to play with one's left *or* right significantly increases the chances of a strong performance and sporting success when the game is on.

## Concluding thoughts and future questions

This text has tried to embrace the sense of ambivalence that emanates from the opportunities and limitations of mobilizing sport to meet the goals of international development. There is, without question, much that remains to be done. It is both my intention and hope that this book be situated much closer to the beginning of a mass of critical research into SDP and its policies, practices, ideologies, discourses and implications than to stand as any kind of steadfast conclusion. Indeed, some of the critical issues that I have raised remain significantly under-explored, both theoretically and empirically, within the burgeoning SDP literature. To conclude, then, I offer some questions for future research into, and critical analyses of, SDP.

1 In what ways does the current mobilization of SFD present an opportunity to rethink and re-imagine the organization and practice of contemporary sport? What would a sporting practice and praxis intimately connected to the politics of unequal development look like? What would be its hallmarks?

2 In what ways can or do sport-based activist groups – or those connected to alter-globalization movements – align with (and diverge from)

the ethos and practices of SDP initiatives? What opportunities for partnership exist?

3 If a goal of SDP research is to enter into relationships with partners in ways that challenge and resist colonial continuities, what would these relationships look like? What would be their constitutive epistemologies and elements?

4 How are sports mega-events, particularly those upcoming in the southern hemisphere, taking up issues of international development within their organization and justification? Is resistance to sports mega-events as catalysts of development being mobilized? What does this resistance look like and what are its effects?

5 How and why are celebrities and celebrity athletes in particular drawn to SDP? What are the implications for those working in the field? How is the dichotomy of charity versus justice implicated in this relationship?

6 How has the changing political economy of development, complicated by the 2008 financial crisis and the responses of states and NGOs, influenced the SDP sector and the ways in which sport is now mobilized to meet development goals?

7 What practices of critical pedagogy, both for the classroom and the research field, are effective for expanding the possibilities of SDP and maintaining an active development imagination in relation to sport?

These questions, and undoubtedly others, remain to be analysed. Yet, based on my recent interactions with colleagues in both the sociology of sport and critical development studies, my work with students both post- and undergraduate, and the plethora of recent presentations at conferences and articles on SDP published recently in scholarly journals, I am confident that the makings of a critical mass of SDP research are in place. Given the possibilities – as well as limitations – of using sport to meet sustainable, egalitarian development, and to contribute to making the world a more just and peaceful place, such interdisciplinary and challenging research is most needed and welcome.

# References

Aboriginal Sport Circle (2008). *Aboriginal Sport Circle*, from http://www. aboriginalsportcircle.ca/main/main.html [accessed 1 November 2011].

Ahmed, S. (2004). *The Cultural Politics of Emotion*. Edinburgh, UK: Edinburgh University Press.

Ahmed, S. (2006). Orientations: Toward a Queer Phenomenology. *GLQ: A Journal of Lesbian and Gay Studies, 12*(4), 543–74.

Akindes, G. & Kirwin, M. (2009). Sport As International Aid: Assisting Development or Promoting Under-development in Sub-Saharan Africa? In R. Levermore & A. Beacom (eds), *Sport and International Development* (pp. 219–45). New York: Palgrave MacMillan.

Alcoff, L. (1991). The Problem of Speaking for Others. *Cultural Critique, 20* (Winter), 5–32.

Alive and Kicking (2011). *Alive and Kicking*, from http://www.aliveandkicking.org.uk/ [accessed 1 November 2011].

Althusser, L. (1969). *For Marx*. New York: Pantheon Books.

Althusser, L. (2001). *Lenin and Philosophy, and Other Essays*. New York: Monthly Review Press.

Amin, S. (2006). The Millennium Development Goals: A Critique from the South. *Monthly Review, 57*(10), from http://www.monthlyreview.org/0306amin2.php [accessed 4 November 2011].

Andrews, D. L. (1993). Desperately Seeking Michel: Foucault's Genealogy, the Body, and Critical Sport Sociology. *Sociology of Sport Journal, 10*(2), 148–68.

Andrews, D. L. (2000). Posting Up: French Poststructuralism and the Critical Analysis of Contemporary Sporting Cultures. In J. Coakley & E. Dunning (eds), *Handbook of Sports Studies* (pp. 106–37). London: Sage.

Andrews, D. L. (2007). Response to Bairner's '*Back to Basics: Class, Social Theory and Sport*'. *Sociology of Sport Journal, 10*(2), 37–45.

Andrews, D. L. & Jackson, S. (eds). (2001). *Sport Stars: The Cultural Politics of Sporting Celebrity*. London: Routledge.

Andrews, D. L. & Loy, J. W. (1993). British Cultural Studies and Sport: Past Encounters and Future Possibilities. *Quest, 45*, 255–76.

Arat-Koc, S. (2010). New Whiteness(es) Beyond the Colour Line? Assessing the Contradictions and Complexities of 'Whiteness' in the (Geo)Political Economy of Capitalist Globalism. In S. Razack, M. Smith & S. Thobani (eds), *States of Race: Critical Race Feminism for the 21st Century* (pp. 147–68). Toronto, ON: Between the Lines.

Ariffin, J. (2004). Gender Critiques of the Millennium Development Goals: An Overview and an Assessment. Paper presented at the International Council on Social Welfare (ICSW), 31st International Conference on Social Progress and Social Justice. Kuala Lumpur, Malaysia, 16 August.

Armstrong, G. (2004) The Lords of Misrule: Football and the Rights of the Child in Liberia, West Africa. *Sport in Society, 7*(3), 473–502.

Asher, K. (2009). *Black and Green: Afro-Colombians, Development and Nature in the Pacific Lowlands*. Durham, NC: Duke University Press.

Baaz, M. E. (2005). *The Paternalism of Partnership: A Postcolonial Reading of Identity in Development Aid*. London and New York: Zed Books.

Bailey, G. & Gayle, N. (2003). *Ideology: Structuring Identities in Contemporary Life*. Peterborough, ON: Broadview Press.

Bairner, A. (2007) Back to Basics: Class, Social Theory and Sport. *Sociology of Sport Journal, 24*(1), 20–36.

Bairner, A. (2009) Re-appropriating Gramsci: Marxism, Hegemony and Sport. In B. Carrington & I. McDonald (eds), *Marxism, Cultural Studies and Sport* (pp. 195–212). New York: Routledge.

Baker, J., Lynch, K., Cantillon, S. & Walsh, J. (2004). *Equality: From Theory to Action*. New York: Palgrave MacMillan.

Baker, W. J. & Mangan, J. A. (eds). (1987). *Sport in Africa*. New York: Holmes & Meier.

Bale, J. & Cronin, M. (2003). *Sport and Postcolonialism*. Oxford, UK: Berg.

Bartoli, H. & Unesco (2000). *Rethinking Development: Putting an End to Poverty*. Management of Social Transformations Program. Paris: *Economica*, UNESCO.

Beasley-Murray, J. (2003). On Posthegemony. *Bulletin of Latin American Research, 22*(1), 117–25.

Berry, A. & Serieux, J. (2007). World Economic Growth and Income Distribution, 1980–2000. In Jomo K. S. & J. Baudot (eds), *Flat World, Big Gaps* (pp. 74–98). New York: Zed Books.

Bhabha, H. K. (1994). *The Location of Culture*. London: Routledge.

Biccum, A. (2010). *Global Citizenship and the Legacy of Empire: Marketing Development*. London and New York: Routledge.

Black, D. (2008). Dreaming Big: The Pursuit of 'Second Order' Games As a Strategic Response to Globalization. *Sport in Society, 11*(4), 467–80.

Black, D. (2010). The Ambiguities of Development: Implications for Development through Sport. *Sport in Society, 13*(1), 121–9.

Bond, P. (2002). The New Partnership for Africa's Development: Social, Economic and Environmental Contradictions. *Capitalism, Nature, Socialism, 13*(2), 151–80.

Boorstin, D. (1961). *The Image: A Guide to Pseudo-events in America*. New York: Harper Colophon.

Bouchier, N. (1994). Idealized Middle-Class Sport for a Young Nation: Lacrosse in Nineteenth-Century Ontario Towns. *Journal of Canadian Studies, 29*(2), 89–110.

Bridel, W. & Rail, G. (2007). Sport, Sexuality and the Production of (Resistant) Bodies: De-/ Re-constructing the Meanings of Gay Male Marathon Corporeality. *Sociology of Sport Journal, 24*(2), 127–44.

Brown, W. (2006). *Regulating Aversion: Tolerance in the Age of Identity and Empire*. Princeton, NJ: Princeton University Press.

Burnett, C. (2006). Building Social Capital through an Active Community Club. *International Review for the Sociology of Sport, 41*(3), 283–94.

Burstyn, V. (1999). *The Rites of Men: Manhood, Politics, and the Culture of Sport*. Toronto, ON: University of Toronto Press.

BW Sportswire (1999). OATH Announces Results of First-Ever Olympic Athlete-Sponsored Symposium on IOC Reform. New York, 11–13 June.

Cameron, J. & Haanstra, A. (2008). Development Made Sexy: How It Happened and What It Means. *Third World Quarterly, 29*(8), 1475–89.

Cammack, P. (2006). U.N. Imperialism: Unleashing Entrepreneurship in the Developing World. In C. Mooers (ed.), *The New Imperialists: Ideologies of Empire* (pp. 229–60). Oxford, UK: Oneworld.

Carrington, B. (2010). *Race, Sport and Politics: The Sporting Black Diaspora*. London: Sage.

Ciochetto, L. (2010). People, Profit, Planet: An Exploration of the Environmental Implications of Development in Brazil, Russia, India and China by 2050, World Congress of Sociology. Gothenburg, Sweden, 12 July.

Clarke, J. (2010). After Neo-liberalism? Markets, States, and the Reinvention of Public Welfare. *Cultural Studies, 24*(3), 375–94.

Coakley, J. & Donnelly, P. (2004). *Sports in Society: Issues and Controversies*. Toronto, ON: McGraw-Hill Ryerson.

Coalter, F. (2008). Sport-in-Development: Development for and through Sport? In M. Nicholson & R. Hoye (eds), *Sport and Social Capital* (pp. 39–67). Oxford, UK: Butterworth-Heinemann.

Coalter, F. (2009). Sport-in-Development: Accountability or Development? In R. Levermore & A. Beacom (eds), *Sport and International Development* (pp. 55–75). London: Palgrave MacMillan.

Coalter, F. (2010a). The Politics of Sport-for-Development: Limited Focus Programmes and Broad Gauge Problems? *International Review for the Sociology of Sport, 45*(3), 295–314.

Coalter, F. (2010b). Sport-for-Development: Going Beyond a Boundary? *Sport in Society,* *13*(9), 1374–91.

Cole, C. L., Giardina, M. D. & Andrews, D. L. (2004). Michel Foucault: Studies of Power and Sport. In R. Giulianotti (ed.), *Sport and Modern Social Theorists* (pp. 207–23). New York: Palgrave MacMillan.

Coleman, J. (1998). Social Capital in the Creation of Human Capital. *American Journal of Sociology,* *94*, 95–120.

Commonwealth Games Canada (2008). *International Development through Sport: Introduction,* from http://www.commonwealthgames.ca/IDS/index_e.aspx [accessed 3 July 2008].

Cooper, A. (2007). *Celebrity Diplomacy and the G8: Bono and Bob As Legitimate International Actors.* Unpublished manuscript, Waterloo, ON.

Cooper, A. (2008). Beyond One Image Fits All: Bono and the Complexity of Celebrity Diplomacy. *Global Governance, 14,* 265–72.

Cornelissen, S. (2008). Scripting the Nation: Sport, Mega-events, Foreign Policy and State-Building in Post-apartheid South Africa. *Sport in Society, 11*(4), 481–93.

Cornelissen, S. (2009). A Delicate Balance: Major Sports Events and Development. In R. Levermore & A. Beacom (eds), *Sport and International Development* (pp. 76–97). New York: Palgrave MacMillan.

Cottle, S. & Nolan, D. (2007). Global Humanitarianism and the Changing Aid-Media Field: Everyone Was Dying for Footage. *Journalism Studies, 8*(6), 862–78.

Cox, R. W. & Sinclair, T. J. (1996). *Approaches to World Order.* Cambridge, UK; New York: Cambridge University Press.

Crabbe, T. (2009). Getting to Know You: Using Sport to Engage and Build Relationships with Socially Marginalized Young People. In R. Levermore & A. Beacom (eds), *Sport and International Development* (pp. 176–97). New York: Palgrave MacMillan.

Da Costa, D. (2010). Introduction: Relocating Culture in Development and Development in Culture. *Third World Quarterly, 31*(4), 501–22.

Darnell, S. C. (2006). International Development and the Sociology of Sport: Exploring a New Research Agenda, North American Society for the Sociology of Sport Conference. Vancouver, BC, 2 November.

Darnell, S. C. (2007). Playing with Race: Right to Play and the Production of Whiteness in Development through Sport. *Sport in Society, 10*(4), 560–79.

Darnell, S. C. (2009). The Steve Nash Foundation: Sporting Celebrity, Politics and Philanthropy, North American Society for the Sociology of Sport Conference. Ottawa, ON, 4 November.

Darnell, S. C. (2010a). Power, Politics and Sport for Development and Peace: Investigating the Utility of Sport for International Development. *Sociology of Sport Journal, 27*(1), 54–75.

Darnell, S. C. (2010b). Race, Sport and Bio-politics: Encounters with Difference in 'Sport for Development and Peace' Internships. *Journal of Sport and Social Issues, 34*(4), 396–417.

Darnell, S. C. (2011a). Sport, Education and Conflict: Responses, Cautions and Questions. *Conflict and Education, 1*(1), from http://conflictandeducation.org/?p=48 [accessed 5 November 2011].

Darnell, S. C. (2011b). Identity and Learning in International Volunteerism: 'Sport for Development and Peace' Internships. *Development in Practice, 21*(7), 974–86.

Darnell, S. C. (in press). Olympism in Action, Olympic Hosting and the Politics of 'Sport for Development and Peace': Investigating the Development Discourses of Rio 2016. *Sport in Society.*

Darnell, S. C. & Hayhurst, L. (2011). Sport for De-colonization: Exploring a New Praxis of Sport for Development. *Progress in Development Studies, 11*(3), 183–96.

Darnell, S. C. & Hayhurst, L. (in press). Hegemony, Post-colonialism and Sport for Development: A Response to Lindsey and Grattan. *International Journal of Sport Policy, 4*(1).

Darnell, S. C. & Sparks, R. (2005). Inside the Promotional Vortex: Canadian Media Construction of Sydney Olympic Triathlete Simon Whitfield. *International Review for the Sociology of Sport, 40*(3), 357–75.

Day, R. J. F. (2005). *Gramsci Is Dead: Anarchist Currents in the Newest Social Movements.* London and Ann Arbor, MI: Pluto Press; Toronto, ON: Between the Lines.

De Lissovoy, N. (2008a). Conceptualizing Oppression in Educational Theory: Toward a Compound Standpoint. *Cultural Studies – Critical Methodologies, 8*(1), 82–105.

De Lissovoy, N. (2008b). *Power, Crisis, and Education for Liberation.* New York: Palgrave MacMillan.

Denzin, N. K. (2001). *Interpretive Interactionism* (2nd edn). Thousand Oaks, CA: Sage.

Desai, A. & Vahed, G. (2010). World Cup 2010: Africa's Turn or the Turn on Africa? *Soccer & Society, 11*(1–2), 154–67.

Develtere, P. & De Bruyn, T. (2009). The Emergence of the Fourth Pillar of Development Aid. *Development in Practice, 19*(7), 912–22.

Dieter, H. & Kumar, R. (2008). The Downside of Celebrity Diplomacy: The Neglected Complexity of Development. *Global Governance, 14*, 259–64.

Domingos, N. (2007). Football and Colonialism, Domination and Appropriation: The Mozambican Case. *Soccer & Society, 8*(4), 478–94.

Donnelly, P. (1993). Democratization Revisited: Seven Theses on the Democratization of Sport and Active Leisure. *Loisir et société/Society and Leisure, 16*(2), 413–34.

Donnelly, P. (2008). Sport and Human Rights. *Sport in Society, 11*(4), 381–94.

Donnelly, P. & Harvey, J. (2007). Social Class and Gender: Intersections in Sport and Physical Activity. In K. Young & P. White (eds), *Sport and Gender in Canada* (2nd edn) (pp. 95–119). Oxford, UK: Oxford University Press.

Donnelly, P., Darnell, S. C., Wells, C. & Coakley, J. (2007). *The Use of Sport to Foster Child and Youth Development and Education.* Toronto, ON: Sport for Development and Peace – International Working Group.

Donnelly, P., Atkinson, M., Szto, C. & Boyle, S. (2011). Sport for Development and Peace: A Public Sociology Perspective. *Third World Quarterly, 32*(3), 589–601.

Dyck, C. (2011). Football and Post-war Reintegration: Exploring the Role of Sport in DDR Processes in Sierra Leone. *Third World Quarterly, 32*(3), 395–415.

Epprecht, M. (2004). Work-Study Abroad Courses in International Development Studies: Some Ethical and Pedagogical Issues. *Canadian Journal of Development Studies, 25*(4), 687–706.

Escobar, A. (1995). *Encountering Development: The Making and Unmaking of the Third World.* Princeton, NJ: Princeton University Press.

Esteva, G. (1992). Development. In W. Sachs (ed.), *The Development Dictionary* (pp. 6–25). London: Zed Books.

Esteva, G. & Prakash, M. S. (1997). From Global Thinking to Local Thinking. In V. Bawtree & M. Rahnema (eds), *The Post-development Reader* (pp. 277–89). London: Zed Books.

Ewing, M., Gano-Overway, C., Branta, C. & Seefeldt, V. (2002). The Role of Sports in Youth Development. In M. Gatz, M. Messner & S. Ball-Rokeach (eds), *Paradoxes of Youth and Sport* (pp. 31–47). Albany, NY: State University of New York Press.

Fain, S. (2008). Celebrities, Poverty, and the Mediapolis: A Case Study of the ONE Campaign, London School of Economics Media and Humanity Conference. London, 21 September.

Farley, A. P. (1997). The Black Body As Fetish Object. *Oregon Law Review, 76*, 457–535.

Felluga, D. (2003). *Modules on Althusser: On Ideology*, from http://www.purdue.edu. guidetotheory/marxism/modules/althusserideology.html [accessed 13 June 2008].

Ferguson, J. (1994). *The Anti-politics Machine: 'Development', Depoliticization and Bureaucratic Power in Lesotho.* Minneapolis, MN: University of Minnesota Press.

FIFA. (2010). *Adidas Exchange Programme Launches in West Africa*, from http://www.fifa. com/aboutfifa/worldwideprograms/news/newsid=1325470.html [accessed 22 June 2011].

FIFA. (2011). Football for Hope, from http://www.fifa.com/aboutfifa/worldwideprograms/ footballforhope/index.html [accessed 1 November 2011].

Fokwang, J. (2009). Southern Perspective on Sport-in-Development: A Case Study of Football in Bamenda, Cameroon. In R. Levermore & A. Beacom (eds), *Sport and International Development* (pp. 198–218). London: Palgrave MacMillan.

Foucault, M. (1978). *The History of Sexuality* (1st American edn). New York: Pantheon Books.

Foucault, M. (1997). *Society Must Be Defended: Lectures at the Collège de France*. New York: Picador.

Foucault, M. (2008). *The Birth of Bio-politics: Lectures at the Collège de France 1978–79*. New York: Palgrave MacMillan.

Fusco, C. (2005). Cultural Landscapes of Purification: Sports Spaces and Discourses of Whiteness. *Sociology of Sport Journal, 22*(3), 283–310.

Gasper, D. (2004). *The Ethics of Development: From Economism to Human Development*. Edinburgh, UK: Edinburgh University Press.

Gasser, P. K. & Levinsen, A. (2004). Breaking Post-war Ice: Open Fun Football Schools in Bosnia and Herzegovina. *Sport in Society, 7*(3), 457–72.

Gilchrist, C. (2005). Local Heroes and Global Stars. In L. Allison (ed.), *The Global Politics of Sport* (pp. 118–39). New York: Routledge.

Giles, D. (2000). *Illusions of Immortality: A Psychology of Fame and Celebrity*. London: MacMillan.

Giulianotti, R. (1999a). *Football: A Sociology of the Global Game*. Cambridge, UK: Polity Press; Malden, MA: Blackwell.

Giulianotti, R. (1999b). Sport and Social Development in Africa: Some Major Human Rights Issues, The First International Conference on Sports and Human Rights. Sydney, Australia, 3 September.

Giulianotti, R. (2004). Human Rights, Globalization and Sentimental Education. *Sport in Society, 7*(3), 355–69.

Giulianotti, R. (2005). *Sport: A Critical Sociology*. Cambridge, UK: Polity Press.

Giulianotti, R. (2011). Sport, Transnational Peacemaking and Global Civil Society: Exploring the Reflective Discourses of 'Sport, Development and Peace' Project Officials. *Journal of Sport and Social Issues, 35*(1), 50–71.

Goldberg, D. T. (1993). *Racist Culture: Philosophy and the Politics of Meaning*. Cambridge, MA: Blackwell.

Gramsci, A. (1971). *Selections from the Prison Notebooks of Antonio Gramsci*. Edited and translated by Q. Hoare and G. Nowell-Smith. London: Lawrence & Wishart.

Grant, J. (2000). The Cultural Turn in Marxism. In J. Dean (ed.), *Cultural Studies & Political Theory* (pp. 132–46). Ithaca, NY and London: Cornell University Press.

Grassroot Soccer (2011). *Grassroot Soccer*, from http://www.grassrootsoccer.org/ [accessed 1 November 2011].

Greig, A., Hulme, D. & Turner, M. (2007). *Challenging Global Inequality: Development Theory and Practice in the 21st Century*. Houndmills, Basingstoke, Hampshire; New York: Palgrave Macmillan.

Grewal, I. (2005). *Transnational America: Feminisms, Diasporas, Neoliberalisms*. Durham, NC: Duke University Press.

Grewal, I. & Kaplan, C. (1994). *Scattered Hegemonies: Postmodernity and Transnational Feminist Practices*. Minneapolis, MN: University of Minnesota Press.

Gruneau, R. (in press). Sport, Development and the Challenge of Slums. In R. Field (ed.), *Scholar, Athlete, Activist: Essays in Honour of Bruce Kidd* [working title]. (Toronto, ON: University of Toronto Press, submitted for review.)

Gruneau, R. S. (1983). *Class, Sports, and Social Development*. Amherst, MA: University of Massachusetts Press.

Guest, A. (2009). The Diffusion of Development-through-Sport: Analysing the History and Practice of the Olympic Movement's Grassroots Outreach to Africa. *Sport in Society, 12*(10), 1336–52.

Guttmann, A. (1978). *From Ritual to Record: The Nature of Modern Sports*. New York: Columbia University Press.

Hall, C. M. (2006). Urban Entrepreneurship, Corporate Interests and Sports Mega-events: The Thin Politics of Competitiveness within the Hard Outcomes of Neoliberalism. In J. Horne & W. Manzenreiter (eds), *Sports Mega-events: Social Scientific Analyses of a Global Phenomenon* (pp. 59–70). Malden, MA: Blackwell.

Hall, S. (1985). Signification, Representation, Ideology: Althusser and the Post-structuralist Debates. *Critical Studies in Mass Communication, 2*(2), 91–114.

Hall, S. (1986). The Problem of Ideology: Marxism without Guarantees. *Journal of Communication Inquiry, 10*(2), 28–44.

Hansen, D., Larson, R. & Dworkin, J. (2003). What Adolescents Learn in Organized Youth Activities: A Survey of Self-reported Developmental Experiences. *Journal of Research on Adolescence, 13*(1), 25–55.

Haraway, D. J. (1991). *Simians, Cyborgs, and Women: The Reinvention of Nature.* New York: Routledge.

Hardt, M. & Negri, V. (2000). *Empire.* Cambridge, MA: Harvard University Press.

Hardt, M. & Negri, V. (2004). *Multitude: War and Democracy in the Age of Empire.* New York: Penguin Press.

Hardy, S. & Ingham, A. (1983). Games, Structures and Agency: Historians on the American Play Movement. *Journal of Social History, 17*(2), 285–301.

Hargreaves, J. & Tomlinson, A. (1992). Getting There: Cultural Theory and the Sociological Analysis of Sport in Britain. *Sociology of Sport Journal, 9*(2), 207–19.

Hargreaves, J. A. & McDonald, I. (2000). Cultural Studies and the Sociology of Sport. In J. Coakley & E. Dunning (eds), *Handbook of Sports Studies* (pp. 48–60). London: Sage.

Hartman, D. & Kwauk, C. (2011). Sport and Development: An Overview, Critique, and Reconstruction. *Journal of Sport and Social Issues, 35*(3), 284–305. Published online: July 29.

Harvey, D. (2005). *A Brief History of Neoliberalism.* Oxford, UK: Oxford University Press.

Harvey, D. (2007). Neoliberalism As Creative Destruction. *The Annals of the American Academy of Political and Social Science, 610*(1), 22–44.

Harvey, J., Horne, J. & Safai, P. (2009). Alterglobalization, Global Social Movements, and the Possibility of Political Transformation through Sport. *Sociology of Sport Journal, 26*(3), 383–403.

Hayhurst, L. & Frisby, W. (2010). Inevitable Tensions: Swiss and Canadian Sport for Development NGO Perspectives on Partnerships with High Performance Sport. *European Sport Management Quarterly, 10*(1), 75–96.

Hayhurst, L., Wilson, B. & Frisby, W. (2011). Navigating Neo-liberal Networks: Transnational Internet Platforms in Sport for Development and Peace. *International Review for the Sociology of Sport, 46*(1), 1–15.

Hayhurst, L. M. C. (2009). The Power to Shape Policy: Charting Sport for Development and Peace Policy Discourses. *International Journal of Sport Policy, 1*(2), 203–27.

Hedges, C. (2009). *Empire of Illusion: The End of Literacy and the Triumph of Spectacle.* Toronto, ON: Knopf Canada.

Hedstrom, R. & Gould, D. (2004). *Research in Youth Sports: Critical Issues Status.* East Lansing, MI: Institute for the Study of Youth Sports, Michigan State University.

Heine, M. (2010). *Four Sad Faces and a Smiley: A Political Topology of Civic and Olympic Spaces at the 2010 Winter Games.* Paper presented at the Rethinking Matters Olympic: Investigations into the Socio-cultural Study of the Modern Olympic Movement. London, ON, 30 October.

Heron, B. (2007). *Desire for Development: Whiteness, Gender, and the Helping Imperative.* Waterloo, ON: Wilfrid Laurier University Press.

Hesse, B. (2002). Forgotten Like a Bad Dream: Atlantic Slavery and the Ethics of Postcolonial Memory. In D. T. Goldberg & A. Quayson (eds), *Relocating Postcolonialism* (pp. 143–73). Oxford, UK: Blackwell.

Heywood, L. (2007). Producing Girls: Empire, Sport and the Neoliberal Body. In J. Hargreaves & P. Vertinsky (eds), *Physical Culture, Power, and the Body* (pp. 101–20). New York: Routledge.

Hickey, S. & Mohan, G. (2005). Relocating Participation within a Radical Politics of Development. *Development and Change, 36*(2), 237–62.

Horne, J. (2006). *Sport in Consumer Culture.* Basingstoke, UK: Palgrave Macmillan.

Horne, J. (2007). The Four 'Knowns' of Sports Mega-events. *Leisure Studies, 26*(1), 81–96.

Huish, R. (2011). Punching above Its Weight: Cuba's Use of Sport for South–South Solidarity. *Third World Quarterly, 32*(3), 417–33.

Hylton, K. (2009). '*Race' and Sport: Critical Race Theory*. London and New York: Routledge.

Ingham, A. & Beamish, R. (1997). Didn't Cyclops Lose His Visions? An Exercise in Sociological Optometry. *Sociology of Sport Journal, 14*(2), 160–86.

Ingham, A. & Hardy, S. (1984). Sport: Structuration, Subjugation and Hegemony. *Theory, Culture & Society, 2*(2), 85–103.

Jacobs, J. M. (1996). *Edge of Empire: Postcolonialism and the City*. London and New York: Routledge.

Jarvie, G. (2006). *Sport, Culture and Society: An Introduction*. London and New York: Routledge.

Jennings, A. (1996). *The New Lord of the Rings: Olympic Corruption and How to Buy Gold Medals*. London: Pocket Books.

Johnson, R. (2007). Post-hegemony? I Don't Think So. *Theory, Culture & Society, 24*(3), 95–110.

Judt, T. (2010). *Ill Fares the Land*. New York: Penguin Press.

Kaplinsky, R. (2005). *Globalization, Poverty and Inequality: Between a Rock and a Hard Place*. Cambridge, UK: Polity Press.

Kapoor, D. (2009a). Subaltern Social Movement Learning: Adivasi (Original Dwellers) and the Decolonization of Space in India. In D. Kapoor (ed.), *Education, Decolonization and Development: Perspectives from Asia, Africa and the Americas* (pp. 7–38). Rotterdam: Sense.

Kapoor, D. (ed.). (2009b). *Education, Decolonization, and Development*. Rotterdam: Sense.

Kapoor, I. (2004). Hyper-self-reflexive Development? Spivak on Representing the Third World 'Other'. *Third World Quarterly, 25*(4), 627–47.

Karagiannis, N. (2004). *Avoiding Responsibility: The Politics and Discourse of European Development Policy*. London and Ann Arbor, MI: Pluto Press.

Kay, T. (2009). Developing through Sport: Evidencing Sport Impacts on Young People. *Sport in Society, 12*(9), 1177–91.

Kerry, D. S. & Armour, K. M. (2000). Sport Sciences and the Promise of Phenomenology: Philosophy, Method and Insight. *Quest, 52*(1), 1–17.

Kidd, B. (1995). Inequality in Sport, the Corporation, and the State: An Agenda for Social Scientists. *Journal of Sport and Social Issues, 19*(3), 232–48.

Kidd, B. (2008). A New Social Movement: Sport for Development and Peace. *Sport in Society, 11*(4), 370–80.

Kidd, B. & Dichter, H. (2011). Introduction: Olympic Reform Ten Years Later. *Sport in Society, 14*(3), 289–91.

Kidd, B. & Donnelly, P. (2000). Human Rights in Sports. *International Review for the Sociology of Sport, 35*(2), 131–48.

Kidd, B. & Eberts, M. (1982). *Athletes' Rights in Canada*. Toronto, ON: Ontario Ministry of Tourism and Recreation.

Kincheloe, J. (2007). Critical Pedagogy in the Twenty-First Century: Evolution for Survival. In P. McLaren & J. Kincheloe (eds), *Critical Pedagogy: Where Are We Now?* (pp. 9–42). New York: Peter Lang.

Klein, N. (2001). *No Logo*. New York: Picador.

Klein, N. (2007). *The Shock Doctrine: The Rise of Disaster Capitalism* (1st edn). Toronto, ON: Knopf Canada.

Klosterman, C. (2009). *Eating the Dinosaur*. New York: Scribner.

Kothari, U. (2005). Authority and Expertise: The Professionalisation of International Development and the Ordering of Dissent. *Antipode, 37*(3), 425–46.

Kruse, S. E. (2006). Review of Kicking AIDS Out: Is Sport an Effective Tool in the Fight against HIV/AIDS? Draft report to NORAD, from http://www.norad.no/en/_attachment/107627/binary/6080?download [accessed 5 November 2011].

Kwon, S.-Y. (2010). The State and Sport Industry in Korea: The Paradox of Korean Globalization, North American Society for the Sociology of Sport Conference. San Diego, CA, 4 November.

Lash, S. (2007). Power after Hegemony: Cultural Studies in Mutation? *Theory, Culture & Society, 24*(3), 55–78.

Lather, P. A. (1991). *Getting Smart: Feminist Research and Pedagogy with/in the Postmodern.* New York: Routledge.

Lefebvre, K. (2010). Sport within Development: Negotiating an Appropriate Role, North American Society for the Sociology of Sport Conference. San Diego, CA, 4 November.

Lenskyj, H. (1986). *Out of Bounds: Women, Sport and Sexuality.* Toronto, ON: Women's Press.

Lenskyj, H. (1993). *Out on the Field: Gender, Sport and Sexualities.* Toronto, ON: Women's Press.

Levermore, R. (2008). Sport: A New Engine for Development? *Progress in Development Studies, 8*(2), 183–90.

Levermore, R. (2009). Sport-in-International Development: Theoretical Frameworks. In R. Levermore & A. Beacom (eds), *Sport and International Development* (pp. 26–54). London: Palgrave MacMillan.

Levermore, R. (2010). CSR for Development through Sport: Examining Its Potential and Limitations. *Third World Quarterly, 31*(2), 223–41.

Levermore, R. (2011). The Paucity of, and Dilemma in, Evaluating Corporate Social Responsibility for Development through Sport. *Third World Quarterly, 32*(3), 551–69.

Levermore, R. & Beacom, A. (eds). (2009). *Sport and International Development.* London: Palgrave MacMillan.

Lewis, S. (2005). *Race Against Time: Searching for Hope in AIDS Ravaged Africa.* Toronto, ON: House of Anansi Press.

Li, T. (2007). *The Will to Improve: Governmentality, Development, and the Practice of Politics.* Durham, NC: Duke University Press.

Lindsey, I. & Grattan, A. (in press). An International Movement? Decentering Sport for Development within Zambian Communities. *International Journal of Sport Policy, 4*(1).

Littler, J. (2009). *Radical Consumption: Shopping for Change in Contemporary Culture.* Berkshire, UK; New York: Open University Press.

Loomba, A. (1998). *Colonialism–Postcolonialism,* from http://link.library.utoronto.ca/eir/EIRdetail.cfm?Resources__ID=448017&T=F [accessed 1 November 2011].

Loy, J. & Booth, D. (2004). Social Structure and Social Theory: The Intellectual Insights of Robert K. Merton. In R. Giulianotti (ed.), *Sport and Modern Social Theorists* (pp. 33–47). New York: Palgrave MacMillan.

MacAloon, J. (1992). The Ethnographic Imperative in Comparative Olympic Research. *Sociology of Sport Journal, 9*(2), 104–30.

MacAloon, J. (1996). Humanism As Political Necessity? Reflections on the Pathos of Anthropological Science in Olympic Contexts. *Quest, 48,* 67–81.

Magubane, Z. (2008). The (Product) Red Man's Burden: Charity, Celebrity, and the Contradictions of Coevalness. *The Journal of Pan African Studies, 2*(6), 134–49.

Maguire, J. (2006). Development through Sport and the Sports Industrial Complex: The Case for Human Development in Sports and Exercise Sciences. In Y. Vanden Auweele, C. Malcolm & B. Meulders (eds), *Sport and Development* (pp. 107–21). Leuven, Belgium: Lannoo Campus.

Maguire, J. (2008). 'Real Politic' or 'Ethically Based': Sport, Globalization, Migration and Nation-State Policies. *Sport in Society, 11*(4), 443–58.

Marcuse, H. (1964). *One-Dimensional Man: Studies in the Ideology of Advanced Industrial Society.* Boston, MA: Beacon Press.

Markula, P. & Pringle, R. (2006). *Foucault, Sport and Exercise: Power, Knowledge and Transforming the Self.* Abingdon, UK: Routledge.

McEwan, C. (2009). *Postcolonialism and Development.* London: Routledge.

McMichael, P. (ed.). (2009). *Contesting Development: Critical Struggles for Social Change.* New York: Routledge.

McQuaig, L. & Brooks, N. (2010). *The Trouble with Billionaires.* Toronto, ON: Viking Canada.

Meier, M. & Saavedra, M. (2009). Esther Phiri and the Moutawakel Effect in Zambia: An Analysis of the Use of Female Role Models in Sport-for-Development. *Sport in Society, 21*(9), 1158–76.

Millington, R. (2010). *Basketball with(out) Borders: Interrogating the Intersections of Sport, Development, and Capitalism.* Kingston, ON: Queen's University.

Mills, S. (1997). *Discourse.* London and New York: Routledge.

Moddelmog, D. (1999). *Reading Desire: In Pursuit of Ernest Hemingway.* Ithaca, NY: Cornell University Press.

Mohanty, C. T. (2003). *Feminism without Borders: Decolonizing Theory, Practicing Solidarity.* New Delhi: Zubaan.

Morgan, W. (1994). Hegemony Theory, Social Domination, and Sport: The MacAloong and Hargreaves-Tomlinson Debate Revisited. *Sociology of Sport Journal, 11*(3), 309–29.

Morgan, W. (1997). Yet Another Critical Look at Hegemony Theory: A Response to Ingham and Beamish. *Sociology of Sport Journal, 14*(2), 187–95.

Mourao, M. (2010). *2014 World Cup Extreme Makeover: The Preparation to Host FIFA's Mega-event. The Case of Porto Alegre/RS – Brazil.* San Francisco, CA: University of San Francisco.

Nederveen Pieterse, J. (2001). *Development Theory: Deconstructions/Reconstructions.* London: Sage.

Nederveen Pieterse, J. (2010). *Development Theory* (2nd edn). Los Angeles: Sage.

Nicholls, S. (2009). On the Backs of Peer Educators: Using Theory to Interrogate the Role of Young People in the Field of Sport-in-Development. In R. Levermore & A. Beacom (eds), *Sport and International Development* (pp. 156–75). New York: Palgrave MacMillan.

Nicholls, S. (2010). *Mainstreaming Sport into International Development.* Considering Youth Agency and Engagement in Sport for Development. Halifax, NS: Dalhousie University.

Nickel, P. & Eikenberry, A. (2009). A Critique of the Discourse of Marketized Philanthropy. *American Behavioral Scientist, 52*(7), 974–89.

Njelesani, D. (2011). Preventive HIV/AIDS Education through Physical Education: Reflections from Zambia. *Third World Quarterly, 32*(3), 435–52.

Nustad, K. G. (2001). Development: The Devil We Know? *Third World Quarterly, 22*(4), 479–89.

Ong, A. (2006). *Neoliberalism As Exception: Mutations in Citizenship and Sovereignty.* Durham, NC: Duke University Press.

Owusu, F. (2003). Pragmatism and the Gradual Shift from Dependency to Neoliberalism: The World Bank, African Leaders and Development Policy in Africa. *World Development, 31*(10), 1655–72.

Payne, A. (2005). *The Global Politics of Unequal Development.* Houndmills, Basingstoke, Hampshire; New York: Palgrave Macmillan.

Peacock, B. (2011). A Secret Instinct of Social Preservation: Legitimacy and the Dynamic (Re)constitution of Olympic Conceptions of the Good. *Third World Quarterly, 32*(3), 477–502.

Perks, T. (2007). Does Sport Foster Social Capital? The Contribution of Sport to a Lifestyle of Community Participation. *Sociology of Sport Journal, 24*(4), 378–401.

Pessoa, C. (2003). On Hegemony, Post-ideology and Subalternity. *Bulletin of Latin American Research, 22*(4), 484–90.

Play Soccer (2011). *Play Soccer,* from http://www.playsoccer-nonprofit.org/ [accessed 1 November 2011].

Ponte, S., Richey, L. A. & Baab, M. (2009). Bono's Product (RED) Initiative: Corporate Social Responsibility that Solves the Problem of 'Distant Others'. *Third World Quarterly, 30*(2), 301–17.

Portes, A. & Landholt, P. (2000). Social Capital: Promise and Pitfalls of Its Role in Development. *Journal of Latin American Studies, 32,* 529–47.

Pringle, R. (2005). Masculinities, Sport and Power: A Critical Comparison of Gramscian and Foucauldian Inspired Theoretical Tools. *Journal of Sport and Social Issues, 29*(3), 256–78.

Pronger, B. (2002). *Body Fascism: Salvation in the Technology of Physical Fitness*. Toronto, ON: University of Toronto Press.

Putnam, R. (2000). *Bowling Alone: The Collapse and Revival of the American Community*. New York: Simon & Schuster.

Putney, C. (2001). *Muscular Christianity: Manhood and Sports in Protestant America, 1880–1920*. Cambridge, MA: Harvard University Press.

Qualter Berna, A. (2006). Sport As a Human Right and As a Means for Development. In Y. Vanden Auweele, C. Malcolm & B. Meulders (eds), *Sport and Development* (pp. 35–9). Leuven, Belgium: Lannoo Campus.

Rail, G. & Harvey, J. (1995). Body at Work: Michel Foucault and the Sociology of Sport. *Sociology of Sport Journal, 12*(2), 164–79.

Rapley, J. (1996). *Understanding Development: Theory and Practice in the Third World*. Boulder, CO: Lynne Rienner.

Razack, N. (2003). *Perils and Possibilities: Racism, Imperialism and Nationalism in International Social Work*. Adelaide, Australia: Flinders University.

Razack, N. (2005). 'Bodies on the Move': Spatialized Locations, Identities, and Nationality in International Work. *Social Justice, 32*(4), 87–104.

Razack, S. (1998). *Looking White People in the Eye: Gender, Race, and Culture in Courtrooms and Classrooms*. Toronto, ON: University of Toronto Press.

Razack, S. (2008). Introduction: Barbara Heron 'Desire for Development' Book Launch: Toronto Women's Bookstore.

Redeker, R. (2008). Sport As an Opiate of International Relations: The Myth and Illusion of Sport As a Tool of Foreign Diplomacy. *Sport in Society, 11*(4), 494–500.

Reed, A. M. (2008). *The Global South: Politics, Policy & Development*, from http://www.yorku.ca/ananya/Globalsouthhome.htm [accessed 3 July 2008].

Rigauer, B. (2000). Marxist Theories. In J. Coakley & E. Dunning (eds), *Handbook of Sports Studies* (pp. 28–47). London: Sage.

Right to Play (2011). Right to Play at a Glance, from http://www.righttoplay.com/International/about-us/Pages/Glance.aspx [accessed 1 November 2011].

Roche, M. (2000). *Megaevents and Modernity: Olympics and Expos in the Growth of Global Culture*. New York: Routledge.

Roche, M. (2006). Mega-events and Modernity Revisited: Globalization and the Case of the Olympics. In J. Horne & W. Manzenreiter (eds), *Sports Mega-events: Social Scientific Analyses of a Global Phenomenon* (Vols 27–40). Malden, MA: Blackwell.

Roman, L. (1997). Denying (White) Racial Privilege: Redemption Discourses and the Uses of Fantasy. In M. Fine, L. Weis & M. Won (eds), *Off White: Readings on Race, Power and Society* (pp. 270–82). New York: Routledge.

Rosaldo, R. (1995). Foreword. In G. Canclini (ed.), *Hybrid Cultures: Strategies for Entering and Leaving Modernity* (pp. XI–XVII). Minneapolis, MN: University of Minnesota Press.

Rose, N. S. (2007). *The Politics of Life Itself: Biomedicine, Power, and Subjectivity in the Twenty-First Century*. Princeton, NJ: Princeton University Press.

Rowe, D. (2004). Antonio Gramsci: Sport, Hegemony and the National-Popular. In R. Giulianotti (ed.), *Sport and Modern Social Theorists* (pp. 97–110). New York: Palgrave MacMillan.

Saavedra, M. (2009). Dilemmas and Opportunities in Gender and Sport-in-Development. In R. Levermore & A. Beacom (eds), *Sport and International Development* (pp. 124–55). London: Palgrave MacMillan.

Sachs, W. (1992). *The Development Dictionary: A Guide to Knowledge As Power*. London and Atlantic Highlands, NJ: Zed Books.

Said, E. W. (1978). *Orientalism* (1st edn). New York: Pantheon Books.

Sardar, Z. (1999). Development and the Locations of Eurocentrism. In D. O'Hearn & R. Munck (eds), *Critical Development Theory: Contributions to a New Paradigm* (pp. 44–62). London: Zed Books.

Saunders, D. (2010). *Arrival City: The Final Migration and Our Next World* (1st edn). Toronto, ON: Knopf Canada.

Saunders, D. (2011). Look East and South: Witness the End of Post-colonialism. *The Globe and Mail*, 8 January.

Schuurman, F. J. (1993). Introduction: Development Theory in the 1990s. In F. J. Schuurman (ed.), *New Directions in Development Theory* (pp. 1–48). London: Zed Books.

Schuurman, F. J. (2001). Globalization and Development Studies: Introducing the Challenges. In F. J. Schuurman (ed.), *Globalization and Development Studies: Challenges for the 21st Century* (pp. 3–16). London: Sage.

Schuurman, F. J. (2009). Critical Development Theory: Moving Out the Twilight Zone. *Third World Quarterly, 30*(5), 831–48.

Scott, J. (1991). The Evidence of Experience. *Critical Inquiry, 17*(4), 773–97.

Sen, A. (2000). *Development As Freedom* (1st edn). New York: Anchor Books.

Shogan, D. A. (1999). *The Making of High-Performance Athletes: Discipline, Diversity, and Ethics*. Toronto, ON: University of Toronto Press.

Shogan, D. A. (2007). *Sports Ethics in Context*. Toronto, ON: Canadian Scholars Press.

Sidoti, C. (1999). Rules Beyond the Game, The First International Conference on Sports and Human Rights. Sydney, Australia, 3 September.

Slater, D. (1993). The Geopolitical Imagination and the Enframing of Development Theory. *Transactions of the Institute of British Geographers, 18*, 419–37.

Slater, D. (2004). *Geopolitics and the Post-colonial: Rethinking North–South Relations*. Malden, MA: Blackwell.

Smith, L. T. (1999). *Decolonizing Methodologies: Research and Indigenous Peoples*. New York: Zed Books; Dunedin: University of Otago Press; distributed in the United States exclusively by St Martin's Press.

Soccer for Peace (2011). *Soccer for Peace*, from http://www.soccerforpeace.com/ [accessed 1 November 2011].

Spaaij, R. (2009). Sport As a Vehicle for Social Mobility and Regulation of Disadvantaged Urban Youth. *International Review for the Sociology of Sport, 44*(2), 247–64.

Spaaij, R. (2010). Using Sport to Engender Social and Cultural Capital in Disadvantaged Communities: The Brazilian Experience, International Sport Sociology Association Conference. Gothenberg, Sweden, 13 July.

Spaaij, R. (2011). *Sport and Social Mobility: Crossing Boundaries*. London and New York: Routledge.

Spivak, G. (1988). Can the Subaltern Speak? In C. Nelson & L. Grossberg (eds), *Marxism & the Interpretation of Culture* (pp. 271–313). London: Macmillan.

Sportanddev.org. (2011). *Developing Local Markets through Sport*, from http://www.sportanddev.org/en/learnmore/sport_and_economic_development/developing_local_markets_through_sport/ [accessed 1 November 2011].

Sport for Development and Peace – International Working Group (2006). *From Practice to Policy*, from http://www.sportanddev.org/newsnviews/search.cfm?uNewsID=27 [accessed 4 November 2011].

Sports Information Resource Centre (2010). *Olympic and Paralympic Medallists to Celebrate Year of Sport Excellence with Corporate Canada in Support of Right to Play – Athlete Helicopter Ball Drop to Kick-Off Sold-Out Golf Tournament in Canmore*, from http://www.sirc.ca/news_view.cfm?id=35784 [accessed 4 November 2011].

Sports Sans Frontières (2011). *Sports Sans Frontières: Qui sommes-nous?* from http://www.sportsansfrontieres.org/ [accessed 1 November 2011].

Stoler, A. L. (1995). *Race and the Education of Desire: Foucault's History of Sexuality and the Colonial Order of Things*. Durham, NC: Duke University Press.

Stoler, A. L. (2002). *Carnal Knowledge and Imperial Power: Race and the Intimate in Colonial Rule*. Berkeley, CA: University of California Press.

Sugden, J. (2006). Teaching and Playing Sport for Conflict Resolution and Co-existence in Israel. *International Review for the Sociology of Sport, 41*(2), 221–40.

Sugden, J. & Tomlinson, A. (2005). Not for the Good of the Game: Crisis and Credibility in the Governance of World Football. In L. Allison (ed.), *The Global Politics of Sport* (pp. 26–45). New York: Routledge.

Sutcliffe, B. (2007). A Converging or Diverging World? In Jomo K. S. & J. Baudot (eds), *Flat World, Big Gaps*. New York: Zed Books.

Swart, K. & Bob, U. (2004). The Seductive Discourse of Development: The Cape Town 2004 Olympic Bid. *Third World Quarterly, 25*(7), 1311–24.

Sylvester, C. (1999). Development Studies and Postcolonial Studies: Disparate Tales of the 'Third World'. *Third World Quarterly, 20*(4), 703–21.

Tamboukou, M. & Ball, S. J. (eds). (2002). *Dangerous Encounters: Genealogy and Ethnography*. New York: Peter Lang.

Targett, M. & Wolfe, E. (2010). Sport for Development and Peace: A Perspective on Defining the Field, from http://www.sportanddev.org/en/newsnviews/news/?2514/Sport-for-Development-and-Peace-A-Perspective-on-Defining-the-Field [accessed 5 November 2011].

Taylor, M. (2010). Conscripts of Competitiveness: Culture, Institutions, and Capital in Contemporary Development. *Third World Quarterly, 31*(4), 561–79.

Teeple, G. (2005). *The Riddle of Human Rights*. Amherst, NY: Humanity Books.

Therien, J. P. (1999). Beyond the North–South Divide: Two Tales of Third World Poverty. *Third World Quarterly, 20*(4), 723–42.

Tiessen, R. (2007). Educating Global Citizens? Canadian Foreign Policy and Youth Study/Volunteer Abroad Programs. *Canadian Foreign Policy, 14*(1), 77–84.

Tiessen, R. (2011). Global Subjects or Objects of Globalization? The Promotion of Global Citizenship in Organisations Offering Sport for Development and/or Peace Programmes. *Third World Quarterly, 32*(3), 571–87.

Tomlinson, A. (2005). Olympic Survivals: The Olympic Games As a Global Phenomenon. In L. Allison (ed.), *The Global Politics of Sport* (pp. 46–62). New York: Routledge.

Tomlinson, J. (2001). Vicious and Benign Universalism. In F. J. Schuurman (ed.), *Globalization and Development Studies: Challenges for the 21st Century* (pp. 45–60). London: Sage.

Torfing, J. (1999). *New Theories of Discourse: Laclau, Mouffe, and Žižek*. Oxford, UK; Malden, MA: Blackwell.

Tucker, V. (1999). The Myth of Development: A Critique of a Eurocentric Discourse. In D. O'Hearn & R. Munck (eds), *Critical Development Theory: Contributions to a New Paradigm* (pp. 1–26). London: Zed Books.

Turner, G. (2004). *Understanding Celebrity*. London: Sage.

United Nations (2003). Sport for Development and Peace: Towards Achieving the Millennium Development Goals. Report from the United Nations Inter-agency Task Force on Sport for Development and Peace. Geneva: United Nations, from http://www.unicef.org/sports/reportE.pdf [accessed 4 November 2011].

United Nations (2004). Universal Language of Sport Brings People Together, Teaches Teamwork, Tolerance, Secretary-General says at Launch of International Year, United Nations.

United Nations (2005). Sport As a Tool for Development and Peace: Towards Achieving the Millennium Development Goals. Report from the United Nations Inter-agency Task Force on Sport for Development and Peace. Geneva: United Nations, from http://www.un.org/sport2005/resources/task_force.pdf [accessed 4 November 2011].

United Nations General Assembly (1987). Report of the World Commission on Environment and Development (Vol. General Assembly Resolution 42/187), 11 December.

United Nations General Assembly (2003). Resolution 58/5: Sport As a Means to Promote Education, Health, Development and Peace.

United Nations General Assembly (2009a). 2010 International Federation of Association Football World Cup Event (Vol. A/64/L.3).

United Nations General Assembly (2009b). Building a Peaceful and Better World through Sport and the Olympic Ideal (Vol. A/64/L.2).

Wainwright, J. (2008). *Decolonizing Development: Colonial Power and the Maya*. Malden, MA: Blackwell.

Walker, I. (2009). Steve Nash Hypes Vancouver NBA Pre-season Game, Charity Soccer Match. *Vancouver Sun*, 23 August.

Weiner, E. (2007). Critical Pedagogy and the Crisis of Imagination. In P. McLaren & J. Kincheloe (eds), *Critical Pedagogy: Where Are We Now?* (pp. 57–78). New York: Peter Lang.

Weisbrot, M., Baker, D. & Rosnick, D. (2007). The Scorecard on Development: 25 Years of Diminished Progress. In Jomo K. S. & J. Baudot (eds), *Flat World, Big Gaps* (pp. 24–47). New York: Zed Books.

West, D. (2007). *Angelina, Mia, and Bono: Celebrities and International Development*. Washington, DC: Brookings Institution.

Whannel, G. (2002). *Media Sports Stars: Masculinities and Moralities*. London: Routledge.

Wieviorka, M. (2005). After New Social Movements. *Social Movement Studies, 4*(1), 1–19.

Wilkinson, R. G. & Pickett, K. (2009). *The Spirit Level: Why Greater Equality Makes Societies Stronger*. New York: Bloomsbury Press.

Willis, O. (2000). Sport and Development: The Significance of Mathare Youth Sports Association. *Canadian Journal of Development Studies, 13*(3), 825–49.

Wilson, B. (2007). New Media, Social Movements and Global Sport Studies: A Revolutionary Moment and the Sociology of Sport. *Sociology of Sport Journal, 24*(4), 457–77.

Wilson, B. & Hayhurst, L. (2009). Digital Activism: Neo-liberalism, the Internet, and 'Sport for Development'. *Sociology of Sport Journal, 26*(1), 115–81.

Wilson, B. & Sparks, R. (1999). Impacts of Black Athlete Media Portrayals on Canadian Youth. *Canadian Journal of Communication, 24*(4), 589–627.

Woodward, D. & Simms, A. (2007). Growth Is Failing the Poor: The Unbalanced Distribution of the Benefits and Costs of Global Economic Growth. In Jomo K. S. & J. Baudot (eds), *Flat World, Big Gaps* (pp. 130–58). New York: Zed Books.

Zea, L. (1970). *América en la historia (Ediciones de la Revista de Occidente)*. Mexico: Fondo de Cultura Económica.

Ziai, A. (2004). The Ambivalence of Post-development: Between Reactionary Populism and Radical Democracy. *Third World Quarterly, 25*(6), 1045–60.

Zirin, D. (2008). *A People's History of Sports in the United States: 250 Years of Politics, Protest, People and Play*. New York: The New Press.

# Notes

## Introduction  Situating sport-for-development and the 'sport for development and peace' sector

1 Aboriginal Canadians are made up of the 630 recognized First Nations in Canada as well as Inuit people and Metis, people of mixed European and Aboriginal ancestry.

2 While this conceptual separation between 'sport development' and 'sport-for-development' (SFD) is generally accepted, the SDP sector sometimes struggles, in practice, to separate itself from elite sports development (Kidd 2008; Maguire 2006: 107–8). Indeed, the dominant 'sports ethic', which privileges and celebrates sacrifice, distinction, risk and pain, and continuously improved performance, is not easily separated from the SDP sector (Maguire 2006: 112).

3 Terminology to describe countries deemed to be 'in need' of development assistance and programmes remains a matter of some debate, particularly given critical perspectives on development from political science, post-colonial theory and anti-racist scholarship. In this text, I use the term 'Global South' to refer to the space(s) – culturally, politically and discursively – that constitute the part of the world which is understood as separate from, and therefore both Othered by and resistant to, the culturally and economically dominant Global North. According to Reed (2008):

> 'Global South' is not just another name for the 'South' or 'the developing world'. The term denotes a community of people at different geographical locations who experience a common set of problems – problems which emanate, by and large, from deep inequities of power within and between nations. (http://www.yorku.ca/ananya/Globalsouthhome.htm)

Despite its strengths in referencing relations of power as they are constituted through space and social relations, the term 'Global South' is not without its problems. Most importantly, it invokes a binary division between North and South that (a) potentially overlooks processes of transculturation in which the colonized take up and remake colonial cultures (Loomba 1998), (b) misinterprets the ubiquity of Empire by referencing its externality (Hardt and Negri 2000) and (c) suggests a Manichean understanding of identity in the post-colonial when ambivalence and hybridity is more accurate (Bhabha 1994). Such criticisms illustrate the difficulty of accurately or effectively transcending the politics of development in post-colonial relations. Similarly, low- and middle-income countries (LMICs) are those nations that are deemed to be at an economic disadvantage relative to the rest of the world. According to the World Bank:

> Low-income and middle-income economies are sometimes referred to as developing economies. The use of the term is convenient; it is not intended to imply that all economies in the group are experiencing similar development or that other economies have reached a preferred or final stage of development. Classification by income does not necessarily reflect development status. (http://data.worldbank.org/about/country-classifications)

'LMIC' is thus a useful term for referring to those nations that are generally understood to be targets of development interventions and logic; at the same time, the use of the term should be accompanied by a critical understanding that it always references and privileges a dominant, yet benign, First World and affords an authority of voice (Said 1978) to speak about southern nations and communities in attempts to better them.

4   In this book, the majority of the discussion and analysis focuses on international development more so than explicit approaches to peace building and conflict resolution. However, sport for peace and conflict resolution is an important dimension of SDP with notable scholarship (see Armstrong 2004; Dyck 2011; Gasser and Levinsen 2004; Sugden 2006 and others). Indeed, as I have argued elsewhere (Darnell, in press) to discuss development is to discuss peace, given that 'the way in which inequality is conceptualized and approached in and through development (through sport or otherwise) is intimately related to the prospects for securing long-term peace and human security'.

5   As a counterpoint to the institutionalization of soccer/football as a tool for development and peace building, scholars of sport have also illustrated how the game is implicated in cultures and institutions of violence, racism, sexism, homophobia and corporatization (see Giulianotti 1999a). It is also important to note that the global recognition and popularity of soccer itself is largely inseparable from its historical colonial utility during which the game was 'introduced' in the Global South by European explorers and settlers. Domingos (2007), among others, argues that the game then underwent a process of 'creolization' where it was taken up by colonized peoples as a form of resistance and cultural expression.

6   http://www.olympic.org/en/content/Olympism-in-Action/Development-through-sport/.

7   http://www.fifa.com/aboutfifa/worldwideprograms/footballforhope/index.html.

8   The millennium development goals (MDGs) were formally recognized by the United Nations General Assembly in September 2000. The goals set a target date of 2015 to achieve lasting and sustainable change, on a global scale, in eight categories related to social and environmental justice, including improved health for mothers and babies, the achievement of universal education, the eradication of extreme poverty and hunger, and the successful erasure of preventative diseases such as HIV/AIDS and malaria. The MDGs also set out to ensure the protection of the physical environment and, in social terms, to 'empower women' towards achieving gender equality (http://www.un.org/millenniumgoals/). The MDGs have been thoroughly scrutinized and significantly critiqued. For example, the MDGs presume that the eradication of poverty is easily compatible with liberal philosophies of social organization and neoliberal policies supporting capital accumulation when these approaches largely serve to exacerbate the poverty to which the MDGs attend (Amin 2006). Furthermore, feminists have critiqued the MDGs for simply restating feminist goals of equity without adequately addressing social causes of sexism and gender marginalization (Ariffin 2004). In other words, the MDGs do very little to support, encourage or demand a political will to effect sustainable social change.

9   In subsequent chapters, I apply these theoretical perspectives to interviews that I conducted in two separate studies – first during a study in which I interviewed 27 young Canadians who had served as volunteers in SDP and second as a researcher in the Department of International Development Studies at Dalhousie University in which I talked to nine policy makers and programme managers from across the SDP sector about the political orientation and challenges of doing this kind of work. The benefits of interviews are that they produce texts that are representative of human performance (Denzin 2001). The interviews that I conducted and analysed lend data to the theoretical connections that I make throughout the text. With that said, in no way can or should the voices captured in these interviews be considered wholly representative of the ideologies or orientations of the entire SDP sector. Particularly considering how many new actors continue to enter the SDP field, it would be problematic and misleading to claim that the interviews I conducted encapsulated the totality of SDP. Still, these voices are methodologically substantial for two reasons. One, they capture the perspectives of people in relative positions of power and privilege, both within

the SDP sector and the broader cultural and political economy, and two, in a post-positivist, post-realist perspective of the manner employed here (see Chapter 2) they offer insights that are relatively deep and broad rather than claims to generalisability. For the purposes of this text, I choose the benefits of the former over the limitations of the latter. I also rely on information for this book gleaned from online sources. The use of Internet materials is a methodology that I have employed and justified previously in critical sociological analyses of SDP (see Darnell 2007), given that they offer a means by which to understand the narratives and world views espoused by key SDP stakeholders (also see Tiessen 2011). Furthermore, recent research by Hayhurst, Wilson and Frisby has illustrated that the Internet, and the online communication that it affords, offers activists, organizations and various other stakeholders in SDP an important means of interaction, engagement and promulgation of their work (see Hayhurst and Frisby 2010; Hayhurst, Wilson and Frisby 2011; Wilson and Hayhurst 2009). In turn, information posted on the Internet becomes an entry point for scholars to make sense of the ways in which SDP programmes and initiatives construct and position themselves, culturally and politically. In sum, while Internet texts and materials rarely yield data as rich, or with as much depth, as ethnographic or interview-based methodologies, they are nonetheless important repositories of cultural and political meaning for the study of SDP, and I employ them in this text when and where appropriate.

10 http://findarticles.com/p/articles/mi_m0EIN/is_1999_June_14/ai_54866551.

11 For example, the Mathare Youth Sport Association (MYSA) in the Mathare slums of Nairobi, Kenya is regularly and rightly held up as an example of a successful, local, grassroots SDP initiative that has improved the lives of youth through the convening interest in football/soccer (see Coalter 2010a; Willis 2000). Arguably, however, MYSA has been 'incorporated' into the broader international SDP fold as a result of its grassroots success and now receives significant international funding from corporate and charitable sources. This limits the extent to which MYSA can be considered representative of a political orientation akin to a Global Movement.

## Chapter 1  Social theory, the sociology of sport and the study of SDP

1 At the same time, Bairner (2007, 2009) has cautioned against the problematic tendency to 'detach' Gramsci from his Marxist roots, to underestimate the class-informed pessimism and revolutionary zeal of Gramsci's writings. This is an important reminder of key Gramscian tenets.

2 Some also suggest that Gramscian hegemony forecloses possibilities of any social and political resistance outside of hegemonic relations and, therefore, increasingly fails to provide a useful account of contemporary agency and resistance such as the Antiglobalization Movement (see Day 2005). This may be a limited reading of Gramsci, however, given that Gramscian scholars such as Raymond Williams took up the hegemony framework specifically to allow and account for emergent struggles. At issue in this chapter is less whether hegemony can account for various radical forms of counter-dominance and more the ways in which commonsense notions of emancipation (such as development through sport) are (re)produced, in many cases, at the expense of relatively powerless groups. Grant (2000), for example, revisited classic critical theory to argue that this process, which Marcuse (1964) described as reason collapsing into 'technological rationality', highlighted the cultural turn in Marxist studies and remains relevant in political theory as a means of investigating the erasure of social possibilities within capitalism. It is such erasures that remain crucial to understanding how current mobilizations of SFD through SDP are constructed, and for maintaining the possibility of alternative and/or radical practices. In this way, hegemony is relevant in SDP to the extent that it helps to illuminate whether and/or how capitalist logic is (re)produced in and through the contemporary use of SFD.

3 Notably, in his lectures at the Collège de France where he explored the 'birth' of bio-politics, Foucault (2008: 28) illustrated how the bio-political state proceeded from an 'epoch of frugal government' in which notions of the market as a site of justice were reified and governmentality organized in such a way as to 'discover' and sustain the principles of the state's own practices. These forms of governmentality were/are not oppressive in the sense of being inherently false, but they did proceed from a particular political economy, one that is arguably more entrenched, or 'true', today. Sport within the neoliberal political economy of contemporary development connects to the bio-political relations that underpin much of the logic, and in many cases the practice, of SDP (see Darnell 2010b).

4 In formulating this approach, Laclau and Moffe drew heavily on Derrida's philosophical criticism of the centre of knowledge and scholarly attempts to essentialize the economic as transcendental.

5 Harvey (2005) also addresses the essentialist residue in the Gramscian approach, arguing that the point may never have been one of privileging the economy as socially fundamental. Rather, at issue is the extent to which capitalist logic based on individuals' 'freedom' to consume has an impact upon the organization of the social and political.

6 In his recent defence, and re-appropriation, of Gramsci for the critical study of sport and physical culture, Bairner (2009: 201) argues that any 'residual economism' in Gramscian theory, such as that identified by Torfing, needs to be recognized as the fundamental anchorage points of key concepts like hegemony (also see Bairner 2007). Bairner therefore argues that analyses of social inequality need to be understood first and foremost in terms of material inequality. I support Bairner's call for a focus on materiality, particularly as it helps to show that much of SDP programming and policy works within the logic of neoliberal globalization and therefore offers little or no resistance to material inequality. Furthermore, I am moved by Bairner's reminder that Gramsci theorized power as both persuasion *and* coercion. At the same time, I am hesitant to accede fundamental explanatory power to economic and class relations; rather I follow Andrews's (2007) response to Bairner in which he argues that connecting class to other forms of oppression (such as race and racism in the post-colonial) is the best way to stem the tide against a retreat from Marxist thought.

7 Sidoti (1999) shows that the social organization and implementation of sport has been complicit in the denial of human rights through institutional racism and sexism, and the denial of opportunities or protection for children and persons with disabilities. However, he concludes that the *potential* for sport to promote social change (as an avenue from poverty, through role modelling and leadership, and as a political catalyst) makes its utility within a human rights framework too important to pass up.

8 Of course, First Nations and Aboriginal persons are not passive in the face of such dismissal. The Aboriginal Sport Circle was established in Canada in 1995 'in response to the need for more accessible and equitable sport and recreation opportunities for Aboriginal peoples' (Aboriginal Sport Circle 2008). The organization develops and facilitates opportunities for youth sport participation, supports the training of coaches and organizes high-performance sporting events.

## Chapter 2 International development studies and SDP: Syntheses and opportunities

1 Byron Peacock (2011) has brought a similar critical analysis to bear on the interest and role of the International Olympic Committee within the SDP sector.

2 A version of this historical overview also appears in Darnell (2010a) in the *Sociology of Sport Journal*.

3 Like most terms in development studies, 'developmentalism' is contestable, insofar as it represents conflicting notions of what development is or should be. For critical

and post-development scholars, in the tradition of Escobar (1995), developmentalism references the modernist compulsion to develop constitutive of globalization and the colonial gaze. For other critical analysts, such as Naomi Klein (2007), state-sponsored developmentalism offers an attractive alternative to unfettered capitalism, particularly supported by militarism, such as Pinochet's Chile of the 1970s and 1980s and the current occupation of Iraq. I use the term here to clarify that the various imaginations of international development, and concomitant interventions, carry political baggage that requires critical scrutiny.

4    'Neoliberalism' as a term and concept has been thoroughly scrutinized in the political and social sciences in recent years (i.e. Harvey 2005; Li 2007; Ong 2006; Slater 2004, among many others). It most often refers to the fundamentalism and privileging of free market economics, often at the expense of state-sponsored social welfare, but has increasingly been taken up to interrogate how discourses of 'individualism' and 'freedom' produce self-regulating and disciplined subjects, most notably in relation to the body (see Fusco 2005; Heywood 2007; Markula and Pringle 2006). In this text, I use the term in both of these ways: to describe the dominant ideology of the global political economy that privileges deregulation and rejects strong state apparatuses, and to refer to the discursive regimes of bio-politics that encourage technologies of self-discipline in order for individuals to successfully participate in the social milieu.

5    Of course, this resiliency of neoliberalism has been tested recently, both politically and socially, by the advocacy, post 9/11, of relatively 'crude' national security models exemplary of the George W. Bush administration that eschewed consensus in favour of exceptionalism (Payne 2005: 1010) and the 2008 economic crisis that exposed the supposed immutable successes of neoliberalism in bringing sustained prosperity to humans. The effects of the economic crisis on the long-term hold of neoliberal philosophy for approaching development remain to be seen (Nederveen Pieterse 2010). As Clarke (2010) has argued, while some aspects of neoliberal logic have come under scrutiny since the economic crisis (such as scepticism of financial institutions and markets and calls for renewed public welfare), the primacy of free enterprise and the 'freedom' to choose, as well as the governmental logic of low-cost efficiency and managerialism, have remained attractive if not central to the dominant political milieu.

6    The notion of hybridity is also relevant to the relativist/universalist debate within development studies. Baaz (2005), in particular, has employed Bhabha's (1994) theory of hybridity that conceptualizes the ways in which language and knowledge fuse within processes of domination, becoming neither dominant nor dominated. This perspective is not intended to reify or essentialize cultural purity but rather reflects processes of transculturation as an ongoing condition of human culture (Rosaldo 1995; cf. Baaz 2005). Hybridity, therefore, challenges both developmentalist and post-development perspectives, in that development practices can be considered neither completely benevolent nor conspiratorial (Baaz 2005: 60).

7    For example, Ziai (2004) has explored the contradictions of the post-development 'school', particularly in (a) illustrating how it largely misappropriates Foucauldian theory and method by retreating to essentialisms and normative models in analysing development politics and (b) summarizing the counter-argument that post-development tacitly supports the unequal development of the status quo. What emerges, though, from Ziai's analysis is that while a brand of neo-populism is possible through post-development thinking, so too is critical post-development thinking that seeks to support more radically democratic development practices. The question, then, is not one of post-development theory *or not* – or even a Foucauldian perspective *or not* – but rather a vigilant reflection on how such methodologies are deployed and to what ends. In this way, I follow Li (2007: 25) in arguing that both a Gramscian approach, attuned to materiality, consciousness and the relationship of dominance/consent, *and* the Foucauldian notion of power as productive through the workings of governmentality are useful to the study of the politics of development and, in turn, to the study of SDP,

particularly given the ways in which they have been used to support critical analyses of sport, sporting bodies and physical culture (see Chapter 1).

8   Gasper (2004) further argues that without equity as a goal, it becomes (increasingly) possible to effectively sacrifice the weak and marginalized. At the same time, he cautions that a commitment to equity needs to be accompanied by critical attention as to whom it is that claims and defines the label equity and recognition that multiple criteria go into equity. Equity is not reducible to one or two elements in a unifying theory. In this way, his conception aligns with Teeple's (2005) political framework for understanding human rights and the transnational feminist argument against the limits of universal feminist essentialisms.

9   Of course, no relations of power are uni-directional or one dimensional, and the post-colonial tradition reminds scholars of development that there is always resistance and agency among people in relatively marginalized positions. Suffice to say that any criticism of post-colonial theorizing, in development studies or elsewhere, for failing to understand the agency of people to resist is a failure of the application of the post-colonial imperative. In fact, foundational post-colonial theorizing has always been concerned, first and foremost, with the complexities of agency (see Spivak 1988) and in deconstructing the tendency for powerful groups to speak for or about Others in ways that preclude agency (Mohanty 2003).

10  For example, D. Kapoor's (2009a) recent research with *Adivasi* (original dwellers) in the south Orissa region of India drew on subaltern studies to (re)position development as the interpretation of, and organized response to, colonizing practices of land dispossession, foreign ownership and exploitation of natural resources. Considering subaltern consciousness against the hegemonic cultural form, and using a radical adult education approach, D. Kapoor (2009b) illustrates that struggles for self-determination in response to the materialism of power *is* the act of development.

11  This focus on the agency of persons to lead their own struggles for development should not be misinterpreted as an invocation of the 'freedom to choose' or freedom from bureaucratic/state constraints that underpins so much of neoliberal thinking. I am not arguing for an overly romanticized notion of subaltern agency or pastoral life, nor suggesting that we should overlook the structural and social reasons why poor people are poor in order to champion their self-determination. Neither am I arguing for a rejection of development, or a limited neo-populist development perspective, as suggested by the most dogmatic post-development perspective and criticized as a result (see Ziai 2004). Rather, development as struggle stands in theoretical and political opposition to the notion that development is primarily a chore of governmentality, in which the conduct of uneducated Others requires improvement. The focus on struggle, as D. Kapoor (2009a: 34) illustrates, also calls for a renewed commitment to Gramscian politics, which recognizes the extent to which people's choices in struggles for development are always produced and constrained within the political economy or the 'structural context' (Payne 2005) of development.

12  In keeping with the framework put forth in Chapter 1, such understandings are best illuminated at the intersection of Foucauldian bio-politics and Gramscian hegemony. For example, as Asher (2009) has illustrated in the struggle for Colombian development, competing cultural notions of ways of life within globalized market politics were established in part by demands of citizens in relation to the actions of the state and corporations. Such insights can certainly be understood in terms of Foucauldian bio-politics but also call for Gramscian analysis of the ways in which such demands effectively served to accelerate state authority (Asher 2009: 93).

## Chapter 3   The SDP intern/volunteer experience

1   Despite its structural reliance on a presumed stable, dominant ideology, Althusserian notions of interpellation continue to be taken up in the social sciences, even in post-structuralist approaches. For example, Bridel and Rail (2007: 139) contend that the gay male marathon runner often constitutes a hybrid social body as subjects are hailed

into athletic competition, often among contradictory discourses of physicality, gender and health. For this study, I follow Heron (2007) and S. Razack (2008) in exploring the extent to which international development volunteer opportunities 'hail' subjects into bourgeois Whiteness.

2   Such insights are, I contend, complementary with the hegemony framework described in the previous section. Indeed, Heron situated the experiences of Canadian development workers against the discursive and material 'colonial continuities' of international development, which, while different in form from colonialism proper, are nonetheless 'recognizable for their similarity to their original colonial manifestations and effects' (Heron 2007: 7). Specifically, these continuities are manifest through an enduring 'planetary consciousness' whereby Others (marked by race and its intersections) require interventions to account for lacks relative to an unmarked standard.

3   I use the term 'placement community' to describe, first and foremost, the communities in which CGC interns were placed during their 8-month service abroad. It is, in this sense, a descriptive term. Of course, the term is also weighted with sociocultural and political meanings and contestabilities that recur throughout this document; it suggests a rather benign sense of transnational entitlement that potentially obscures post- and neocolonial relations and overlooks the ways in which being placed in a community with a mandate of development and social change is an entirely political act. These politics are central to this text and attended to throughout this chapter.

4   Ewing et al. (2002) conclude that sport does not, in and of itself, foster positive behaviours and character among youth; in fact, sport may undermine positive behaviour traits by privileging aggression and violence. Furthermore, Hansen, Larson and Dworkin's (2003) study of youth activities found that young people reported sport to be one of the only social domains in which they experienced negative peer interaction and inappropriate adult behaviour.

5   Bouchier (1994) argues that in nineteenth-century Canada, the use of sport to facilitate character was a particularly pernicious form of social control in which social elites solidified their racist, sexist and classist vision of an 'emerging' nation through the organization of sport and its connections to a national identity. In the case of SDP, the logic of sport as a facilitator of young persons' development continues in a similar fashion, even if the discursive underpinnings are less about securing a social hegemony and more akin to absolving responsibility for geopolitical privilege and power in ways that align with Biccum's (2010) critique.

## Chapter 4  Development history and politics: Investigating SDP

1   Spaaij's (2011) recent monograph on sport and social mobility makes good use of Bourdieusian notions of capital to analyse the processes by which sport facilitates meeting development goals for poor and marginalized people. For example, he points out that in the tradition of Bourdieu, social capital may support upward mobility but that it is also 'border-creating and maintaining, hence exclusionary and laden with power' (Spaaij 2011: 31).

2   Nederveen Pieterse (2010: 205) argues that shifts in the political economy in the past 10 years have resulted in inequality between the North and South being overtaken in importance and relevance by inequality within newly industrializing economies; nevertheless, issues of distributive justice and relations of power, either inter- or intra-national, remain quintessential development issues.

## Chapter 5  Sport, international development and mega-events

1   In July 2011, Pyeongchang, South Korea was awarded the rights to host the 2018 Winter Olympic Games.

2   The recommendations also acknowledged the importance of a range of international development issues that ostensibly recognize the importance of moving the SDP

policy agenda beyond the traditional development focus of growth and infrastructure. Specifically, the recommendations advocated for combating the spread of HIV/AIDS (Recommendation #7) spoke to the role that sport can play in achieving gender equality (#12), outlined a responsibility for protecting the environment through sustainable practices (#9) and asserted the role of sport in creating a climate for peace (#15) and reconciliation from conflict and disaster (#17). In addition, and particularly important from the perspective of sociocultural studies of SFD, Recommendation #3 made reference to the importance of thinking 'beyond the competitive character of sport to maximize its contribution to development'. This appears to acknowledge, at least to some degree, that the dominant discourse of elite sport is particularly susceptible to dependency theories of development whereby the success of the few constructs and affirms the dependence of the relatively marginalized, and to neoliberal development philosophy, which positions competitiveness as a necessary basis for success.

3 http://www.fifa.com/aboutfifa/socialresponsibility/footballforhope/mission.html.
4 Still, FIFA's official campaign for the 2010 World Cup in South Africa was the development of 20 Football for Hope Centres focused on 'public health, education and football in disadvantaged communities across Africa'. Such infrastructure development, even as a way to reach out to youth, is exemplary of neoliberal development and may come at the expense of a focus on social issues and redressing inequality (Levermore 2009).

## Chapter 6 International development and sporting celebrity

1 While I understand that the slave relationship as described by Klosterman (2009) is appealing for (a) offering a critical basis of the cultural construction of celebrity athletes through media and (b) sympathizing with the plight of celebrities who are hailed into filling a cultural void, I am suggesting that his framework does not have full explanatory power *vis-à-vis* the typical northern consumer of celebrity. Still, this framework does illustrate accurately and meaningfully the cultural contexts in which celebrities operate as they attempt to do good work. The tendency towards celebrity athlete development activism proceeds, at least in part, from the inequitable political economy that privileges some at the expense of the many. If Klosterman's slave metaphor works to the extent that celebrities are endowed with money at the expense of a meaningful relationship with culture, then it is reasonable that the justification of this relationship can be strengthened and reinforced in and through the act of 'giving back' through a commitment to development. For celebrity athletes this is likely appealing, and in turn admired by their fans and consumers, because of the oft-perpetuated notion that sport, and professional sport in particular, is culturally vapid at the worst or at the least detached from the rigours and import of hardened, everyday, political experience. It makes sense, therefore, that a person like Steve Nash – fortified with a celebrity persona at his ready disposal – would use such cultural and material capital to work for good; seeking development through celebrity justifies the athlete/fan relationship and makes his celebrity experience not only more important but also more dynamic and weighty. In this way, the meanings regularly and somewhat loosely ascribed to the *power* of sport-in-development refer not (only) to the power of change through sport but to the power of sport as a visual, accessible, media-savvy, fun and relatively low-stakes political enterprise inextricably connected to media, marketing and celebrity culture. Celebrity athletes like Nash can build on the goodwill and affection afforded his position, and the consumption of his celebrity status, to contribute to the betterment of the world, a world in which he disproportionately benefits.

2   Nash, in fact, has regularly stood out in North American professional sport as a particularly engaged political thinker. In 2003, amidst talk of a US-led war in Iraq, he received significant attention for wearing a T-shirt to the NBA all-star game that read 'No War – Shoot for Peace'. According to a Steve Nash fansite, 'Nash explained his position by saying that the United States had provided insufficient evidence that Iraq was a threat and that the UN inspectors should be allowed to complete their mission'. Although Nash did get positive support from teammate Nick Van Exel among others, he also drew criticism from David Robinson, a former naval officer and fellow NBA player. Some journalists like Skip Bayless also criticized Nash as being uninformed and advised him to 'just shut up and play' (http://www.steve-nash.info/steve-nash-off-the-court.htm).

# Index